SPORTS LAW

IN A NUTSHELL

SECOND EDITION

By

WALTER T. CHAMPION, JR.
Professor,
Texas Southern University
School of Law

WEST
GROUP

ST. PAUL, MINN.
2000

To
Crunch, City, Lamisha, Tina and Wally

*

PREFACE

The world of sports law is a world full of mystery and intrigue. Welcome to this world. This slim volume is your road map on a perilous journey replete with contracts, torts, antitrust, constitutional implications, labor law and taxes—all elements that appear to be mutually contradictory. Still, in the chaotic universe through which sports law ruminates, these diverse strands peaceably coincide.

The world of sports law is also a somewhat nascent one struggling to develop its own identity. It is torn between "academic" fields (e.g., labor and antitrust) and practical areas (e.g., contracts and agents); at best it is an unholy alliance. It is not quite in diapers anymore, but it might still be an adolescent bumbling about at the sophomore hop. However, there are enough texts and treatises and apologies in the area that the field has now earned its first distillation into a Nutshell. This book is not intended to be a full-blown treatise, but it will serve as a readable outline to a field that has many divergent subtopics. In Sports Law, you really can't tell the forest from the trees, because there are just so many trees, and the "trees" themselves are all readily recognizable as separate forests in their own right (e.g., contracts, torts, constitutional law, labor law, etc.).

This Nutshell will explain all elements of Sports Law in an organized, reasonably coherent manner. Sports Law flows through our lives in many different formats and impacts on many different people: from agents to lawyers to athletic directors to fans. This book is a review of sports law; it can also be used as a course book, a student outline, a primer for would be professionals (whether agent, athletic director, athlete or coach), or just a nice way to mull away an afternoon.

As regards the second edition, after tightening up a few loose metaphors, refining some legal definitions, bulking up the appendices, and cajoling my colleagues and friends to review a key chapter or two, I decided to concentrate on the interaction among intellectual property, marketing, and sports. The Big Bertha™ trade dress wars was an impetus to review this incredibly litigious tempest-in-a-teapot. To SWOOSH or not to SWOOSH, that is the question.

WALTER CHAMPION

Friendswood, Texas
July, 1999

ACKNOWLEDGMENTS

A good book needs good contributors. To begin with, I was lucky enough to have coerced two exemplary sports professionals to write introductions, namely, Steve Patterson, former General Manager of the Houston Rockets and currently the point guard to bring back an NFL franchise to Houston, and Nick Nichols, the "father" of participant litigation.

I was also lucky to secure contributions, advice, revisions, and consultations from several outstanding legal scholars, namely: Greg Simmons (malpractice), McKen Carrington (taxes), Gita Bolt (NCAA), Patrick Thornton (intellectual property, contracts, and agents), Ricky Anderson (negotiating contracts and marketing), Rey Ramirez (sovereign immunity), Gary Smith (facility liability), Joe Corrigan (financial planning), James Nafziger (international law), and Enrique Juarez (workers' compensation).

A good book needs good people behind it, and that we have in abundance. Special thanks goes to Steve Kauffman, sports agent extraordinaire, for being my pulse to the concerns of fans and athletes alike; Ricky Anderson, who has been with me from the beginning; Steve Underwood, counsel to the Tennessee Titans for his constant support and especially for his assistance in compiling the appendices; and my crackerjack Bomber Squadron of Sports Law afficianados who have assisted me the past five years in bringing the Good News of Sports Law to the unwashed masses through continuing education seminars (they are, in no particular order, Ricky Anderson, Pat Thornton, the Hon. Frank Rynd, Carl Poston, Steve Herskowitz, Steve's Dad, Ed Fowler, Steve Underwood, Bill Frizzell from Tyler, Texas, Steve Patterson, Nick Nichols, and the Hon. Harold Dutton).

WALTER CHAMPION

Friendswood, Texas
July, 1999

INTRODUCTION TO FIRST EDITION

BY STEVE PATTERSON, ESQ.
General Manager of the Houston Rockets

Twenty-five years ago, in 1968, my father was the President and General Manager of the then expansion team, Milwaukee Bucks. The National Basketball Association played most of its games in dingy old gyms without signage, fancy sky boxes, instant replay screens, or sushi bars. There was no cable television or pay-per-view, no Turner Network Television or nightly highlight shows on CNN and ESPN. ABC, NBC and CBS dominated the telecasting of all sports. There were no independents or superstations to carry local teams to regional or national audiences.

Players unions were in their infancy and agents were almost unheard of. Vince Lombardi, Coach and General Manager of the Green Bay Packers, had only recently traded away one of his starting linemen just because the player had retained an agent to help negotiate his contract. Many players had off-season jobs because they couldn't exist on the salaries they made playing sports.

The Bucks were in a contract battle with their starting center who was threatening to hold out unless his monetary demands were met (so what's new?). The player was asking for $35,000. The Club was offering $32,500. Once a contract was agreed to, there was as much chance that it would be written on a restaurant placemat as anything else since there was no Uniform Player Contract. In such an environment the very thought of a book about sports law was unheard of at least, a joke at best.

Today, NBA superstars are paid in excess of $3,500,000 per year plus millions more in endorsements and appearance fees. Sports programming is omnipresent on radio, cable and over-the-air television. Pay-for-view television is a growing reality with direct broadcast-satellite availability just around the corner. Professional sports leagues, the NCAA, the Olympics and even single franchises sign billion dollar television deals. Teams are valued in excess of $200,000,000. Strongly entrenched unions and thriving agency firms battle management over Labor Laws, Antitrust, Medical Malpractice, Trademark Laws and countless other issues. Tort Law, Worker's Compensation, Criminal Law, Equal Protection issues and many other "real world" problems have now become inextricably woven into the fabric of American Sports.

In its new world of sports, Professor Walter Champion's *Sports Law in a Nutshell* is a timely and important addition to the sports law field's burgeoning list of publications. From the nuts and bolts of contract issues and financial considerations, to the hotly contested antitrust arguments absorbing all four major sports leagues, Professor Champion's work gives great insight for the professional involved with major league sports on a day-to-day basis.

Students of sports law will find this work very useful as Professor Champion enlightens us on the full breadth and depth of the field of Sports Law. Tort Law issues for participants, spectators and facilities is a growing area of legal involvement. Worker's Compensation is an increasing burden on professional franchises and a new "gold mine" for plaintiffs' attorneys.

Even the "amateur sports" area does not escape Professor Champion's watchful eye. The old days of college sports as fun and recreation are long gone, replaced by big budgets, TV ratings battles, and daily stories on legal issues outside the playing field. Whether you are interested in eligibility issues like Proposition 48, scholarship issues, Title IX or the "Death Penalty", they are all here in a clear and concise overview with reference cases and citations for more detailed investigation.

All in all, *Sports Law in a Nutshell* is insightful, informative and fun to read for the professional, the student, and the sports fan who wants a better understanding of today's professional and amateur sports world. I intend to use it and hope you do too.

> STEVE PATTERSON
> July, 1992
> Houston, Texas

*

INTRODUCTION TO SECOND EDITION

BY NICK NICHOLS, ESQ.

Abraham, Watkins, Nichols, Sorrels, Matthews & Friend

Sports Law in a Nutshell, the latest edition of Professor Walter Champion's treatise on sports law brings to the education table a valuable publication which covers an enormous territory in every aspect on the subject of sports law.

The numerous subjects covered, provide valuable information and material from a legal standpoint in every area of the modern day sports industry. The legal responsibility of every party involved in the sports field is clearly discussed by Professor Champion with pertinent examples concerning responsibility of sports organizations, participants, spectators, schools, coaches, and referees. Very few modern treatises on sports law today carry the depth and range of the subject matter covered in this publication. The amateur sports arena is portrayed in detail and information on such topics as the "no pass, no play" rule is given attention in this publication. The legal porthole is opened in response to subjects such as defamation, criminal liability and drug testing. This is one of the few treatises in sports law that offers information on the disabled athlete, as well as the power and discipline of the National Collegiate Athletic Association.

For the student with an interest in a future in sports management, valuable information is presented regarding the sports agent, contracts, and pension plans, with explanations on collective bargaining, strikes, lock-outs, arbitration, antitrust, eligibility and mediation.

A panoramic view is given to the legal sports enthusiast with a full cup of sports law topics and information on issues relating to involvement in sports by various participants, spectators, referees, as well as a stable insight into sports facilities. Very few, if any, sports torts topics in the sports legal field are missing in this publication.

Besides playing point for the Rice Owls, my personal journey into sports law began in 1977 when Laker forward Kermit Washington punched Rocket forward Rudy Tomjanovich during a National Basketball Association regular season game. Washington sighted Tomjanovich's red jersey out of the corner of his eye; he pivoted and threw a right-hand punch that literally exploded with Rudy's face. Although he recovered (and led his Rockets as coach to two championships), he had suffered fractures of the nose, jaw, and skull; facial lacerations, a brain concussion, and leakage of spinal fluid from the brain cavity. It was easily the most horrific shot ever fired in a professional basketball game. I have personally forced Professor Champion to sit through a gory tape of the incident on at least 20 occasions. And although a robust lad, Professor Champion still Pavlovianly squirms at the mention of The Punch. I was

Rudy's trial lawyer; the jury awarded an unprecedented $3.3 million on the theory that the Lakers knew or should have known (and then taken steps to prevent) Washington's dangerous tendencies as a self-described enforcer. At the time of the trial, our theory of the case that the Lakers were liable for the actions of their employee, even though it was not a basketball injury per se, was viewed as semi-revolutionary. Now, with *Sports Law in a Nutshell* an established tradition, the once-nascent field of participant injuries has been transformed into a solid brick in the keystone of sports law.

The Second Edition also adds insight to the burgeoning field of sports marketing and intellectual property. Today, the trademark is more recognizable than the event or the athlete; whether it is the Shark's Shark or "Rudy T." or "3–peat" or "March Madness." The insignia is the engine that drives the multi-billion dollar sports marketing phenomenon.

Sports Law in a Nutshell presents an interesting, detailed and thoroughly covered review on all legal aspects of sports law. This could be classified as "required reading" for the sports fan and student, young and old. Professor Champion displays his tenure in the legal sports arena in well-organized and easy-to-read chapters that clearly depict the principal topics in the modern sports field today. The result is great reading material for all those interested in sports law. His excellent research and pertinent case examples further the interest of all readers. As the sports commentator would say "a home run with bases loaded in the bottom of the ninth inning."

NICK C. NICHOLS

Houston, Texas
August 1999

OUTLINE

———

Page

PREFACE -- V
ACKNOWLEDGMENTS --------------------------------- VII
INTRODUCTION TO FIRST EDITION ------------------ IX
INTRODUCTION TO SECOND EDITION -------------- XIII
TABLE OF CASES ------------------------------------- XXVII

Chapter 1. Contracts ----------------------------- 1
A. Formation -- 1
    1. Offer -- 1
    2. Acceptance ------------------------------------ 2
    3. Interpretation -------------------------------- 2
B. Standard Player's Contract-------------------- 3
C. Specialty Clauses ------------------------------- 6
    1. Option -- 6
    2. Reserve --- 7
    3. No–Cut --- 7
D. Collateral Agreements ------------------------- 8
E. Terminations-------------------------------------- 9
F. Assignments-------------------------------------- 9
G. Remedies -- 10
H. Defenses -- 11
    1. Unclean Hands------------------------------- 12
    2. Unconscionability -------------------------- 12
    3. Mutuality ------------------------------------- 13
I. Negotiating the Contract------------------------ 13

OUTLINE

		Page
Chapter 2. Agents		15
A.	Background	15
B.	Standard Representation Agreements	15
C.	Duties	16
D.	Conflicts of Interest	18
E.	Registration of Agents	19
	1. State Legislation	19
	2. Union Regulations	20
	3. NCAA–Based	22
F.	Criminal Liability	23
G.	Representing the Athlete	24
Chapter 3. Financial Considerations		26
A.	Taxation	26
	1. Gross Income	27
	2. Planning	27
B.	Assignment of Income	28
C.	Deferrals	29
	1. By Contract	29
	2. By Pension Plans	29
	3. Substantially Non–Vested Property	31
D.	Tax–Sheltered Investments	32
E.	Incorporation	33
F.	Financial Planning	34
	1. Preservation of Capital	34
	2. Tax Minimization	35
	3. Protection Against Risk	36
	4. Estate Planning	36
Chapter 4. Labor Law		39
A.	National Labor Relations Act	39
B.	Unions and Management	41
C.	Collective Bargaining Generally	44
D.	The Collective Bargaining Agreement	45

		Page
E.	Concerted Actions	45
	1. Strikes	46
	2. Lockouts	46
F.	Arbitration and Mediation	47
	1. Grievance	50
	2. Salary	50
Chapter 5. Antitrust		52
A.	Generally	52
B.	Exemptions	56
	1. Baseball	56
	2. Labor Exemption	57
	3. NFL Exemptions	58
	4. Non–Statutory Labor Exemption	58
C.	Player Restraints	61
D.	Franchise Movement	62
E.	League Versus League	64
F.	TV Packaging	65
G.	Cable TV	66
H.	Amateur Sports	68
I.	Miscellaneous	69
Chapter 6. Torts		71
A.	Negligence	71
	1. Duty of Care	72
	2. Standard of Care	72
	3. Breach of Duty	73
	4. Proximate Cause	74
	5. Damages	74
B.	Medical Malpractice	75
	1. Duty of Care	76
	2. Duty to Disclose and Informed Consent	77
	3. Fraudulent Concealment	79
	4. Team Physicians	82
	5. Failure to Refer and Vicarious Liability	86

Page

C. Product's Liability 87
D. Strict Liability 88
E. Warranty Liability 89
F. Facility Liability 90
   1. Status of Injured Party 90
   2. Invitees 91
   3. Minors 92
   4. Unreasonably Hazardous Conditions 93
   5. Design, Construction, Maintenance and
       Repair 93
G. Professional Sports 94

Chapter 7. Participant Injuries 95
A. Generally 95
B. Violation of Safety Rules 97
C. Unsportsmanlike Conduct 98
D. Professional Sports 99
E. Contact Sports 100
F. Third Persons 101

Chapter 8. Spectator Injuries 104
A. Generally 104
B. Baseball 105
C. Golf 108
D. Hockey, Car Races and Wrestling 109
E. Minors 111
F. Facilities 113

Chapter 9. School Liability 115
A. Negligence 115
B. Vicarious Liability 117

		Page
C.	Failure to Warn	118
D.	Failure to Instruct	118
E.	Failure to Hire Competent Coaches	118
F.	Failure to Properly Supervise	119
G.	Failure to Maintain Equipment and Facilities	120

Chapter 10. Coach Liability		122
A.	Generally	122
B.	Qualifications	125
C.	Preparation of Participants	128
D.	Supervision	132

Chapter 11. Referee Liability		134
A.	Duty to Enforce Rules	135
B.	Duty to Protect Participants	136
C.	Duty to Warn	136
D.	Anticipating Reasonably Foreseeable Dangers	137
E.	Failure to Control Game	138

Chapter 12. Defamation		140
A.	Sportswriters	140
B.	Per se	141
C.	Public Figures	143
D.	Rule of Repose	148
E.	Invasion of Privacy	149
F.	Defenses	151

Chapter 13. Tort Defenses		156
A.	Generally	156
B.	Assumption of Risk	156
	1. Expressed	159
	2. Implied	160

Page

B. Assumption of Risk—Continued
   3. Jockeys and Car Racers 161
   4. Skiing, Golf and Baseball 163
   5. Minors 166
C. Contributory Negligence 166
D. Comparative Negligence 169
E. Warnings 170
F. Waivers 171
   1. Foot Races 174
   2. Car Races 176
   3. Minors 177
G. Sovereign Immunity 178
   1. Discretionary Acts 181
   2. Policy Considerations 183
H. Charitable Immunity 184
I. Recreational Use Statutes 185

Chapter 14. Workers' Compensation 186
A. Professional Sports 186
B. Collegiate Sports 189
C. Employer–Based Sports 189
D. Non–Participants 191

Chapter 15. Criminal Liability 193
A. Violence in Sports 193
B. Criminal Action Generally 195
C. Inherently Violent Sports 196
D. Battery 198
E. The Canadian Approach 199

Chapter 16. Amateur Sports 201
A. Generally 201
B. Administration 201

Page

C. Status of Athlete 202
D. Rule-making 203
E. NCAA 204

Chapter 17. Eligibility 207
A. Generally 207
B. Scope of Eligibility Rules 207
C. Participation as a Right or Privilege 208
D. State Actors 211
E. Due Process and Equal Protection 213
F. Types of Rules 216
    1. Red Shirting 216
    2. No Transfer Rules 217
    3. Anti-marriage 218
    4. "No-agent" Rule 219
G. Proposition 48 and Progeny 221
H. No Pass, No Play Statutes 223

Chapter 18. The Disabled Athlete 227
A. Generally 227
B. Eligibility to Participate 228
C. Section 504 of the Rehabilitation Act 231
D. Americans With Disabilities Act 233

Chapter 19. College Scholarships 236
A. The Nature of Scholarships 236
B. Scholarships as Contracts 238
C. Workers' Compensation 242
D. Taxation 244
E. Employee Status 246

Chapter 20. International Sports 248
A. Olympics 248
B. Amateur Sports Act of 1978 249

Page

C. Boycotts... 252
D. Drug Testing 253

Chapter 21. Discipline and Penalties...... 256
A. Power to Discipline and Penalize General-
    ly 256
B. NCAA... 257
    1. Power to Sanction......................... 257
    2. Death Penalty 258
C. High School Sports 259
D. Professional Sports........................... 260

Chapter 22. Drug Testing 263
A. Generally 263
B. Professional Sports........................... 263
C. Amateur Sports 265
D. Right of Privacy 268
E. Reasonableness of Search 269
F. Due Process and Equal Protection 270

Chapter 23. Sex Discrimination 272
A. Discrimination Generally 272
B. Separate but Equal........................... 274
C. Contact and Non-contact Sports 275
D. Title IX... 276
    1. Application 277
    2. Grove City and Civil Rights Restoration
       Act of 1987 278
E. Equal Protection 281
F. State ERA's...................................... 284

Chapter 24. Intellectual Property............ 286
A. Generally 286
B. The Nature of Marketing 286

OUTLINE

	Page
C. Athletes as Entertainers	287
D. Patents	288
E. Copyrights	289
F. Trademarks	290
G. Trade Dress	293
Appendices	295
INDEX	403

*

TABLE OF CASES

References are to Pages

Akins v. Glens Falls City School Dist., 441 N.Y.S.2d 644, 424 N.E.2d 531 (N.Y.1981), *92*

Alabama Football, Inc. v. Greenwood, 452 F.Supp. 1191 (W.D.Pa. 1978), *6*

Alabama Football, Inc. v. Stabler, 294 Ala. 551, 319 So.2d 678 (Ala.1975), *6*

Ali v. Playgirl, Inc., 447 F.Supp. 723 (S.D.N.Y.1978), *150*

American Football League v. National Football League, 323 F.2d 124 (4th Cir.1963), *64*

American League of Professional Baseball Clubs, 180 N.L.R.B. 190 (1969), *39*

Arnold v. City of Cedar Rapids, 443 N.W.2d 332 (Iowa 1989), *107*

Ashcroft v. Calder Race Course, Inc., 492 So.2d 1309 (Fla.1986), *162*

Associated Students, Inc. of California State University–Sacramento v. National Collegiate Athletic Ass'n, 493 F.2d 1251 (9th Cir.1974), *221*

Atlanta, City of v. Merritt, 172 Ga.App. 470, 323 S.E.2d 680 (Ga.App.1984), *92, 112*

Averill v. Luttrell, 44 Tenn.App. 56, 311 S.W.2d 812 (Tenn. Ct. App.1957), *95*

Bailey v. Truby, 174 W.Va. 8, 321 S.E.2d 302 (W.Va.1984), *225*

Baker v. Mid Maine Medical Center, 499 A.2d 464 (Me.1985), *109*

Banks v. National Collegiate Athletic Ass'n, 746 F.Supp. 850 (N.D.Ind.1990), *219*

Bartmess, State ex rel. v. Board of Trustees of School Dist. No. 1, 223 Mont. 269, 726 P.2d 801 (Mont.1986), *224*

Bayless v. Philadelphia Nat. League Club, 472 F.Supp. 625 (E.D.Pa.1979), *188*

Begley v. Corporation of Mercer University, 367 F.Supp. 908 (E.D.Tenn.1973), *239, 240, 243*

Bell v. Lone Oak Independent School Dist., 507 S.W.2d 636 (Tex.Civ.App.–Texarkana 1974), set aside and cause dismissed on other grounds Lone Oak Independent School Dist. v. Bell, 515 S.W.2d 252 (Tex.1974), *214, 219*

Blair v. Washington State University, 108 Wash.2d 558, 740 P.2d 1379 (Wash.1987), *285*

Blancher v. Metropolitan Dade County, 436 So.2d 1077 (Fla.App. 3 Dist.1983), *94, 103*

Board of Trustees of School Dist. No. 1, State ex rel. Bartmess, 223 Mont. 269, 726 P.2d 801 (Mont.1986), *224*

Board of Trustees of University of Arkansas v. Professional Therapy Services, Inc., 873 F.Supp. 1280 (W.D.Ark.1995), *292*

Bourque v. Duplechin, 331 So.2d 40 (La.App. 3 Cir.1976), *95, 98, 157*

Boyd v. Board of Directors of McGehee School Dist. No. 17, 612 F.Supp. 86 (E.D.Ark.1985), *210*

Brahatcek v. Millard School Dist., School Dist. No. 17, 202 Neb. 86, 273 N.W.2d 680 (Neb.1979), *127*

Brenden v. Independent School Dist. 742, 342 F.Supp. 1224 (D.Minn.1972), affirmed 477 F.2d 1292 (8th Cir.1973), *282*

Brewer v. Memphis Pub. Co., Inc., 626 F.2d 1238 (5th Cir.1980), *146*

Brooks v. Paige, 773 P.2d 1098 (Colo.App.1988), *141*

Brosko v. Hetherington, 16 Pa. D. & C. 761 (Pa.Com.Pl.1931), *111*

Carabba v. Anacortes School Dist. No. 103, 72 Wash.2d 939, 435 P.2d 936 (Wash.1967), *102, 119, 135, 137, 138*

Centennial Turf Club, Inc., 192 N.L.R.B. 698 (1971), *40*

Churilla v. School Dist. for City of East Detroit, 105 Mich.App. 32, 306 N.W.2d 381 (Mich.App.1981), *181*

Chuy v. Philadelphia Eagles Football Club, 595 F.2d 1265 (3rd Cir.1979), *146*

Chuy v. Philadelphia Eagles Football Club, 431 F.Supp. 254 (E.D.Pa.1977), affirmed 595 F.2d 1265 (3rd Cir.1979), *85*

City of (see name of city)

Clark v. Goshen Sunday Morning Softball League, 129 Misc.2d 401, 493 N.Y.S.2d 262 (N.Y.Sup.1985), affirmed 122 A.D.2d 769, 505 N.Y.S.2d 655 (N.Y.A.D. 2 Dept.1986), *107*

Colorado Seminary (University of Denver) v. National Collegiate Athletic Ass'n, 570 F.2d 320 (10th Cir.1978), *209*

Connecticut Professional Sports Corp. v. Heyman, 276 F.Supp. 618 (S.D.N.Y.1967), *12*

Craig v. Boren, 429 U.S. 190, 97 S.Ct. 451, 50 L.Ed.2d 397 (1976), *282*

Crocker v. Tennessee Secondary School Athletic Ass'n, 735 F.Supp. 753 (M.D.Tenn.1990), *230*

Crocker v. Tennessee Secondary School Athletic Ass'n, 873 F.2d 933 (6th Cir.1989), *230*

Cureton v. National Collegiate Athletic Ass'n, 1999 WL 118667 (E.D.Pa.1999), *222*

DeFrantz v. United States Olympic Committee, 492 F.Supp. 1181 (D.D.C.1980), *253*

Dempsey v. Time Inc., 43 Misc.2d 754, 252 N.Y.S.2d 186 (N.Y.Sup.1964), affirmed 22 A.D.2d 854, 254 N.Y.S.2d 80 (N.Y.A.D. 1 Dept.1964), *148*

Dent v. Texas Rangers, Ltd., 764 S.W.2d 345 (Tex.App.–Fort Worth 1989), *107*

Detroit Football Co. v. Robinson, 186 F.Supp. 933 (E.D.La.1960), affirmed 283 F.2d 657 (5th Cir.1960), *1*

Detroit Lions, Inc. v. Argovitz, 580 F.Supp. 542 (E.D.Mich.1984), *16, 18*

Dimeo v. Griffin, 924 F.2d 664 (7th Cir.1991), *264*

Dodson v. Arkansas Activities Ass'n, 468 F.Supp. 394 (E.D.Ark. 1979), *282*

Doe v. Marshall, 459 F.Supp. 1190 (S.D.Tex.1978), vacated 622 F.2d 118 (5th Cir.1980), *233*

Doyle v. Bowdoin College, 403 A.2d 1206 (Me.1979), *178*

Duffy v. Midlothian Country Club, 135 Ill.App.3d 429, 90 Ill.Dec. 237, 481 N.E.2d 1037 (Ill.App. 1 Dist.1985), *108*

Everett v. Bucky Warren, Inc., 376 Mass. 280, 380 N.E.2d 653 (Mass.1978), *89, 125, 126*

Fagan v. Summers, 498 P.2d 1227 (Wyo.1972), *119*

Falls v. Sporting News Pub. Co., 834 F.2d 611 (6th Cir.1987), *153, 155*

Fawcett Publications, Inc. v. Morris, 377 P.2d 42 (Okla.1962), *142*

Federal Base Ball Club of Baltimore v. National League of Professional Baseball Clubs, 259 U.S. 200, 42 S.Ct. 465, 66 L.Ed. 898 (1922), *39, 57*

Fila U.S.A., Inc. v. Kim, 884 F.Supp. 491 (S.D.Fla.1995), *292*

Flood v. Kuhn, 407 U.S. 258, 92 S.Ct. 2099, 32 L.Ed.2d 728 (1972), *56, 57*

Florida High School Activities Ass'n, Inc. v. Bradshaw, 369 So.2d 398 (Fla.App. 2 Dist.1979), *212*

Friedman v. Houston Sports Ass'n, 731 S.W.2d 572 (Tex.App.–Hous. (1 Dist.) 1987), *113, 171*

Gary v. Party Time Co., Inc., 434 So.2d 338 (Fla.App. 3 Dist. 1983), *169*

Gaspard v. Grain Dealers Mut. Ins. Co., 131 So.2d 831 (La.App. 3 Cir.1961), *96, 166*

Gertz v. Robert Welch, Inc., 418 U.S. 323, 94 S.Ct. 2997, 41 L.Ed.2d 789 (1974), *154*

Green, Regina v., 16 D.L.R.3d 137 (1970), *200*

Griffin High School v. Illinois High School Ass'n, 822 F.2d 671 (7th Cir.1987), *212*

Griggas v. Clauson, 6 Ill.App.2d 412, 128 N.E.2d 363 (Ill.App. 2 Dist.1955), *95*

Grisim v. TapeMark Charity Pro–Am Golf Tournament, 394 N.W.2d 261 (Minn.App.1986), reversed 415 N.W.2d 874 (Minn.1987), *108*

Grove City College v. Bell, 687 F.2d 684 (3rd Cir.1982), affirmed 465 U.S. 555, 104 S.Ct. 1211, 79 L.Ed.2d 516 (1984), *279, 280*

Grube v. Bethlehem Area School Dist., 550 F.Supp. 418 (E.D.Pa. 1982), *228, 231*

Gulf South Conference v. Boyd, 369 So.2d 553 (Ala.1979), *209, 240*

Hackbart v. Cincinnati Bengals, Inc., 435 F.Supp. 352 (D.Colo. 1977), reversed 601 F.2d 516 (10th Cir.1979), *99*

Haffer v. Temple University, 524 F.Supp. 531 (E.D.Pa.1981), affirmed and remanded 688 F.2d 14 (3rd Cir.1982), modified 678 F.Supp. 517 (E.D.Pa.1987), *280*

Hall v. University of Minnesota, 530 F.Supp. 104 (D.Minn.1982), *209*

Hampton v. Orleans Parish School Bd., 422 So.2d 202 (La.App. 4 Cir.1982), *120*

Hemphill v. Sayers, 552 F.Supp. 685 (S.D.Ill.1982), *129*

Hennigan v. Chargers Football Co., 431 F.2d 308 (5th Cir.1970), *7*

Hill v. National Collegiate Athletic Assn. (Hill II), 26 Cal.Rptr.2d 834, 865 P.2d 633 (Cal.1994), *266, 269*

Hill v. National Collegiate Athletic Ass'n (Hill I), 230 Cal.App.3d 1714, 273 Cal.Rptr. 402 (Cal.App. 6 Dist.1990), review granted, opinion superseded 276 Cal.Rptr. 319, 801 P.2d 1070 (Cal.1990), *266, 268*

Home Box Office v. Champs of New Haven, Inc., 837 F.Supp. 480 (D.Conn.1993), *289*

Indianapolis Colts, Inc. v. Metropolitan Baltimore Football Club Ltd. Partnership., 34 F.3d 410 (7th Cir.1994), *292*

In re (see name of party)

Johnson v. Green Bay Packers, 272 Wis. 149, 74 N.W.2d 784 (Wis.1956), *4*

Johnston v. Time, Inc., 321 F.Supp. 837 (M.D.N.C.1970), affirmed in part, vacated in part Time, Inc. v. Johnston, 448 F.2d 378 (4th Cir.1971), *148*

Jones v. Three Rivers Management Corp., 483 Pa. 75, 394 A.2d 546 (Pa.1978), *106, 166*

Kabella v. Bouschelle, 100 N.M. 461, 672 P.2d 290 (N.M.App. 1983), *100*

Kampmeier v. Nyquist, 553 F.2d 296 (2nd Cir.1977), *229*

Kansas City Royals Baseball Corp. v. Major League Baseball Players Ass'n, 532 F.2d 615 (8th Cir.1976), *47*

Keller v. Mols, 156 Ill.App.3d 235, 108 Ill.Dec. 888, 509 N.E.2d 584 (Ill.App. 1 Dist.1987), *96, 101*

Kircos v. Goodyear Tire and Rubber Co., 108 Mich.App. 781, 311 N.W.2d 139 (Mich.App.1981), *177*

Kite v. Marshall, 661 F.2d 1027 (5th Cir.1981), *214*

Kleinknecht v. Gettysburg College, 989 F.2d 1360 (3rd Cir.1993), *72*

Krueger v. San Francisco Forty Niners, 234 Cal.Rptr. 579 (1987), *79*

Laing v. Minnesota Vikings Football Club, Inc., 372 F.Supp. 59 (D.Minn.1973), *69*

Leavell v. Commissioner, 104 T.C. 140 (1995), *34*

Los Angeles Memorial Coliseum Com'n v. National Football League, 726 F.2d 1381 (9th Cir.1984), *55, 63*

Los Angeles Rams Football Club v. Cannon, 185 F.Supp. 717 (S.D.Cal.1960), *1*

Mackey v. National Football League, 543 F.2d 606 (8th Cir.1976), modifying info. 407 F.Supp. 1000 (D.Minn.1975), *54, 55, 59*

Maki, Regina v., 14 D.L.R.3d 164 (1970), *200*

Martin v. PGA Tour, Inc., 994 F.Supp. 1242 (D.Or.1998), *234*

McCourt v. California Sports, Inc., 600 F.2d 1193 (6th Cir.1979), *60*

Milkovich v. Lorain Journal Co., 497 U.S. 1, 110 S.Ct. 2695, 111 L.Ed.2d 1 (1990), *141*

Minnesota Muskies, Inc. v. Hudson, 294 F.Supp. 979 (M.D.N.C. 1969), *8, 12*

Mogabgab v. Orleans Parish School Bd., 239 So.2d 456 (La.App. 4 Cir.1970), *122*

Molinas v. National Basketball Ass'n, 190 F.Supp. 241 (S.D.N.Y. 1961), *5, 262*

Molinas v. Podoloff, 133 N.Y.S.2d 743 (N.Y.Sup.1954), *5, 262*

Munchak Corp. v. Cunningham, 457 F.2d 721 (4th Cir.1972), *8*

Munday v. Churchill Downs, Inc., 600 S.W.2d 487 (Ky.App.1980), *187*

Murphy v. Steeplechase Amusement Co., 250 N.Y. 479, 166 N.E. 173 (N.Y.1929), *71*

Nabozny v. Barnhill, 31 Ill.App.3d 212, 334 N.E.2d 258 (Ill.App. 1 Dist.1975), *72, 95, 97, 98, 157*

National Basketball Ass'n v. Motorola, Inc., 105 F.3d 841 (2nd Cir.1997), *290*

National Collegiate Athletic Ass'n v. Board of Regents of University of Oklahoma, 468 U.S. 85, 104 S.Ct. 2948, 82 L.Ed.2d 70 (1984), *55, 65, 66, 67*

National Collegiate Athletic Ass'n v. Tarkanian, 488 U.S. 179, 109 S.Ct. 454, 102 L.Ed.2d 469 (1988), *211, 257, 270*

National Football League v. Governor of Delaware, 435 F.Supp. 1372 (D.Del.1977), *70*

National Football League v. Rondor, Inc., 840 F.Supp. 1160 (N.D.Ohio 1993), *289*

National Football League Management Council, 203 N.L.R.B. 165 (1973), *40*

National Football League Players Ass'n v. N.L.R.B., 503 F.2d 12 (8th Cir.1974), *43*

National Football League Properties, Inc. v. Wichita Falls Sportswear, Inc., 532 F.Supp. 651 (W.D.Wash.1982), *291*

Neeld v. National Hockey League, 594 F.2d 1297 (9th Cir.1979), *231*

New York Football Giants, Inc. v. Los Angeles Chargers Football Club, Inc., 291 F.2d 471 (5th Cir.1961), *12*

New York Times Co. v. Sullivan, 376 U.S. 254, 84 S.Ct. 710, 11 L.Ed.2d 686 (1964), *146, 148, 149, 152*

Niemczyk v. Burleson, 538 S.W.2d 737 (Mo.App.1976), *96*

North American Soccer League v. National Football League, 505 F.Supp. 659 (S.D.N.Y.1980), affirmed in part, reversed in part 670 F.2d 1249 (2nd Cir.1982), *69*

North American Soccer League v. N.L.R.B., 613 F.2d 1379 (5th Cir.1980), *42*

Novak v. Lamar Ins. Co., 488 So.2d 739 (La.App. 2 Cir.1986), *96*

Nussbaumer v. Time, Inc., 1986 WL 12640 (Ohio App. 8 Dist. 1986), *146, 147, 151*

Nydegger v. Don Bosco Preparatory High School, 202 N.J.Super. 535, 495 A.2d 485 (N.J.Super.L.1985), *132*

O'Halloran v. University of Washington, 679 F.Supp. 997 (W.D.Wash.1988), *266*

Ordway v. Superior Court, 198 Cal.App.3d 98, 243 Cal.Rptr. 536 (Cal.App. 4 Dist.1988), *161*

Oswald v. Township High School Dist. No. 214, 84 Ill.App.3d 723, 40 Ill.Dec. 456, 406 N.E.2d 157 (Ill.App. 1 Dist.1980), *98*

Outlaw v. Bituminous Ins. Co., 357 So.2d 1350 (La.App. 4 Cir.1978), *169*

Palmer v. Kansas City Chiefs Football Club, 621 S.W.2d 350 (Mo.App. W.D.1981), *188*

Pape v. State, 90 A.D.2d 904, 456 N.Y.S.2d 863 (N.Y.A.D. 3 Dept.1982), *135, 136*

Pasquel v. Owen, 186 F.2d 263 (8th Cir.1950), *2*

Pebble Beach Co. v. Tour 18, Ltd., 942 F.Supp. 1513 (S.D.Tex. 1996), *293*

Philadelphia Ball Club v. Lajoie, 202 Pa. 210, 51 A. 973 (Pa. 1902), *4, 10*

Piazza v. Major League Baseball, 831 F.Supp. 420 (E.D.Pa.1993), *57*

Poole v. South Plainfield Bd. of Ed., 490 F.Supp. 948 (D.N.J. 1980), *229, 231*

Powell v. National Football League, 888 F.2d 559 (8th Cir.1989), *60*

Radovich v. National Football League, 353 U.S. 931, 77 S.Ct. 716, 1 L.Ed.2d 724 (1957), *64*

Radovich v. National Football League, 352 U.S. 445, 77 S.Ct. 390, 1 L.Ed.2d 456 (1957), *57*

Regents of University of California v. American Broadcasting Companies, Inc., 747 F.2d 511 (9th Cir.1984), *66*

Regina v. _____ (see opposing party)

Rensing v. Indiana State University Bd. of Trustees, 444 N.E.2d 1170 (Ind.1983), *241, 242, 243, 244, 247*

Rensing v. Indiana State University Bd. of Trustees, 437 N.E.2d 78 (Ind.App. 4 Dist.1982), vacated 444 N.E.2d 1170 (Ind. 1983), *241, 242, 243, 244*

Robillard v. P & R Racetracks, Inc., 405 So.2d 1203 (La.App. 1 Cir.1981), *163*

Rosen v. LTV Recreational Development, Inc., 569 F.2d 1117 (10th Cir.1978), *171*

Salerno v. American League of Professional Baseball Clubs, 429 F.2d 1003 (2nd Cir.1970), *57*

San Francisco Seals, Ltd. v. National Hockey League, 379 F.Supp. 966 (C.D.Cal.1974), *63*

Schaill v. Tippecanoe County School Corp., 864 F.2d 1309 (7th Cir.1988), *267, 268*

Schaill v. Tippecanoe County School Corp., 679 F.Supp. 833 (N.D.Ind.1988), affirmed 864 F.2d 1309 (7th Cir.1988), *212, 271*

Scheff v. Homestretch, Inc., 60 Ill.App.3d 424, 18 Ill.Dec. 152, 377 N.E.2d 305 (Ill.App. 3 Dist.1978), *174*

Schentzel v. Philadelphia Nat. League Club, 173 Pa.Super. 179, 96 A.2d 181 (Pa.Super.1953), *105*

Schwilm v. Pennsylvania Sports, 84 Pa. D. & C. 603 (Pa.Com.Pl. 1952), *110*

Score Group, Inc. v. Dad's Kid Corp., In re, 1994 WL 794773 (C.D.Cal.1994), *290*

Scott v. News–Herald, 25 Ohio St.3d 243, 496 N.E.2d 699 (Ohio 1986), *149, 152*

Scott v. W.C.A.B. (Packaging Corp. of America), 113 Pa.Cmwlth. 80, 536 A.2d 492 (Pa.Cmwlth.1988), *191*

Seal–Flex, Inc. v. Athletic Track and Court Const., 870 F.Supp. 753 (E.D.Mich.1994), *290*

Seymour v. New Bremen Speedway, Inc., 31 Ohio App.2d 141, 287 N.E.2d 111, 60 O.O.2d 236 (Ohio App. 3 Dist.1971), *163, 177*

Shoemaker v. Handel, 795 F.2d 1136 (3rd Cir.1986), *264, 269*

Shubert, United States v., 348 U.S. 222, 75 S.Ct. 277, 99 L.Ed. 279 (1955), *57*

Smith v. Pro Football, Inc., 593 F.2d 1173, 193 U.S.App.D.C. 19 (D.C.Cir.1978), *61*

Southeastern Community College v. Davis, 442 U.S. 397, 99 S.Ct. 2361, 60 L.Ed.2d 980 (1979), *229*

Spahn v. Julian Messner, Inc., 274 N.Y.S.2d 877, 221 N.E.2d 543 (N.Y.1966), vacated Julian Messner, Inc. v. Spahn, 387 U.S. 239, 87 S.Ct. 1706, 18 L.Ed.2d 744 (1967), *150*

Sports Authority, Inc. v. Prime Hospitality Corp., 877 F.Supp. 124 (S.D.N.Y.1995), *292*

Spring Branch I.S.D. v. Stamos, 695 S.W.2d 556 (Tex.1985), *210, 215, 224*

State Compensation Ins. Fund v. Industrial Com'n, 135 Colo. 570, 314 P.2d 288 (Colo.1957), *243*

State ex rel. v. _____ (see opposing party and relator)

Stehn v. Bernard McFadden Foundations (1959), *126*

Stepien v. Franklin, 39 Ohio App.3d 47, 528 N.E.2d 1324 (Ohio App. 8 Dist.1988), *152*

Sullivan v. University Interscholastic League, 616 S.W.2d 170 (Tex.1981), *215, 218*

Tavernier v. Maes, 242 Cal.App.2d 532, 51 Cal.Rptr. 575 (Cal. App. 1 Dist.1966), *96*

Taylor v. Wake Forest University, 16 N.C.App. 117, 191 S.E.2d 379 (N.C.App.1972), cert. denied 282 N.C. 307, 192 S.E.2d 197 (N.C.1972), *239, 243, 244*

Taylor Made Golf Co., Inc. v. Carsten Sports, Ltd., 175 F.R.D. 658 (S.D.Cal.1997), *293*

Taylor Made Golf Co., Inc. v. Trend Precision Golf, Inc., 903 F.Supp. 1506 (M.D.Fla.1995), *294*

Thomas v. Barlow, 5 N.J. Misc. 764, 138 A. 208 (N.J.Sup.1927), *96*

Thomas v. Chicago Bd. of Ed., 77 Ill.2d 165, 32 Ill.Dec. 308, 395 N.E.2d 538 (Ill.1979), *130*

Three Blind Mice Designs Co., Inc. v. Cyrk, Inc., 892 F.Supp. 303 (D.Mass.1995), *292*

Tiemann v. Independent School Dist. # 740, 331 N.W.2d 250 (Minn.1983), *121*

Tiffany v. Arizona Interscholastic Ass'n, Inc., 151 Ariz. 134, 726 P.2d 231 (Ariz.App. Div. 1 1986), *210, 216*

Tillman v. New Orleans Saints Football Club, 265 So.2d 284 (La.App. 4 Cir.1972), *5*

Time, Inc. v. Firestone, 424 U.S. 448, 96 S.Ct. 958, 47 L.Ed.2d 154 (1976), *146*

Time Warner Sports Merchandising v. Chicagoland Processing Corp., 1995 WL 107145 (N.D.Ill.1995), *292*

Toolson v. New York Yankees, Inc., 346 U.S. 356, 74 S.Ct. 78, 98 L.Ed. 64 (1953), *57*

Toone v. Adams, 262 N.C. 403, 137 S.E.2d 132 (N.C.1964), *102*

Tose v. First Pennsylvania Bank, N.A., 648 F.2d 879 (3rd Cir. 1981), *70*

United States v. _____ (see opposing party)

United States Football League v. National Football League, 644 F.Supp. 1040 (S.D.N.Y.1986), affirmed 842 F.2d 1335 (2nd Cir.1988), and related reference 704 F.Supp. 474 (S.D.N.Y. 1989), *65*

University of Denver v. Nemeth, 127 Colo. 385, 257 P.2d 423 (Colo.1953), *243, 247*

University of Pittsburgh v. Champion Products Inc., 686 F.2d 1040 (3rd Cir.1982), *291*

Van Horn v. Industrial Accident Commission, 219 Cal.App.2d 457, 33 Cal.Rptr. 169 (Cal.App. 2 Dist.1963), *243*

Vendrell v. School Dist. No. 26C, Malheur County, 233 Or. 1, 376 P.2d 406 (Or.1962), *128, 129*

Vernonia School Dist. 47J v. Acton, 515 U.S. 646, 115 S.Ct. 2386, 132 L.Ed.2d 564 (1995), *269, 271*

TABLE OF CASES

Wagenblast v. Odessa School Dist. No. 105–157–166J, 110 Wash.2d 845, 758 P.2d 968 (Wash.1988), *174*

Walters, United States v., 711 F.Supp. 1435 (N.D.Ill.1989), *68*

Welch v. Dunsmuir Joint Union High School District, 326 P.2d 633 (Cal.App. 3 Dist.1958), *86*

Whitfield v. Cox, 189 Va. 219, 52 S.E.2d 72 (Va.1949), *111*

Wilkinson v. Hartford Acc. and Indem. Co., 411 So.2d 22 (La. 1982), *93, 132*

Williams v. Cox Enterprises, Inc., 159 Ga.App. 333, 283 S.E.2d 367 (Ga.App.1981), *175*

Wood v. National Basketball Ass'n, 602 F.Supp. 525 (S.D.N.Y. 1984), affirmed 809 F.2d 954 (2nd Cir.1987), *53, 55, 61*

Woodson v. Irvington Board of Education (1987), *124*

Woy v. Turner, 573 F.Supp. 35 (N.D.Ga.1983), *146*

Wright v. Columbia University, 520 F.Supp. 789 (E.D.Pa.1981), *232*

Yonkers Raceway, Inc., 196 N.L.R.B. 373 (1972), *40*

Zacchini v. Scripps–Howard Broadcasting Co., 433 U.S. 562, 97 S.Ct. 2849, 53 L.Ed.2d 965, 5 O.O.3d 215 (1977), *151*

Zinn v. Parrish, 461 F.Supp. 11 (N.D.Ill.1977), reversed 582 F.2d 1282 (7th Cir.1978), appeal after remand 644 F.2d 360 (7th Cir.1981), *15, 17*

*

SPORTS LAW
IN A NUTSHELL
SECOND EDITION

*

CHAPTER 1

CONTRACTS

A. FORMATION

A valid contract is formed only if both parties intend the act of signing to be the last act in the formation of a binding contract. In evaluating contract validity, first identify the offeror and the offeree and then ascertain whether there was a proper acceptance. If the player's response includes a variance, it is a counter-offer.

In earlier versions of the contract between players and management, the wording of the contract was such that the commissioner's signature in approving the agreement was a condition precedent to the formation of a binding contract. Without that approval the player's signature was merely a counter-offer. The failure to obtain the commissioner's signature was deemed a material breach of the agreement pursuant to the contractual language of the contract. *Los Angeles Rams v. Cannon* (1960). Without the commissioner's signature, the player's signing was merely a revocable offer. *Detroit Football Co. v. Robinson* (1960).

1. Offer

A player's contract is drafted by the team, and it is the team that seeks out the services of the player.

The team makes the offer and the player expresses his acceptance by signing the contract. However, if the signing is not accompanied by consideration and a withdrawal is advanced to the team before an acceptance then the signing is an authentication of a revocable offer as opposed to the formation of a binding contract. It is the intent of the parties that will determine this conflict.

2. Acceptance

The problem that arises with an acceptance is the timeliness of the alleged acceptance. Acceptance is indicated by any showing that expresses the player's willingness to be bound by the offer's exact terms.

3. Interpretation

In determining the meaning of an indefinite or ambiguous term in a contract, the language should be read in light of all the surrounding circumstances. The interpretation that is placed on a contract by the parties prior to the time that it becomes a matter of controversy is entitled to great, if not controlling influence in ascertaining the intent and understanding of the parties.

In *Pasquel v. Owen* (1950), the ambiguous term in question was "player-manager." The defendant, Mickey Owen, a major league baseball player, abandoned his contract to play baseball in the Mexican League when he was relieved of his duties as manager but still continued as a player. The question is whether the removal of Owen as either a player or a manager constituted a breach of contract by one party that was of such a character as to warrant abandonment of the contract by the other party. But to permit abandonment, the failure to perform by the defaulting party must go to the substance of the contract. In this case, although the contract referred to defendant as a "player-manager," it did not indicate at what time he was to function as either a player or a manager or both. Therefore, the act of relieving Owen as a manager but continuing to pay his whole salary resulted in no financial loss to the player and thus did not constitute a breach of contract sufficient to warrant the player's abandonment of the contract.

B. STANDARD PLAYER'S CONTRACT

Contracts in sports define the rights and responsibilities of the various participants in the business of professional sports. The so-called Standard Player's Contract (SPK) (see Appendix), is an employment contract which specifies the player's rights. The SPK will state that the player has unique skills and that the team will control the activities of the player.

The average player has little job security. For him the SPK is a contract of adhesion. However, the SPK can be modified if that particular player has "juice". "Juice" is the ability to write your own ticket based on unique skills or rampant popularity (e.g., Michael Jordan). Sammy Sosa or Mark

McGuire has juice; Bobby Nobody, a free agent from Slippery Rock, does not. The more juice a player possesses, the greater his ability to modify his SPK by attaching standard modifications such as no-cut, no-trade or attendance clauses. Management will usually not give their players anything.

The SPK can be modified through collateral agreements, e.g., the incorporation of the collective bargaining agreement (c.b.a.) and the League's By-Laws and Constitution into the contract.

The parol evidence rule is incorporated into the SPK. If the agreement is written and it is their final expression then the contract as it stands cannot be modified by other agreements or promises. In the interpretation of ambiguous terms, the contract will be interpreted against the writer of the contract. Handwritten provisions will prevail over printed provisions. *Johnson v. Green Bay Packers, Inc.* (1956).

The club's responsibility for liability for injuries is limited by the terms of the SPK.

There is no right by the team to demand performance of a player for a player's non-performance as exhibited by his jumping to another team, however, they can obtain equitable performance by way of injunctive relief through a contractual clause. *Philadelphia Ball Club v. Lajoie* (1902).

The SPK calls for annual physical examinations. In these examinations, the club can ascertain if the player suffered an off-season injury. If a player passes this examination, then the club cannot later claim that a current (under contract) injury is a result of a previous (non-contract) injury. *Tilman v. New Orleans Saints* (1972). The player further promises to be in "good physical condition" and to swear "loyalty" to the club.

The SPK includes a termination clause which gives the team the right to terminate the athlete's contract. The termination must be "for cause," but "for cause" could be simply that the employee no longer fits the team's needs. There is also a no-tampering clause which avers that one player cannot attempt to entice another employee to enter negotiations with another club while under contract to a different team. The SPK demands that a copy of the contract must be filed by the team with the office of the league's commissioner within 48 hours of the execution of the contract. The wording of current SPKs contain language such that the filing of a copy is merely a condition precedent to the execution of the contract.

The SPK further provides that the Commissioner possesses the ability to fine players for infractions of league rules. The Commissioner, in his sole discretion, can expel a player for gambling on a game's outcome if the player is a participant in that game. *Molinas v. National Basketball Association* (1961) and *Molinas v. Podoloff* (1954).

The SPK merges all the peculiarities of contract formation into one document that must be signed before an athlete can participate. The SPK, since it is drawn by the team, is drawn in their favor and, therefore, if ambiguities arise, they are interpreted against the team. However, since the particular wording of each SPK is essential, it must be carefully read and completely understood.

C. SPECIALTY CLAUSES

The more juice a player possesses, the more specialty clauses he can add to his SPK so as to enhance it. This is where negotiation skills come in handy; negotiation-wise, the SPK is a dead issue.

The preeminent specialty clause is the signing bonus. To secure this bonus, a player at a minimum, must appear in training camp in good shape and ready to play. It is not considered salary. The employee may receive it for merely signing and not actually playing. If he is "cut" later on, he will still keep the signing bonus. To secure the bonus, the player must at least try to perform. Or, in the case of a team folding before camp, the signed player must show his willingness to perform by allowing the team to use his good name for public relations purposes. *Alabama Football, Inc. v. Stabler* (1975) and *Alabama Football, Inc. v. Greenwood* (1978).

1. Option

Another part of the SPK is the so-called option clause which allows the team to unilaterally bind the player for another year at a stated per cent (usually ten per cent less) of the prior year's salary. Since this clause restrains trade, it often exhibits antitrust implications. However, the option year is usually softened through collective bargaining. As an agent, when an option clause is sent to a player, advise him not to sign it, since it may be interpreted as yet another signed contract and if so, will include another mandatory option year. Also, make sure that all the benefits of the original contract are carried over to the option year. See *Hennigan v. Chargers Football Co.* (1970).

2. Reserve

Baseball's former infamous reserve clause was truly unconscionable since it gave management a perpetual option year. Under baseball's old reserve system a player belonged to a team for life. The only alternatives left to a player was to either request a trade or retire from the sport. However, the team could at their whim, release a player or trade him without consent to another team. This hated version of the option clause was eradicated from baseball's lexicon in 1975 as a result of a bargained-for grievance procedure.

3. No–Cut

This type of clause assures the player that he will not be "cut" during the life of the contract. There are many ways and reasons that a player can be terminated: skill, physical condition, off-season injuries, suspension, death, etc. Because of this, a standard no-cut clause does not exist since each clause only protects the player from a certain type of termination.

The basic types of no-cut clauses are the *Cunningham* model, the standard NFL clause and the *Hudson* model. In *Munchak Corp. v. Cunningham* (1972), the parties agreed to a "no-cut contract" using that term and anticipating that this clause would protect the player from a cut based on a lack of skill. This clause would still not protect the player from "cuts" due to bad physical or mental condition, inability to perform as a result of off-field injuries and suspension without pay for disciplinary reasons. The standard NFL "no-cut" clause is comparable to the *Cunningham* model except that it is more specific concerning the necessity of the player to maintain a superior physical condition. The best for the player, is the *Hudson* Model (*Minnesota Muskies, Inc. v. Hudson* (1969)), which employs the following language: "salary payable in any event." Even with this language, the club will still not waive its right to suspend a player; nor will it protect a player who fails to exhibit a good faith effort. Any no-cut clause, however, only guarantees that the player will continue to be paid; it does not correspondingly guarantee a player an automatic spot on the roster.

D. COLLATERAL AGREEMENTS

A sports contract can also be modified through inclusion of collateral agreements by way of an incorporation clause. The standard collateral agreements are collective bargaining agreements and the league's constitution and by-laws; these additional documents will then be incorporated into the SPK as if they were a part of the contract. Less standard agreements can also be incorporated into the contract, for example, drug usage guidelines, player-agent standards, etc. When a player signs an SPK he not only agrees to abide by the ten pages in that contract but he also impliedly agrees to abide by the some 300 pages of responsibilities and obligations contained within the collateral documents.

E. TERMINATIONS

The termination of an athlete will be construed as a breach of contract if the termination is not justified. An employer can terminate an athlete if he is physically unable to perform. If a team terminates an employee on the basis of an injury there is usually a procedure that will cover this situation in the collective bargaining agreement.

A club must act within its rights when it terminates a contract. A player can be rightfully terminated for being out of shape, a lack of skill, defying club and league rules or a material breach of the SPK. In reality, a player with unique and proven skills will not be released, whereas, a marginal player will be released due to a lack of skills judged solely by the club.

F. ASSIGNMENTS

A necessary evil of a professional sports environment is the assignment of contracts, that is, trading players. SPK's contain a clause that allows the team to trade players at will. Players can, of course, negotiate "no trade" contracts; another alternative is that c.b.a.'s can also provide certain agreed-upon no-trade provisions.

G. REMEDIES

A breach of contract can usually be remedied by either money damages, restitution or specific performance. In the typical scenario, a party will seek the benefit of that bargain, that is, that which was promised in relation to what was received. If the legal remedy is inadequate then the aggrieved party may seek specific performance if the services are unique.

As regards specific performance, a court will not force an athlete to play against his will. But because an athlete's particular skills are unique and the addition of his participation to the chemistry of a team can never be successfully delineated, divided or understood, a court will allow the prevailing team to enjoin the athlete from playing for another team.

The use of injunctions as a remedy in professional sports was established in *Philadelphia Ball Club v. Lajoie* (1902) which allowed a ball club to enjoin a professional baseball player, a future Hall of Fame member, one Napoleon Lajoie, when he attempted to play for another team. The injunction was authorized to restrain Lajoie from rendering services to another team since his services were of a unique character which would render them of peculiar value to the baseball club. In short, it would be difficult to find a substitute for the services of Napoleon Lajoie.

Because of this uniqueness, the first team can enjoin the player from playing for another team during the continuation of the contract. The provisions in the contract which prohibited the athlete from jumping to another team were a part of the consideration for the employer's agreement to pay the athlete his salary. These promises were not lacking mutuality of remedy or were they so unreasonable as to prevent the issuance of an injunction. Another rationale was that the contract was already partially performed and the employer was desirous of its continuance.

H. DEFENSES

When there is an alleged breach of contract, there are several defenses that can be posited. Of course, when an employer terminates the contract due to an injury, the c.b.a. will spell out the appropriate procedures. Usually, the team doctor's diagnosis will be submitted to arbitration after a review by a neutral physician. Club's defenses that can be raised in arbitration are: failure to pass the preseason physical exam, failure to make complete disclosure of a physical or mental condition, injury occurring prior to exam, a non-sport injury, no new sports-related injury after exam and no aggravation of prior injury after exam.

1. Unclean Hands

It is axiomatic that one cannot request a remedy in equity if he comes to court with unclean hands. Players have successfully used the doctrine of unclean hands in defending against suits by management for negative injunctions. A court of equity will not grant injunctive relief to a plaintiff who has acted in bad faith as regards the problem to be litigated. See *New York Football Giants, Inc. v. Los Angeles Chargers Football Club, Inc.* (1961).

In *Minnesota Muskies, Inc. v. Hudson* (1969), plaintiff was not entitled to enjoin defendant basketball player from joining another team during the life of his contract since plaintiff professional basketball team had already soiled its hands in negotiating a contract with the player while the player was still bound by contract to another professional basketball club in a different basketball association. Therefore, plaintiff club was not entitled to enjoin breach of that contract by the player, who after signing with plaintiff then signed a new contract with the original club and honored that contract by performing under it.

2. Unconscionability

Another defense could be that the contract was illegal or unfair. A court, for example, will not permit equitable enforcement if the terms of the contract are too harsh and one-sided. *Connecticut Professional Sports Corp. v. Heyman* (1967). Historically some form of the reserve clause might well have been unconscionable and thus unenforceable. At present, the once overly harsh player retention systems have all been, to a certain extent, ameliorated by collective bargaining; as a result, they are now more narrowly drawn and less likely to be viewed as unfair, illegal or unconscionable.

3. **Mutuality**

Another defense to a club's suit for a negative injunction is the lack of mutuality. That is, either inequality between the player's obligation of many years and the team's obligation for a minimal amount of time or the fact that the club can avail itself of an opportunity to obtain the specific performance of an athlete's negative promise, whereas, specific performance is unavailable to a player.

I. NEGOTIATING THE CONTRACT

The art of negotiating a contract in sports is very similar to the art of negotiating in other more standard venues. Although the SPK is in many ways a contract of adhesion, there are ways to flesh out the contract in an attempt to get the best deal for your client. As an overview, the more money up front the better; the more money in the signing bonus the better. Also, management will usually not object to the addition of incentive clauses (e.g., bonus money for achieving "all-rookie" status, attendance clauses, etc.).

The unions have greatly improved an agent's ability to successfully negotiate by providing players and agents with a complete statistical file of the relative worth of each potential professional athlete. This way, the athlete and his agent will have a clear idea of the contracts that similarly-positioned athletes were able to obtain. This takes the guess work out of ascertaining the "bottom line" and shows the athlete his market place comparative worth figure.

As an aside, much of the athlete's would be negotiation strengths are defined and refined through collective bargaining. Therefore, it would behoove the good agent to immerse himself into the c.b.a. before attempting contract negotiation. Although the SPK and c.b.a. include rules and benefits that automatically accrue to a player there are still certain concerns that reside completely in the domain of the individual contract negotiator. For example, signing bonus amount, time of payment of the bonus, desirability of a loan, insurance, contract length, injury or skill guarantees, ascertaining the appropriate mix of initial year salary and annual installments, option clauses, salary adjustments, roster bonuses, individual and team incentives, etc.

CHAPTER 2

AGENTS

A. BACKGROUND

With the great increases in salaries and benefits in professional sports, a need developed for athletes to have personal representatives, or agents, to manage their affairs. This representation includes the negotiation of a personal services contract with a professional sports team. There is a fiduciary relationship between agents and athletes; therefore, agents are under an obligation to exercise the utmost care and good faith in their dealings with athletes.

B. STANDARD REPRESENTATION AGREEMENTS

The main connection between player and agent is the standard representation contract (SRK). This contract establishes the rights and responsibilities between the parties. It only calls for a good faith effort. The actions of the agent do not necessarily have to prove successful. *Zinn v. Parrish* (1977).

However, the agent does have the obligation to make a full and complete disclosure of all areas of potential conflicts of interest and must receive prior

consent from the athlete if representation is continued after this disclosure. *Detroit Lions, Inc. v.
Argovitz* (1984). Like any other contract, the key
to an SRK is its particular wording. There are at
least four essential clauses within an SRK: notice
in writing of potential conflicts, a negotiation in
good faith clause, an arbitration provision, and a
clause that stipulates which state's law will govern
if interpretation of the contract is necessary.

The basic responsibility of an agent is to exercise
good faith effort overall and to act as a trustee for
his client's money when investing it. Investments
must be similar to those that a prudent investor
would engage in for his own account, keeping in
mind both safety and income.

C. DUTIES

The most essential part of the SRK is the agent's
obligation to negotiate a contract. Implied in this
obligation is the understanding that the agent possesses the necessary background, skills, experiences,
and expertise to perform this task to a degree that
corresponds with the skills and knowledge that are
standard to the profession. An agent does not have
to secure the best contract, he must only negotiate
the contract in good faith using his best abilities.

The responsibilities of the agent will usually include contract negotiation, investments, taxes and
public relations. The number of functions that an
agent can perform is limited only by the agent's

imagination. The list of functions that might be covered include: 1) contracts, 2) taxes, 3) financial planning, 4) money management, 5) investments, 6) income tax preparation, 7) incorporation, 8) estate planning, 9) endorsements, 10) sports medicine consultations, 11) health and physical training consultations, 12) career and personal development counseling, 13) post-career development, 14) insurance and 15) legal consultations.

Zinn v. Parrish (1977), established the obligations that an agent must meet in his effort to satisfy his client. Plaintiff, an agent, brought an action to recover commissions that were allegedly due under an SRK. The agent secured three professional football team contracts for his client and pursuant to the SRK was entitled to a 10% agency fee. The agent was to negotiate contracts, furnish advice on business and tax matters, seek endorsements and assist with off-season employment. The plaintiff performed some of these obligations; he solicited some investment advice and assisted defendant in investing a small amount of his money in buying a house. No jobs, though; no endorsements; no off-season employment and, for tax advice, plaintiff sent his client to H & R Block.

Defendant alleged that his agent acted as an investment advisor under 15 U.S.C.A. § 80(b)–2(a)(11) and since he was not registered, the contract was void. However, the court held that the investment advice was merely an incident to the primary purpose of the management contract which was to negotiate a professional contract. In short, defendant alleged that plaintiff failed to perform his duties competently. However, plaintiff satisfied his obligations by performing these duties in good faith.

D. CONFLICTS OF INTEREST

The agent must not have any conflicts of interest that might influence or affect his ability to do the best job for his client. The agent must inform the principal of all facts that come to his knowledge which may be material or might affect his principal's rights or interests or influence the actions that the athlete may or may not take. *Detroit Lions, Inc. v. Argovitz* (1984).

An agent should err on the side of a complete and detailed disclosure of any possible or potential conflicts of interest that might occur between the agent and the athlete.

Avoidance of conflicts of interest is even more important if the agent is also an attorney. Under the rules of professional conduct, an attorney must decline representation if it will be directly adverse to the interests of another client or if the attorney's personal interests materially limit his responsibilities to his client.

An attorney must perform his legal duties with unabated loyalty. This loyalty is necessarily questioned if the agent has conflicting interests that appear to be adverse to the interests of the athlete, e.g., representation of a competing athlete or ties with management. The attorney-agent is under the restriction of the attorney-client privilege of confidentiality. He cannot use confidential information to the athlete's disadvantage.

E. REGISTRATION OF AGENTS

Although their relationship is fiduciary in nature, sports agents were unregulated for many years. As a result of this, there were many infamous cases of abuse on the part of the agents. The perceived need for reform created a public outcry that resulted in attempts to regulate agents by both the states and the professional sports unions.

1. State Legislation

Many state legislatures entered into the controversy by enacting legislation that requires that agents register with that state if they are from that state or if they sign an athlete from that state. Registration must occur before they proceed with contract negotiations for an athlete.

The earliest registration model came from California. It requires that any agent who represents an athlete in an attempt to gain an employment contract with a professional sports team must register with the state labor commission. The act does not include "advisors" who do not negotiate contracts nor does it include California attorneys that act as legal counsel. Non–California attorneys are not exempted, they're treated as non-attorney agents. The act requires that agents must register and post a $10,000.00 surety bond to satisfy any damages for misrepresentation or fraud. The labor commissioner acts as an arbitrator for agent-athlete disputes. Any violation of the statute is a criminal misdemeanor. West's Ann.Cal. Labor Code § 1546.

A newer, "tougher" approach is represented by a Florida statute which targets both the agent and the athlete for criminal and civil penalties for violations. This act requires registration of all agents who do business in Florida. However, the registration itself is routine and is accompanied by only a minimal fee. The act applies to all agents who communicate with any Florida athlete regardless of whether the athlete is or is not ultimately signed. Failure to register is a third-degree felony with penalties of up to five years incarceration and a $5,000.00 fine. The athlete and the agent must notify the college's athletic director within 72 hours of the signing of an SRK. There are sanctions involved which include voiding the SRK as unenforceable, subjecting both the athlete and the agent to criminal penalties and allowing the school an opportunity to bring a civil suit against the athlete and the agent. West's Fla.St.Ann. § 468.451 et seq.

2. Union Regulations

Another way to curb abuses is through mechanisms provided by the sports unions. Basically, the unions created their own plan so that any agent who wanted to represent a union member must first register with, or be certified by, the union. This gives the union a certain amount of control.

They can keep out unsavory would be agents while also mandating continuing education to improve the overall caliber of representation. All major sports unions currently maintain some form of agent registration.

However, the seminal model is from the National Football League Players' Association (NFLPA), which in 1983 established guidelines requiring agents to become certified as contract advisors. To gain certification, an agent must apply, pay a fee and submit an application providing information about education, employment, membership in business and professional associations, criminal history, etc. Two major aspects of the qualification process are 1) full disclosure and 2) an absence of a prior history that reveals incidents of serious misconduct. A procedure such as this, however, only excludes those whose conduct is egregious.

After they become contract advisors, the newly certified agents must use an NFLPA SRK, agree to abide by NFLPA limits to the percentage of the athlete's compensation that the agent can receive for representation, attend annual NFLPA continuing education seminars, pass a test, agree not to give a player anything of value in exchange for the opportunity to secure representation, fully comply with applicable state and federal rules and regulations, and agree to avoid potential conflicts of interests by not having any financial interest in a professional sports teams. A violation of these rules will subject the agent to fines and penalties along with the possibility of a revocation of his contract advisor status.

The purpose of this type of regulation is to provide quality control in representation and to limit the fees that agents can charge NFLPA members for contract negotiation. However, its protective umbrella will not cover charlatans that might masquerade as financial advisors or publicity consultants or marketing experts, rather than act as contract negotiators. All other union-orchestrated, agent-certification schemes copy to a large extent the NFLPA model.

3. NCAA–Based

The National Collegiate Athletic Association (NCAA), an unincorporated association of individual schools; is the primary regulator of intercollegiate athletics. It also promulgates regulations that attempt to police agents. Athletes will lose their remaining collegiate eligibility if they accept gifts or enter into contracts with agents. In 1984, the NCAA established a voluntary "Player Agent Registration Plan" which urges agents to register with the NCAA. Once the agent chooses to register with the NCAA, the agent must provide information on his employment and education background. In addition he must notify the athlete's coach or athletic director before contacting an athlete who still possesses NCAA eligibility. Through this process, the agent's name is placed on a list of registered agents that is then provided to NCAA schools. An agent is removed from this list if he provides gifts to a still eligible athlete or if he fails to contact the school's athletic director before contacting either the athlete or the athlete's coach.

Many states have designed their regulatory legislation so that it facilitates and corresponds to the NCAA rules. These statutes are considered NCAA-based in that they put teeth into the NCAA eligibility rules. Although these statutes vary greatly, many are similar in that they provide for 1) a written notice regarding the possibility of losing eligibility upon the signing of an SRK and 2) a cooling off period which allows the athlete an opportunity to rescind the contract. Usually an SRK which violates the statute is void. Also, an agent must notify the school of a potential contract. Some statutes require that notice be given to the university prior to the proposed signing. Other statutes simply prohibit the signing of an athlete before the expiration of his NCAA eligibility.

F. CRIMINAL LIABILITY

Some state statutes regulate the conduct of professional sports agents by the imposition of criminal sanctions. For example, in Alabama, an agent can be prosecuted under a statute that prohibits tampering with a sporting event. Ala.Code § 13A–11–143 (1982). Criminal sanctions are applicable. Ala.Code § 8–26–1 to 8–26–41 (Supp.1989). The penalty provisions of the Alabama act establish that all offenses under the act are felony violations. These offenses range from failure to properly register to failure to provide a ten-point type on the face of the SRK warning that the athlete's amateur standing might be jeopardized by entering into the contract.

G. REPRESENTING THE ATHLETE

The agent-athlete agreement typically demands that the agent will be the exclusive representative for the athlete. The fee for these services can range from 3% to 50% of the athlete's contract; the specific share will depend on the agent's responsibilities, the sport, etc. The athlete should expect that the agent's results will be comparable to the results of other agents. The agent has an affirmative duty to be aware of the customs and practices that are relevant to that particular professional sport. Also, as regards publicity, the agent must use his best efforts in a good faith attempt to find employment opportunities outside of the sporting arena.

As regards negotiating a contract, it is essential to acquire the necessary background and then map the most appropriate strategies. One must also possess the flexibility to counter management's negotiation thrusts.

Other aspects of representation may include counseling, managing the athlete's assets, marketing his image through personal appearances and commercial endorsements, assisting the athlete to resolve his disciplinary or salary disputes through mediation or arbitration, and planning life-time strategies that will guarantee the athlete financial, mental and emotional security at the time of the athlete's retirement from the work force.

The goal is to spread income from a short period of time so that it extends through a long period of time, and/or to create employment and business opportunities after retirement from the playing field in order to continue the athlete's standard of living past his days as an athlete.

CHAPTER 3

FINANCIAL CONSIDERATIONS

The astute agent of a professional athlete, through tax and financial planning, should maximize the athlete's income and minimize the tax bite on his earnings. Success is measured by the athlete's financial security at the time of his retirement from the work force rather than at the end of his playing career. One must strive to preserve capital and lessen any adverse tax consequences during the peak income period.

A. TAXATION

Taxation is the application of tax rates to taxable income during a given tax year. To determine an athlete's tax liability one must calculate the gross amount of all income attributed to the athlete-taxpayer during the taxable year. After that, subtract from this gross amount, all deductions; that amount is the taxable income figure which will be used to determine the athlete's tax liability by the application of rates.

Income is a gain derived from any source whatsoever. It includes not only salary, but also bonuses, prize money, the value placed on interest-free loans, endorsement revenues, sportswear companies' gift products, gifts for radio or TV appearances, employer-provided insurance benefits in excess of $50,-000.00, "free use of an automobile," etc.

1. Gross Income

An athlete's gross income is where many of the athlete's expenses can be deducted. Gross income can be reduced by deductions for business-related expenses. Business-related expenses are all the ordinary and necessary expenses that are incurred by reason of an athlete's performance in an athletic event including the cost of tools of his trade, expenses related to maintaining a good physical condition, travel, professional services, business entertainment and necessary gratuities. In order to prove the deductibility of an expense, the athlete must maintain a system of record-keeping of expenditures so that the business expense deduction can be maximized and all expenses can be monitored to determine if they are excessive.

2. Planning

The crux of the "problem" is that, typically, athletes receive a large amount of income in a very short amount of time. Therefore, tax planning is imperative. The purpose of this planning is to maximize the benefit from those years in which a high income is recognized by spreading the tax liability to those years of lower income. There are many different ways that one can arrange a tax plan. These arrangements can include deferred compensation plans, tax sheltered investments, and other contractual arrangements that spread out the receipt of income over a period longer than the playing period of the athlete.

B. ASSIGNMENT OF INCOME

The idea behind income assignment is to avoid realization of income from professional services as an athlete by assigning a portion of that income to a third person. This assignment would reduce overall tax liability by spreading the income to another person who is in a lower marginal tax bracket than the athlete.

It is a good strategy; however, an attempted assignment will be nullified unless it avoids the assignment of income doctrine which stipulates that he who is entitled to income cannot circumvent tax liability by causing it to be paid to another through an anticipatory assignment. There must be a legitimate basis for the other person to receive the assigned income from the athlete. The way to establish this basis is to show that the recipient performed valuable services which aided in the production of the income so as to be entitled to the assignment. Because the highest tax rate is now just 31 percent, any technique that required the assignment of $1.00 to save 31 cents will be of dubious value. This technique is advisable only if tax rates increase.

C. DEFERRALS

The principle behind deferring income is to lessen tax liability by prolonging the incident of taxation from the years in which the athlete earns income to a time in the future. An employee can arrange income deferral through his employer by way of the contract or it can be arranged separately by either the athlete or the athlete's agent. Income can be deferred through pension plans, by contract or by the receipt of restricted property. The latter technique can be accomplished through "substantially nonvested property." That is, property that is not required to be included as income until the first time that the beneficial percentage in the property becomes substantially vested.

1. By Contract

Deferral of the receipt of income can be arranged by way of contract through the SPK. The contract can stipulate that the payment of income will be extended over a period of years and paid in equal sums during each year of that period.

2. By Pension Plans

An extremely popular deferral plan is one arranged by a pension plan that can be created by or for the benefit of a professional athlete. These plans can be individually negotiated or they can be the result of a collective bargaining agreement. A qualified pension plan will provide several benefits including deferring the income to later years to the extent of the employer's contributions; making the employer's contribution deductible; and tax-deferring the pension income.

For relatively high-paid athletes, the most important fact of a qualified pension plan is the extent of the tax reduction on current income. Usually, the athlete will receive monthly payments on retirement or disability. These payments are a part of the athlete's income. The athlete, however, can exclude an amount equal to a portion of the higher payment into the plan. This portion is determined by the exclusion ratio which is determined by dividing the athlete's investment by its expected return. The amount to be excluded will equal the figure that is produced by multiplying payment by the percentage. Since most athletes do not personally contribute to the pension plan, then all of the payments will be included as income.

Another option is that the athlete can receive his benefits in a lump-sum which will qualify for special averaging. One other option is a pension plan that is available to the athlete who does not participate in team or league plans. These plans usually cover non-team sports, such as tennis or golf, and allows the athlete as a self-employed person to be treated as both employer and employee for pension plan purposes.

The final option concerns individual retirement accounts. These accounts are for those people who are not active in a qualified plan and could be established by the athlete for a non-working spouse. The athlete then can contribute and deduct a maximum of $2,000 of the compensation included in the gross income for the taxable year. However, for the typical athlete, no deduction will be permitted because the deduction is available for individuals that earn $35,000 or less; married couples are allowed a deduction for those who earn $50,000 or less. The nondeductible contribution is still advisable because the income earned on the contribution is tax-deferred until final withdrawal. Penalty-less withdrawals are not permitted prior to age 59½ and do not qualify for the five year forward averaging rule for lump sums under qualified plans. Currently, the most attractive option appears to be the Roth IRA; this is yet another retirement vehicle that affluent athletes can utilize. A tax advisor should suggest the appropriate retirement option.

3. Substantially Non–Vested Property

Another deferral technique concerns substantially non-vested property which is property that is transferred in connection with the performance of services. The value of this property does not have to be included in the athlete's income until the first time its beneficial interest becomes substantially vested; that is, until it is transferable or no longer possesses a substantial risk of forfeiture. This mechanism can provide the athlete with a means of deferring income recognition while providing some security.

The athlete can acquire possession of property at the time services are rendered while allowing taxation deferral until the time when there is a lapsing of a substantial risk of forfeiture. For this to work, the athlete must have the party to whom the services are to be rendered take the deferred amount and purchase the type of property that is preferred by the athlete, e.g., corporate stock or real property. This property then must be transferred to the athlete with a restriction that would qualify as a substantial forfeiture risk such as a provision that would require the athlete to transfer the property to the other party in the event that the athlete ends his athletic services during a particular period of time.

D. TAX–SHELTERED INVESTMENTS

Another method to lessen taxes is through tax-sheltered investments. These investments are those that through appropriate deductions shelter the athlete's income from tax liability. Although such investments vary in kind and activity, they often possess the following tax-minimizing characteristics: leveraging, tax-deferral and tax-free cash flow.

Leveraging: Some tax-shelters offer the investor the use of someone else's money to finance an investment. This is called leveraging.

Tax-deferral: When an investment permits deductions to be accelerated in the early years of the investment and applied to the investor's other income, such an investment offers tax-deferral.

Positive cash flow: When a tax-sheltered investment combines deductions with investment income and generates both simultaneously; the investor receives all the cash that exceeds actual expenses.

Two programs that remain viable are real estate investments especially in low income housing, and oil and gas. However, as with any investment, these programs involve a degree of risk. Thus, a professional athlete must carefully evaluate each program prior to making the investment.

E.   INCORPORATION

Another form of temporary tax planning is to create a personal services corporation based on the athlete's athletic participation, commercial endorsements, etc. This type of corporation is organized for the purpose of using the athlete's abilities. The athlete will form the corporation and then become its major shareholder. He is obliged to perform specialized services with the corporation which would then contract with the sports team. This type of corporate structure allows a deferral of income by the adoption of a corporate pension and profit sharing plan along with a corporate fiscal year.

The corporation can adopt corporate fringe benefits programs and can also allow the creation of various estate planning advantages that are offered by the corporate form of organization. The corporation, though, must have some other purpose than merely avoiding taxes. See *Leavell v. CIR* (1995).

F. FINANCIAL PLANNING

The aims of planning should be capital preservation, tax minimization, protection against risk and an orderly estate plan. The primary objective of financial planning is to increase long-term capital at the expense of current income.

The four basic ways of managing an athlete's assets are to let him decide his own choices, invest in mutual funds, turn the account over to a broker or retain an investment manager. The latter is the most preferred since the investment manager acts as a personal agent and is not a broker.

An investment manager makes decisions on an investor's behalf based upon research of the investment's potential. Rather than receiving payment for each stock transaction, the manager is paid an annual fee for structuring an investment portfolio. As part of this structure, the manager will invariably attempt to achieve financial security for the athlete's investments.

1. Preservation of Capital

The number of years the average professional athlete can compete is extremely short: for example, approximately two years in football and four and a half in baseball. Since the athlete will probably have 40 or so years until retirement age it is imperative that a strategy be adopted to maximize his investment portfolio. There are many products that can assist in achieving the goal of capital preservation such as certificates of deposit, common stock and annuities. An annuity is a contract between the athlete and an insurance company for fixed payments at regular intervals over some period of time. An example would be a 30–year–old athlete who purchases an annuity for $100,000 with payments of money per month beginning at age 45.

2. Tax Minimization

The planner also should consider the following tax measures to minimize the income tax burden of the athlete:

1. Making a contribution to an IRA for a non-working spouse. Although no deduction is allowed for the couple making in excess of $60,000 per year, all income earned on the IRA is tax-deferred until final distribution.

2. Making Keogh contributions: for athletes with substantial endorsement income, contributions of up to the lesser of $30,000 or 25% of this self-employment income are allowable. Endorsement income is normally self-employment income. This presents an opportunity for savings.

3. Converting taxable income into tax-exempt income.

4. Making family gifts so that earnings can be removed from income.

5. Making contributions to a college fund for the athlete's children.

6. Converting personal non-deductible interest into qualified residence income.

3. Protection Against Risk

There is an ongoing struggle between investing in assets that appreciate rapidly and investing in assets that protect against risk. Since the money that the athlete can earn from his skills is finite, it is imperative that he does not lose money. Therefore, investment plans should be balanced against his risk. Conservative instruments such as certificates of deposit and money market funds are available but the skilled investment professional should be capable of structuring a more profitable conservative plan while retaining emphasis on preservation of capital. This approach can achieve a higher return at little risk to the athlete/investor.

4. Estate Planning

Estate planning is important for athletes since they risk accidental death with every tackle or misplaced fast ball. An athlete should have a will to pass title to property on death. A will can be used to place funds in a trust for the benefit of others unable to manage property. For example, a trust can be used to educate and care for the deceased athlete's children and when they reach maturity, provide for the principal to be paid out as specified in the will.

Another aspect of estate planning is the creation of a revocable trust. A trust takes effect at the time of its creation and operates as a will substitute. A trust is an agreement between grantor and trustee which contains instructions to the trustees so as to assist in the disposition of the property that is transferred to the trustee. Revocable trusts seldom establish a workable asset management arrangement during the athlete's life; a durable power of attorney provides for continued action on behalf of the athlete upon disability that renders him incompetent. An added advantage of trust is that trust property is not subject to probate upon the owner's death. The trust can be freely revoked or amended during the owner's life and the cost and delays are less than those in an administration of a will.

Estate tax is the government's tax on the value of property that passes from a person who has died to his beneficiaries. The tax is assessed against the fair market value of all property that was owned by the decedent upon death. Estate tax is calculated on the taxable estate which is the gross estate less deductions and credits. There is a marital deduction which allows an unlimited deduction for property passing from the decedent to the surviving spouse. There is also a charitable deduction which can benefit the athlete in his estate plan by providing a deduction from estate taxes. Like property that passes to a spouse, property that passes to a qualified charity is also deductible from the gross estate. While spousal and charitable deductions are deducted from the athlete's gross estate, the "unified credit" is applied to reduce the tax itself. This credit can currently eliminate estate taxes on $700,-000 worth of property.

There is also a generation skipping tax which is a separate tax designed to prevent avoiding estate or gift taxes which would have been applicable if the property in question had first been given to the intervening generation and then transferred to the grandchildren. However, there's a significant exemption from generation-skipping taxes which allows each individual to transfer up to $1,000,000 of property, free from this tax.

Life insurance is yet another aspect of many financial plans. Because of their age and robust physical condition life insurance is readily obtainable at a reasonable price by professional athletes. Insurance proceeds can be important to his family if the athlete does die young. These proceeds can be used to pay debts, taxes, bequests, and/or provide funds for trusts for family members of the athlete.

CHAPTER 4

LABOR LAW

A. NATIONAL LABOR RELATIONS ACT

Union-management relations in professional sports are controlled under the auspices of the National Labor Relations Act (NLRA), 29 U.S.C.A. §§ 151–166. However, sports for many years was viewed as an anomaly that was not a business, and it thus escaped the protection of the NLRA during those years. Baseball, for example, in the early days was a classic case of management abuse. Yet, in *Federal Base Ball Club, Inc. v. National League of Professional Baseball Clubs* (1922), the Supreme Court excepted baseball and the reserve clause from antitrust regulations, thus stagnating any attempts by the players to organize as a union.

But, professional sports include other employees than just athletes. There are also the relatively low-paid club house attendants, bat boys, traveling secretaries, physical therapists, ushers, ticket sellers, etc. Collective bargaining and the umbrella protection of the NLRA finally came to baseball in 1969.

In *American League of Professional Baseball Clubs* (1969), the National Labor Relations Board (NLRB) moved to take jurisdiction over professional baseball. The NLRB can decline jurisdiction when a particular industry's impact on interstate commerce is deemed to be insubstantial. The NLRB has accordingly declined jurisdiction over some forms of recreational activity, for example, harness racing. *Yonkers Raceway, Inc.* (1972); See also *Centennial Turf Club, Inc.* (1971). However, the NLRB will generally take jurisdiction of all organized team sports.

American League of Professional Baseball Clubs involved baseball umpires. The NLRB held that since baseball is an industry that affects commerce it is subject to the coverage and the jurisdiction of the NLRB. The policy of the NLRB is to encourage collective bargaining through the protection of the rights of employees to self-organize and choose the representation of their choice. These goals were felt to be best served by asserting jurisdiction over professional baseball and thus subjecting all labor disputes to determination under the NLRA. The NLRB also specifically took jurisdiction over professional football in *National Football League Management Council* (1973).

The NLRB's § 7 demands that "employees should have the right to self-organization, to bargain collectively through representatives of their own choosing, and to engage in other concerted activities for the purpose of collectively bargaining or other mutual aid or protection." The NLRB was formed to administer and police these § 7 rights: the NLRA applies to all employers whose business

affects commerce, although the NLRB can decline
to intervene if the effect on commerce is minimal.
Today, there is no question that professional sports
and the corresponding collective bargaining relationship between players and management falls
firmly under the NLRA's protection.

B. UNIONS AND MANAGEMENT

It was a tough struggle for unions to organize in
professional sports: management was especially ad-
amant in the defense of what they considered their
personal and private fiefdom. For many years,
labor groups were not sufficiently organized to be
recognized as unions by the NLRA. Even after
recognition, the relationship between unions and
management was stormy, with the owners' behavior
characterized by a demeanor that was both pro-
crastinating and bullying.

The first question the NLRB must decide when
considering if a particular industry is eligible for
protection under the NLRA is whether the coverage
of the NLRA is broad enough to include that industry. The NLRB answered in the affirmative regarding the sports industry, since the affect of professional sports on commerce is not minimal.

Next, the NLRB must determine the appropriate
bargaining unit. In most sports, the unit is determined to be the sport as a whole instead of individual teams or particular positions (e.g., not a union
for catchers only). Once a union is recognized it

becomes the exclusive bargaining representative for all members of the unit.

In *North American Soccer League v. NLRB* (1980), the court found the bargaining unit to be all professional soccer players on clubs that are based in the United States. The court held that the league and its member clubs are joint employers. The key to the decision was the joint employer status of the individual teams and the league. The court, however, was momentarily swayed by the apparent individuality of each team: "Contrary to our first impression, which was fostered by the knowledge that teams in the League compete against each other on the playing fields and for the hire of the best players, * * *." However after further consideration, the court agreed with the NLRB that there was a joint employer relationship among the league and its member clubs; they then designated the league as the appropriate bargaining unit.

The NLRB is not required to select the most appropriate bargaining unit, but only to choose an appropriate unit under the circumstances. The NLRB's decision not to exercise jurisdiction over the three Canadian clubs did not undermine its evidentiary base for their finding that there was a joint employer relationship between the league and the clubs.

There is one caveat. The duty to bargain requires that both sides must bargain in good faith. Section 8(d) of the NLRA states that both parties must meet at reasonable times and confer on mandatory subjects of collective bargaining. The failure to do so is an unfair labor practice. This duty to bargain in good faith can be defined as a willingness to enter in negotiations with an open and fair mind and with a sincere desire to find a basis of agreement. The duty to bargain calls for sincerity, not results.

An example of the above process was revealed in *NFLPA v. NLRB* (1974). In the case, various National Football League owners and their management council unilaterally promulgated and implemented a rule that provided for an automatic fine against any player who left the bench while there was a brawl or altercation on the playing field. The unilateral enactment of this rule without the benefit of collective bargaining was an unfair labor practice. This rule was an unfair labor practice since it involved a mandatory subject of collective bargaining and should have been sifted through the collective bargaining process. Also, the c.b.a. itself provided that any change in current practices that affect the players' employment conditions shall be negotiated in good faith.

The union has the responsibility to fairly represent all members of the bargaining unit, even those who are not members. This is the duty of fair representation. In order to prove a violation of this duty one must show that the union acted arbitrarily or in bad faith. For example, a union always defends any of its players when they are disciplined for clubhouse brawls, but then the union ignores one particular player who happened to be anti-union. This case would reflect a violation of the duty of fair representation.

C. COLLECTIVE BARGAINING GENERALLY

Collective bargaining is the process under the NLRA where owners and the players' union participate in a give-and-take that produces a document which is called the collective bargaining agreement (c.b.a.). This document establishes the rules and regulations of their relationship. Once they have entered into collective bargaining, they are obliged to bargain in good faith. The failure of either party to bargain in good faith is an unfair labor practice.

The subject matter of collective bargaining, that is, what must be discussed at the bargaining table, includes wages, hours and conditions of employment. There are also permissive subjects of bargaining which include anything other than wages, hours and conditions. The parties must bargain in good faith about mandatory subjects, but they may refuse to bargain about permissive subjects. A party may insist that the other party agree to their proposal on a mandatory subject, even to the point of impasse. If an agreement does not materialize, a party then may resort to economic pressure, i.e., strikes or lock-outs, without risking NLRA §§ 8(a)(5) or 8(b)(3) unfair labor practice charges.

This is important because if a strike is an unfair labor practice, it can be enjoined.

D.　THE COLLECTIVE BARGAINING AGREEMENT

Collective bargaining agreements express the complete range of relationships between management and their athlete employees. This document will specify the scope of the union—management agreement and will prohibit the use of either strikes or lockouts. Although the collective bargaining agreement will vary with the sport, it will cover at a minimum the following: club discipline, non-injury grievances, commissioner discipline, injury grievances, the SPK, college draft, option clauses, waivers, base salaries, access to personnel files, medical rights, retirement, insurance and the duration of the c.b.a.

E.　CONCERTED ACTIONS

The process of collective bargaining only works because of the threat of concerted action that each party can legally invoke if negotiation reaches an impasse. This is especially true in professional sports where the season is only so long and the athlete's career is limited in duration. Even though the history of collective bargaining in professional sports is not very long, there is an almost annual ritual in the major sports of either concerted actions, the threat of concerted actions or accusations of unfair labor practices.

1. Strikes

The NLRA guarantees employees, and thus professional athletes, the right to engage in strikes and in other concerted activities. If collective bargaining reaches an impasse then the players' union is legally allowed to strike. A strike is the failure to report to training camp or to the playing field. The strike is the players' primary weapon in coercing the owners to either adhere to the players' demands, compromise, or at least get back to the bargaining table and continue to negotiate in good faith. All strikes are a double-edged sword with the "winner" being the side that can most easily withstand the economic hardships that concerted actions by nature bring.

This right to strike cannot generally be diminished or thwarted and will receive considerable legal protection. Even though there is a right to strike, the union must still continue to bargain in good faith. The union will also lose their legal right to strike if it agrees to a no-strike clause in the c.b.a., if the players' union engages in an activity that has an unlawful objective or if the union uses improper means. The owners can impose sanctions on the strikers; however, they are still employees and cannot be punished for any unfair labor practices committed by management during a strike.

2. Lockouts

On the other hand, the owners have the ability to lockout the players, that is, to not allow the athletes to report to training camp. The lockout is the owners' primary economic weapon; it is the power to withhold employment. It is used as a means to economically coerce the players to either return to the bargaining table and/or rekindle their desire to continue good faith negotiations. Lockouts are legal as long as bargaining continues in good faith and the lockout occurs only after impasse.

F. ARBITRATION AND MEDIATION

The arbitration and mediation procedures in professional sports are probably the most important result and ingredient in the collective bargaining process. In fact, in baseball, the grievance procedure which began in the 1970 c.b.a. helped to end the reserve clause; and salary arbitration which began in the 1973 c.b.a. is perhaps the greatest additive to the players' quest for higher salaries.

If there is an applicable clause, arbitration will be the exclusive remedy for achieving peace. Courts rarely reverse an arbitrator's decision if the party seeking arbitration makes a claim that on its face is governed by the arbitration provisions of the c.b.a. The basic issue in arbitration is whether the dispute is arbitrable, that is, is it within the range of matters that were intended to be arbitrated through the grievance procedure.

The seminal case of *Kansas City Royals Baseball Corp. v. MLBPA* (1976), is a good illustration of how grievance arbitration works in sports. In this case, a major league baseball team brought an action against the players' association to overturn an arbitration award that ruled in favor of two professional baseball players who played out their option years and then sought to be declared free agents. The court's review was limited to the legitimacy of the arbitration process. The court's favorable ruling was predicated on the following: The arbitration provision of the c.b.a. was broad enough to cover the dispute in question; there was nothing in the history of their collective bargaining relationship that showed a strong intent not to arbitrate grievances that involved the reserve clause, that is, there was nothing to overcome the presumption that the question of free agency was arbitrable; that the documents in question (e.g., the c.b.a.) were at least susceptible of the arbitration panel's interpretation; that the decree was not impermissible against other entities that were not party to either the arbitration or the court proceedings; and that the decree was not vague and indefinite as regards the granting of free agency.

In an SPK a party has certain rights. The question becomes how to enforce these rights; the answer generally is arbitration. An agreement to arbitrate is a promise to resolve disputes by nonjudicial means. Arbitration is preferred to judicial remedies because it is more informal, less costly and less time-consuming. It is also more private, which is important in an industry which is concerned with its public image and constantly under intense media scrutiny. The parties can pick the person who will hear the case which can guarantee that that person is at least familiar with the peculiarities of the particular sport.

As regards determining what controversies are subject to arbitration, one must look to the actual wording of the SPK. Most sports contracts contain a very broad arbitration clause: it will cover nearly all disputes. However, in most agreements the club will still retain the right to seek judicial redress as regards the players' promise to perform exclusively for that club during the term of the contract. Clubs want the power of an injunction to stop players from club or league jumping.

Matters that are not subject to arbitration include controversies not covered in the agreement, situations when the breaching party waived his arbitration rights (e.g., initiating a law suit instead of proceeding with arbitration) and cases where the court recognizes certain claims that they believe require direct judicial enforcement because of public policy reasons (e.g., equal employment or antitrust).

There are few grounds for vacating an arbitrator's award. A court will set aside awards only in extreme cases; therefore, agents should not approach arbitrations with a cavalier attitude. The rationale behind the "finality" of the award is that the parties have freely bargained away their rights to seek judicial remedies and presumably each party has received something in return. Therefore, the parties should be made to keep their bargain. Also, arbitration is deemed to be a desirable mechanism for dispute resolution and as a result, arbitration decisions should be maintained and honored.

1. Grievance

The standard grievance arbitration clause will usually stipulate that all problems that arise out of a dispute or grievance that emanates from an interpretation or misinterpretation of the c.b.a. or SPK must be handled through agreed upon arbitration procedures.

Arbitration procedures are relatively standard in most SPK's and c.b.a.'s. Usually they deal only with grievance or contract disputes, but, as in professional baseball, they can be formulated to deal with other concerns, such as salary disputes.

The grievance arbitration procedure as usually stipulated in the c.b.a. is an extremely practical method for both parties to settle their differences. The purpose of this clause is to provide an orderly and expeditious procedure for the handling and resolving of certain disputes, grievances and complaints. Although it is similar to all other sports, baseball's arbitration procedure specifically excludes the benefit plan, union dues check-off and complaints involving the integrity of the sport.

2. Salary

In baseball, a player or a club is allowed to submit a dispute over a player's salary to binding arbitration without the consent of the other party after a certain number of years in service have been accumulated by the player. (It was two years, then it was three, now, it falls between two and three years; more precisely, as a result of the 1990 lock-out, 17% of the two to three year players are eligible for salary arbitration). The technique that is used in this type of arbitration is called "high-low," which means that both parties must submit proposed salary figures to the arbitrator who then must choose only one figure, without modification or compromise. The tool of the arbitrator and also the tool for both the players and owners, is statistics: the player's statistics covering productivity, longevity, potential and comparable worth as compared to like-situated players. Each party will offer statistics in order to prove their contention that their salary figure is most correct. The arbitrator must then decide the significance of mutually contradictory figures and choose the one that he feels is most correct. A major complaint about this type of arbitration is that the arbitrator who is chosen (under mutual agreement by both the union and the owners) is often lacking in the requisite baseball expertise to properly decipher the often confusing statistics.

CHAPTER 5

ANTITRUST

A. GENERALLY

The Sherman Antitrust Act, 15 U.S.C.A. § 1 et seq., makes illegal every combination in the form of a conspiracy that restrains interstate commerce. Every person who monopolizes or combines to monopolize is guilty of a felony. The goal of the antitrust acts is to stop monopolies and protect fair competition.

These laws are the major mechanism available to effect change in sports. That is because the basic leitmotif in organized sports is summarized by the oxymoron of competitive cohesion. In sports one competes in some respects and cooperates in others. Organized sports must have honest competition to be attractive, but to be organized it must establish rules to assure fair play, arrange schedules, punish wrongdoers, etc. "Cooperation" is necessary for the college draft, cable TV, roster limitations, player restraints, preseason games, season tickets, franchise movement and league competition.

The antitrust laws have been used by various groups: e.g., players, owners, colleges, etc. The goal of these antitrust plaintiffs was to achieve some result at the expense of management, whether it was better wages, better conditions, a new location or less control.

The typical situation involves players who contend that they are victims of anti-competitive practices. The thrust of the Sherman Act is to protect the public interest from anti-competitive practices. (Interestingly, these players, or victims of anti-competition, are paid millions a year to play sports.)

Monopolies are deemed to be against public interest: the concern is that a monopolized industry can result in exorbitant prices because it is unchallenged by free competition. However, as a result of antitrust court victories by players, especially by baseball players, salaries have been inflated. This in turn inflates ticket prices. A realistic and legal approach to public interest concerns is exemplified by the National Basketball Association's (NBA) salary cap which limits salaries to 53% of the NBA's gross. See *Wood v. NBA* (1984).

There are two basic ways to interpret an antitrust controversy: either as a "per se" violation or through a rule of reason approach. Professional sports usually will merit the rule of reason analysis rather than a mechanical "per se" review.

The per se approach is most applicable to overt antitrust violations. Throughout the years, the courts have gained enough experience with antitrust problems to identify certain types of agreements that are so consistently unreasonable that they may be deemed to be illegal per se without further inquiry into their purported rationales.

Among the practices that are so pernicious that they are illegal per se are group boycotts and concerted refusals to deal. A concerted refusal to deal is an agreement by two or more persons either not to do business with other persons or to do business with them only on particular terms. Group boycotts are refusals to deal or inducements to others not to deal or to have business relations. *Mackey v. NFL* (1976).

In the district court's opinion in *Mackey,* which analyzed the legality of the Rozelle Rule (allowing the commissioner, one Pete Rozelle, to require the club that acquires a free agent to compensate the free agent's former club in the form of money, players and/or valuable draft picks), the court held that the Rule significantly deterred clubs from negotiating with and signing free agents. Because of the Rule, a club would only sign free agents if it was able to reach an agreement to compensate the player's former team or when it was willing to risk the commissioner's awarding of unknown compensation. The court held that the rule as enforced constituted a group boycott and a concerted refusal to deal and thus a per se violation of the Sherman Act.

The Court of Appeals in *Mackey,* however, acknowledged that it was inappropriate to declare the Rozelle Rule illegal per se without reviewing the purported justifications behind the Rule. The per se approach is typically used with agreements between business competitors in the traditional sense.

Professional sports combines aspects of both competition and cooperation; also, the NFL does assume some characteristics of a joint venture in that each member club has a stake in the success of the other teams. That is, no one club is interested in driving any other team out of business, since if the league fails then no one team can survive.

The *Mackey* appellate ruling reviewed the Rozelle Rule under a rule of reason analysis. The focus of inquiry under a rule of reason approach is whether the restraint as imposed is justified by legitimate purposes and it is no more restrictive than necessary. A rule of reason analysis poses the question of whether the restraint is reasonable under all the circumstances.

Most of the obvious antitrust infractions, for example, certain onerous player restriction procedures that were a part of the SPK, have now been ameliorated through collective bargaining so that currently these procedures can either pass antitrust examination or they are protected by an exemption to the antitrust laws. However, antitrust actions are still very much part of attempts to regulate and readjust both amateur and professional sports. For example, the NBA salary cap was attacked but found to be legal. *Wood v. NBA* (1984). The NCAA violated the antitrust laws by restricting college football broadcasts. *NCAA v. Board of Regents* (1984). The NFL violated antitrust laws by restricting franchise movement. *Los Angeles Memorial Coliseum Commission v. NFL* (1984).

B. EXEMPTIONS

Although many of the policies, rules, regulations and procedures of organized sports appear on the surface to violate both the letter and the spirit of the antitrust laws, they are deemed to be legal because they fall under certain exemptions to these laws. Usually, an allegedly underpaid professional athlete claims that league rules have financially disadvantaged him because he cannot achieve free agent status and test the market. Facially, this appears to be an antitrust violation; however, this procedure might be protected by an exemption. In this hypothetical, the exemption used by management would be the non-statutory labor exemption which protects agreements that are a product of good faith union-management negotiation.

1. Baseball

Professional baseball is exempt from the antitrust laws. Baseball's exemption is an anomaly that was categorized by Justice William Douglas as "a derelict in the stream of law." *Flood v. Kuhn* (1972) (Douglas, J., dissent). The Supreme Court realized its mistake but preferred for Congress to formulate a solution: "If there is any inconsistency or illogic in all this, it is an inconsistency and illogic of long standing that is to be remedied by the Congress and not by this court."

Baseball's exemption began in 1922 when Justice Holmes declared that professional baseball was not a business that involved interstate commerce. *Federal Base Ball Club of Baltimore, Inc. v. National League of Professional Base Ball Clubs* (1922). Even though it was freely acknowledged "that *Federal Baseball* was not one of Mr. Holmes' happiest days." *Salerno v. American League of Professional Baseball Clubs* (1970). No court would dare overrule Holmes and a unanimous court. In fact *Federal Baseball* was affirmed in 1953 and again in 1972. *Toolson v. New York Yankees* (1953); *Flood v. Kuhn* (1972). However, *Piazza v. Major League Baseball* (1993) redefined the exemption to apply solely to baseball's reserve system. *Piazza*, an opinion by the Eastern District of Pennsylvania, has limited precedential merit; it involved an attempt to purchase and relocate the S.F. Giants.

There is no chance that baseball's exemption will be extended to any other sport. Professional football was specifically denied immunity despite the obvious similarities between the two sports. *Radovich v. NFL* (1957). Baseball's exemption then is just "a narrow application of *stare decisis*." *United States v. Shubert* (1955).

2. Labor Exemption

The "statutory" labor exemption originated in certain provisions of the Clayton Act (15 U.S.C.A. § 12 et seq.) and the Norris–La Guardia Act (29 U.S.C.A. §§ 101–115) in which unions are allowed to enter into agreements, *inter se,* which might eliminate competition from other unions and create monopolies of all union organizational activities. Businesses cannot claim this privilege.

3. NFL Exemptions

Other "minor" exemptions to the antitrust laws in professional sports are those that were specifically created for the National Football League (NFL). One allows agreements between the NFL and the TV networks to pool and sell a unitary video package. 15 U.S.C.A. § 1291. Another allows blackouts of non-local games telecasted into home territories when the home team is playing. It will also permit the blackout of home games in the home territory. 15 U.S.C.A. § 1292. Also, when the two major leagues (NFL and AFL) were merged the merger of their two draft systems was specifically excluded from antitrust scrutiny. 15 U.S.C.A. § 1291.

4. Non–Statutory Labor Exemption

The non-statutory labor exemption is a derivative of the labor exemption that protects union activity from antitrust scrutiny. It is the crux of nearly all antitrust actions in professional sports. Basically, any union-management agreement that was a product of good faith negotiation will receive protection from the antitrust laws.

The goal of this exemption is certainly laudable; however, it is increasingly used by management as a means of legitimating certain agreements that were clearly forced on a weak union. Management attempts to wrap their anti-competitive policies with the mantle of this exemption. This is not the intent of the original Supreme Court decisions.

The non-statutory labor exemption is based on the policy that favors collective bargaining and gives it preference over the antitrust laws. The exemption will apply where the restraint on trade primarily affects only the parties to the collective bargaining agreement; where the restraint concerns a mandatory subject of collective bargaining; and where the agreement that is sought to be exempted is a product of bona fide arms' length bargaining. *Mackey v. NFL* (1976).

In *Mackey,* although the Rozelle Rule did not deal with a mandatory subject of collective bargaining on its face, since it was neither wages, hours or conditions of employment; however, since the Rule operated to restrict a player's ability to move from one team to another and thus depress salaries, the court held that the rule constituted a mandatory subject of collective bargaining. Id. at 615.

Regarding the Rozelle Rule in *Mackey,* it was established that there was no bona fide arm's length bargaining over the Rule. The Rozelle Rule imposed significant restraints on player mobility. The form of the Rule was unchanged since it was unilaterally promulgated by management in 1963. Also, there was no evidence to suggest that the players received any benefits from the Rule. Because of this, the Rule did not qualify for an exemption from the antitrust laws.

However, in *McCourt v. California Sports, Inc.* (1979), an action by a professional hockey player challenging the National Hockey League's reserve system, the court held that the nonstatutory labor exemption applied since the reserve system was incorporated into the c.b.a. as a result of good faith, arms' length bargaining. In this case, good faith bargaining was deemed to exist even though one of the parties to the negotiation did not yield on its initial bargaining position. The fact that one party's position on a mandatory subject prevailed unchanged does not necessitate the conclusion that there was no bargaining over the issue. A failure to succeed is not the same thing as a failure to negotiate.

However, recent court decisions which have sought to decipher the National Football League's labor-management imbroglio have expanded the protection of the non-statutory labor exemption to continue not only after the expiration of the c.b.a., but even after the parties have reached an impasse. *Powell v. NFL* (1989). In *Powell*, the policies under question were the "free agent" and draft procedures. These policies are protected by the nonstatutory labor exemption even though they are actively opposed by the union and its constituents. This opposition exists regardless of the fact that these policies carry an alleged favorable imprimatur by way of an earlier (1982) c.b.a.

At the same time, there have been situations where labor and management have compromised enough to create policies that reflect bona fide, good faith collective bargaining. For example, in *Wood v. NBA* (1984), a district court analyzed the legality of the NBA's salary cap provision which limits the total amount that each team can annually pay to their players. This procedure could limit the salary that a particular player could negotiate from his club. But, the cap was agreed to by both labor and management and became a part of their c.b.a. The court held that the cap was exempt from antitrust regulations and that the player in question, Leon Wood, came under the coverage of the agreement even though as a rookie he only entered the bargaining unit after the agreement was negotiated. The exemption was applicable since the salary cap affected only the parties to the c.b.a. (management and players), involved mandatory subjects of bargaining and was the result of bona fide, arms' length negotiations.

C. PLAYER RESTRAINTS

The use of antitrust litigation as a means to force change in professional sports historically developed from policies that restrain the movement of the athletes. Player restraint mechanisms limit the player's ability to negotiate the best dollar from the highest bidder and thus restrict the player's commerce; these procedures appear on their face to violate antitrust laws.

For example in *Smith v. Pro Football, Inc.* (1978), football's draft of collegiate talent was held to violate the antitrust laws. The draft is a procedure where negotiating rights to graduating college seniors are allocated each year among the NFL teams in reverse order of the club's finish in the previous year. The NFL draft as it existed in 1968 had a severely anticompetitive impact on the market for player's services; also, this type of restraint was not reasonably necessary to accomplish whatever legitimate business purposes that might be asserted as a rationale for a 17–round draft. In short, it was anticompetitive in both its purpose and its effect.

However, many of the earlier player restraint mechanisms have been modified through collective bargaining so that they are no longer considered to be an antitrust violation. As in the NBA salary cap dispute, the current generation of player restraints will now be decided under the purview of the nonstatutory labor exemption.

D. FRANCHISE MOVEMENT

Antitrust strategies in professional sports have shifted in recent years. Once the sole domain of relatively underpaid athletes, they are now used by the team owners themselves to gain advantage from the league, usually in the form of attempts to relocate their franchise. Professional sports is a big business; the precise geographical location of a team at a particular moment in time can be essential to that team's economic life or death. Franchise movement, however, is regulated by league regulations.

In *San Francisco Seals, Ltd. v. NHL* (1974), an individual NHL team brought suit against the league when they denied their request to relocate from San Francisco to Vancouver, British Columbia. The court held that the team was not competing economically with the league and the other teams. Because of this, the league's relocation rules did not restrain trade within the relevant market. Also, the Seals did not have standing to sue the league and the other teams for an alleged § 2 Sherman Act violation of monopolizing the business of major league hockey, since an individual team was not within the target area with respect to the claimed conspiracy.

However, in *Los Angeles Memorial Coliseum Commission v. NFL* (1984), the applicable league regulation directed that ¾'s of all NFL teams must approve any franchise relocation into the home territory of another team. The court held that the NFL's rule violated antitrust laws as the NFL was not a "single entity" and the regulation was an unreasonable restraint of trade. If it was not a single entity, the NFL could be held liable under a rule of reason analysis for unreasonably restraining the trade of the Oakland Raiders by thwarting their plans to relocate in Los Angeles. However, if the league was viewed as a single entity, it would be immune from suits against it by individual teams.

The NFL was not a single entity since each team had a separate identity independent from the league; the teams competed with the others for revenue and personnel; and each team was independently owned and operated. If the league was a single entity, it would be logically and legally unable to conspire with itself to restrain trade. However, since that is not the case, the league is simply a group of individual competitors whose joint votes on league matters could constitute an illegal group boycott.

E.   LEAGUE VERSUS LEAGUE

Antitrust conflicts also arise in professional sports when a nascent league claims that the dominant, established league is guilty of unfair competition. There is a cyclical history in professional sports: when it appears that there is money to be made a new league will form to compete against the established league. The end result is either that the older league conquers the new league upstart or they compromise and the two leagues merge as one (e.g., the NFL–AFL merger).

Many of the famous law suits that have shaped the current state of antitrust in professional sports have involved interleague rivalry. *Radovich v. NFL* (1957), which declared that football is not exempt from antitrust laws, involved the blacklisting of a football player by an NFL affiliate for playing with a competing league.

In *AFL v. NFL* (1963), the American Football League (AFL) sued the more established NFL on grounds that the older league monopolized all the best markets. The court found that the older league did not have the power to monopolize the relevant market; and did not attempt a conspiracy to monopolize the market. That is, the court found that any monopoly that the NFL might have possessed over the AFL was a natural monopoly.

A natural monopoly does not violate antitrust laws unless the natural monopoly was misused to gain a competitive advantage. Basically, the NFL acquired markets that the latecomer thought desirable. But, the first league is not required to surrender any, or all, of its advantageous sites to the second league simply to enable the latecomer to compete more effectively with the NFL. However, one must acquire a natural monopoly by means which are neither exclusionary, unfair, nor predatory.

In *USFL v. NFL* (1986), although the USFL won treble damages ($3.00), and attorney fees, the USFL is now defunct. The court held that the NFL's superiority in the bidding war was due to the USFL's poor management and the NFL's natural superiority and not entirely the result of illegal antitrust violations; therefore, the jury award of nominal damages was not in error.

F. TV PACKAGING

Although antitrust litigation is endemic in professional sports, it has also arisen in amateur sports, especially in the area of the NCAA's packaging of television broadcasts of college football games. In *NCAA v. Board of Regents* (1984), the court held that the NCAA's plan of packaging these broadcasts was unlawful under a rule of reason analysis since, *inter alia,* the plan was not intended to equalize competition, it did not regulate the money that the schools spent on their football programs, and it gave control of the packaging to schools that either did not have football programs or would not be affected by the restrictions (i.e., small-time collegiate football).

The NCAA's TV package was an unreasonable restraint of trade since the plan restricted the total number of football games that an NCAA member could televise, and further, the plan did not allow the member schools to sell their TV rights except in accordance with the NCAA's stipulations. By limiting the output and curtailing the big schools' ability to respond to network offers the NCAA was found to restrict the trade of these colleges. The *Board of Regents* decision set the networks free to negotiate TV contracts with the major college football teams; as a result, two large groups of universities were formed under the auspices of the two major television networks. See *Regents of University of California v. ABC* (1984).

G. CABLE TV

Sports has become an increasingly noticed phenomenon because of the advent and prosperity of cable TV. During recent years a number of prime time regular season professional football games and the National Hockey League's TV package have shifted from the major TV networks to cable TV, i.e., football to ESPN and hockey to Sportschannel America. Cable TV is limited access TV, in that viewers must pay for the pleasure of enjoying their programming. Many fans who once watched sports programming without payment are now forced to pay for that privilege. ESPN is a basic cable network whereas Sportschannel America costs more than the basic cable rate and thus reaches far less viewers.

There is also the emerging technology of pay-per-view broadcasts of one-of-a-kind sports spectaculars, e.g., the Holyfield–Foreman professional boxing match billed as the "Battle of the Ages". Does this migration of sports programming from the major networks to cable TV violate the antitrust laws? There is a court defined methodology that can deduce whether a package sale of broadcast rights increases or decreases the viewing of sports events. When these agreements diminish viewership, then they will constitute an unreasonable restraint of trade and thus can be enjoined. *NCAA v. Board of Regents of the University of Oklahoma* (1984).

These package sales are agreements among individual teams who would otherwise sell their rights to broadcast their own games. Package sales are agreements among competitors and as such will often invoke a per se analysis. However, courts have consistently reaffirmed that the special needs of professional sports leagues demand the more careful analysis of a rule of reason review.

Broadcast rights agreements when analyzed under a rule of reason analysis will be found to be anticompetitive and thus illegal if the prices become higher and the output lower. Cable TV, by definition, increases the costs and reduces the number of potential viewers since not everyone is covered by cable. Therefore, the phenomenon of the transfer of sports broadcasts from the major networks to cable TV may well be determined to be anticompetitive when it comes under judicial analysis.

H. AMATEUR SPORTS

TV packaging is not the only area in which antitrust litigation has arisen in amateur sports. The typical situation involves the National Collegiate Athletic Association (NCAA) as a defendant versus either a college, an athlete or another athletic governing organization. The plaintiffs will claim that NCAA policies and regulations have acted as an illegal restraint on their trade and commerce. Although the court found against the NCAA as regards their television packaging regulations, that is not the case for their eligibility requirements. Neither the NCAA eligibility rules that restrict compensation to athletes nor the enforcement of these rules are violations of the antitrust laws. These eligibility rules are justifiable means of encouraging competition among amateur teams and therefore, are pro-competitive since they enhance public interest in intercollegiate sports. See *United States v. Walters* (1989).

I. MISCELLANEOUS

Other than the primary arenas of antitrust litigation discussed above, there are also some peripheral areas of litigation. Most of these miscellaneous antitrust actions coalesce around tie-ins, rival sports and business-type problems.

A tie-in is the practice of tying the purchase of preseason tickets to the purchase of season tickets. Fans do not like this practice and have sued on antitrust grounds. This practice is legal since there is no consumer compulsion and there are always individual seats left for all home games. *Laing v. Minnesota Vikings Football Club, Inc.* (1973).

A corollary of the more famous league versus league suits, are those that involve rival sports. In *North American Soccer League v. NFL* (1980), a soccer league sued the NFL for its cross-ownership ban which stipulated that an NFL team owner could not own a part of another sports franchise. The court stated that, if there was a limited subgroup of sportsmen/entrepreneurs, then plaintiff had the burden of proving that that somewhat illusory fraternity did indeed exist. A rule of reason analysis was applied with the caveat that not every concerted action of professional sports league members possessed antitrust implications.

In another area, the NFL sued a state for trademark infringement concerning a state lottery that was based on the outcome of NFL games. The state claimed that the NFL's restrictions on trademark usage was violative of the antitrust laws since all NFL licenses were only obtainable through a package arrangement. The state lost, even though the scores, etc., were not property. However, since there was an illusion of sponsorship the state must issue a disclaimer. *NFL v. Governor of Delaware* (1977).

Business-related antitrust implications also arose when the owner of a controlling partnership in a professional football franchise brought an action against certain banks for allegedly attempting to force a distress sale of the club. This claim failed in part because plaintiff failed to establish that this alleged action by the banks violated the rule of reason. *Tose v. First Pennsylvania Bank, N.A.* (1981).

CHAPTER 6

TORTS

A. NEGLIGENCE

The tort action of choice for sports-related injuries is negligence. Negligence is any conduct that falls below the reasonable man standard. In sports, there is a myriad of possible variations of what that standard is as it relates to the varieties of sporting conduct. Negligence is measured against the particular facts and circumstances in each and every case.

The burden is on the plaintiff to show that a negligent act or omission occurred on the part of the defendant and that it was the proximate cause of that injury. That is, there must be an established duty of care, a breach of that duty, a proximate cause between defendant's action and the injury, and damages that resulted from that breach.

Negligence in sports is a relatively new phenomenon. In earlier days, the law was dominated by Justice Cardozo's maxim that "the timorous may stay at home." *Murphy v. Steeplechase Amusement Company* (1929). Basically, the law did not want to place an unreasonable burden on active participation in sports. One was assumed to voluntarily embrace any danger that might occur in a sporting

71

activity. However, the courts slowly began to understand that athletic competition did not exist in a vacuum; "some other restraints of civilization must accompany every athlete onto the playing field." *Nabozny v. Barnhill* (1975).

1. Duty of Care

The inquiry of whether the defendant owed a duty to the injured party is one of law. Whether that duty has been breached or whether there is a causal connection between breach and injury are questions of fact.

A duty is an expression of the sum total of policy considerations that would lead an adjudicator to find that a particular plaintiff is entitled to some sort of protection. A duty can be created by either common law, statute, contract or policy. If no duty is evident then an action in negligence will be unsuccessful.

A duty of care can also arise through a special relationship. Duty is predicated on the existing relationships between the parties at the relevant times. *Kleinknecht v. Gettysburg College* (1993) held that a recruited lacrosse player who suddenly collapsed and died during practice was owed a duty of care by the college to provide prompt emergency medical service. The special relationship here was the active recruitment of the player.

2. Standard of Care

The key to discovering a breach of a duty is to determine whether defendant's conduct falls below an applicable standard of care. For example, a violation of a league safety rule could constitute an actionable duty, if that rule is recognized as a standard of care created for the protection of participants.

In some instances a school is held to the same degree of care as the children's parents. The school is in loco parentis, and the applicable standard is that of reasonably prudent parents acting under similar and comparable circumstances.

The level of care will vary with the plaintiff's situation. The more foreseeable the injury, the higher the standard. An example of this would be an injured football player who is carried off the field in a stretcher in an unreasonable and dangerous manner. The standard of care for an already injured player is one of extreme caution. An absence of a specific standard of care as created by a safety rule or a physical education standard does not defeat negligence. Without a specific applicable rule, the standard of a reasonable man acting under similar circumstances will be applicable. Established rules and regulations will merely assist the plaintiff in his or her burden of proof.

3. Breach of Duty

A breach will occur when there is sufficient evidence for a jury to conclude that defendant breached a duty; and if so whether the jury could reasonably infer that defendant's breach was the proximate cause of the injury. When a duty exists, the question of breach is one for the trier of fact to resolve unless the evidence is so obvious that reasonable minds could not differ in their conclusions. Since the question of breach is one of facts, the determination must be on a case-by-case basis.

4. Proximate Cause

The next factor is whether there is a connection between the negligence and the resulting injury. The question is whether the breach of a duty was the proximate cause of the injury. This is a fact question and must be decided by a jury on a case-by-case basis.

Proximate cause is that cause which in a natural and continuous sequence, unbroken by an efficient intervening cause, produces the injury and without which the injury would not have occurred. In proving proximate cause, the plaintiff is not required to eliminate all of the other potential causes. One needs only to prove a sufficient evidentiary basis from which causation could reasonably be inferred, and the causation must only be a substantial factor in bringing about the injury.

5. Damages

Negligence requires that the plaintiff must suffer some damages. The phenomenon of a sporting activity is such that it is action-oriented and creates a situation in which the participant is extremely prone to injuries as a result of physical contact.

Therefore, damage is usually easy to prove. The only requirement is that actual loss or damages must result to the interest of another. Nominal damages alone where no actual loss has occurred will be insufficient. Likewise, the threat of future loss without more is also insufficient.

The question of damages is intertwined with the requirement of proximate cause. If the negligence in question is the proximate cause of the injury then it follows that the resulting damages, if more than nominal, would be sufficient to complete the negligence cause of action.

B. MEDICAL MALPRACTICE

Malpractice is a bad or unskilled practice by a physician or other medical professional. As in other negligence actions, the element of duty is essential to malpractice. Duty is an obligation to conform to a particular standard of conduct towards another. In the medical sports area, this duty can include the duty to disclose, the duty to instruct, the duty to disclose whether the physician is employed by a third party, e.g., a sports team, and a duty to disclose medical negligence. The duty is evaluated by a standard of conduct taking into account the skill and knowledge of the medical community as a whole.

A key element in any suit against a team for potential malpractice is whether the doctor in question was a team physician. The problem is that there is great deal of flexibility and variety among the possible relationships between doctor and team. The problem will usually translate into a question of whether the doctor is an employee of the team or an independent contractor. A doctor-patient relationship requires mutual acceptance between a doctor and an athlete (or an athlete's agent or parents or guardians). When mutual acceptance has occurred, a doctor-patient relationship is established. Then consent to treat must be obtained. Consent must come from either the adult patient himself or from the parents of a minor athlete, since a minor is deemed incapable of giving valid consent.

1. Duty of Care

Like in any other negligence action, there must be a duty, breach of duty, causation and damages. The most typical potential for malpractice will come from the medical examination. Examinations, however, are conducted for a variety of purposes with various degrees of thoroughness: for example, pre-participation exams, determination of fitness to participate, and examinations to prevent subsequent injury and to assess rehabilitation status. Since each type of examination calls for a different degree of analysis by the attending physician, it is difficult to establish a precise standard by which a physician's conduct may be evaluated. However, as in all medicine, a physician must act with the skill and knowledge that will be utilized by other doctors acting in similar circumstances.

In analyzing a physician's duty of care for medical examinations, one factor that must be considered is whether this particular physician is acting for the benefit of the team or for the benefit of the athlete. When a team physician acts for the benefit of the athlete, the duty of care owed will also include a duty not to increase the risk of other, foreseeable losses. Therefore, a missed diagnosis would be subject to liability for any lost opportunities that the athlete could prove were resulting losses.

2. Duty to Disclose and Informed Consent

A physician must disclose any material information regarding the athlete's physical condition. This duty to inform emanates both from the fiduciary nature of the relationship and from the athlete's right to determine the procedures that will be performed on his own body. A failure to disclose any medical information that ultimately results in damages to the athlete will create tort liability for the physician. The duty to disclose includes the duty to inform the athlete that he must seek further medical advice. Since an athlete is expected to perform at his highest obtainable level, a doctor's concealment or failure to disclose might cost the athlete his career through the aggravation of an injury.

A duty to disclose will remain even in the case where the doctor is hired by a party other than the athlete: the duty will exist regardless of who pays or even whether the doctor is paid or has an expectation of payment.

A corollary to the duty to disclose, at least as regards who needs the information to make a well-reasoned decision, is the doctrine of informed consent. A patient's consent to treatment is valid if it is informed. An athlete is informed when the doctor has released an amount of medical information relevant to the proposed treatment and sufficient to allow the athlete to make an intelligent choice as whether he should continue that treatment. This includes the reasonable disclosure of available alternative procedures as well as the dangers that correspond with each and an indication of whatever applicable advantages might ensue. The consent by the athlete should always be in writing and should be clear and understandable in terms and in scope.

Finally, in the world of sports, physicians' disclosure of information relative to the physical or even mental condition of the athlete is unusually important since any disclosure to the media could severely damage an athlete's potential to successfully continue his career. For example, if a team's doctor communicates any information on an athlete's conditions to the media, with or without consent, the doctor may be subject to liability for defamation, invasion of privacy or breach of a confidential relationship. Also, disclosure in the absence of consent may subject that doctor to potential liability if the team relies upon the physician's statement and it is subsequently proved inaccurate.

3. Fraudulent Concealment

The Charlie Krueger case revolved around allegations that the team physicians for his professional football team fraudulently concealed medical information about his injuries, the extent of his injuries and his ability to continue to play. *Krueger v. San Francisco Forty Niners* (1987). Mr. Krueger was an exemplary defensive lineman for the San Francisco 49ers from 1958 until 1973 when he retired; he missed only parts of two seasons due to injuries. During his career he suffered numerous injuries but continued to play through the pain: for example, a broken arm, broken ring fingers on each hand, numerous broken noses, multiple dislocations of fingers and thumbs on both hands, a blow-out fracture of the right ocular orbit, an eye infection, a sprained right knee and hypertension.

Those injuries, however, were somewhat minor compared to the problems that befell his left knee. It was operated on in college and in 1963 he ruptured his medial collateral ligament; the team operated on it at that time and told him it was in "good repair". He continued to play with the help of rehabilitative therapy from the team trainer and a brace which he wore while playing until 1967. The team physician noted that Krueger's anterior cruciate ligament, which prevents the tibia from shifting forward on the femur, appeared to be absent. An injury like this produces instability in the knee, particularly when combined with other injuries; Krueger was never told of this injury.

His left knee continued to hurt and swell; in 1964, he received further treatment from the team physicians in the form of an aspiration of bloody fluids by syringe and a contemporaneous injection of novocaine and cortisone, a steroid compound. Krueger testified to 50 such treatments in 1964 and a 14 to 20 average per year from 1964 to 1973; through all this he was never informed of the dangers that are associated with steroids: possible rupturing of tendons, weakening of joints and cartilage, and destruction of capillaries and blood vessels. In 1971, he underwent another operation on his left knee by the team doctor to remove "loose bodies" as a result of chronic chondromalacia, thinning and loss of cartilage on the knee cap's undersurface; this condition is fully consistent with steroid abuse. Also, x-rays from 1964 to 1971 revealed degenerative post-traumatic changes in the knee; he was not informed of any of these afflictions by the 49ers medical staff. Added to this, in 1971, Krueger felt a hit on his knee with a resulting feeling that a piece of substance dislodged on the outside of his knee joint; still, he played the five remaining games. During this time period he was never advised by the team doctors that he risked permanent injury by continuing to play without surgery.

Finally, five years after retirement, he was shown x-rays and was advised for the first time that he suffered from a chronic and permanent disability. He now suffers from traumatic arthritis and a crippling degenerative process in the left knee; he cannot stand up for prolonged periods; he cannot run; he is unable to walk up stairs without severe pain; his condition is degenerative and irreversible.

Under the informed consent doctrine an integral part of the physician's overall obligation is to the patient: there is a duty of reasonable disclosure of the available choices with respect to the proposed therapy and of the dangers that are inherently and potentially involved in each procedure. The physician must disclose all information that is necessary to make a knowledgeable decision about the proposed treatment. This duty is imposed so that the patient can meaningfully exercise their right to make decisions that affect their own bodies; therefore, even if the patient rejects the recommended treatment the duty will still continue. The failure to make this type of disclosure not only constitutes negligence, but, where the requisite intent is shown, fraud or concealment can also be established. A physician, especially a team doctor, cannot avoid responsibility for failure to fully disclose simply by claiming that information was not specifically withheld. Krueger was never advised of the adverse effects of the injection of steroids or the continued medical risks that would occur as a result of his continuing in football; therefore, the requisite disclosure was not forthcoming.

Intent also must be established for fraudulent concealment; plaintiff must show that at the time of the concealed information defendant intended to induce the patient to adopt or abandon a course of action. In this case, the intent was to induce

Krueger to continue to play despite his injuries. The team in its desire to keep their player on the field consciously failed to make full, meaningful disclosure as to the magnitude of the risk he took in continuing to play a violent contact sport with a profoundly damaged left knee. It is axiomatic in the situation of an athlete and a team doctor that the element of reliance was also present.

4. Team Physicians

The major conflict inherent in analyzing potential medical malpractice claims in athletics is the role or roles of the team physician. The question is what is the doctor's relationship to the athlete's employer and how does that relationship affect the physician's relationship with the patient, the athlete.

Since most claims against team physicians will be based on negligence, the first hurdle will be to establish a duty and a standard of care. The duty to act will usually be predicated on the existence of a physician-patient relationship. A standard of care, on the other hand, will be based upon society's expectations that physicians act reasonably under the circumstances.

Usually, the existence of a physician-patient relationship is a given; however, it is much more complicated when the physician works for a school or a professional sports team. It is clear that when the primary purpose of the medical service is actual care and treatment, then a relationship will be deemed to exist; however, it is less clear when a doctor is hired for non-therapeutic purposes, for example, a preparticipation physical exam. Traditionally, no duty will exist for non-therapeutic examinations. However, many states currently hold that doctors may owe a duty of care to discover dangerous conditions and then to report these conditions to the athlete, even if the physician is paid by a third party.

There is also the question of the extent to which the medical doctor may limit the scope of his relationship to the athlete/patient. The physician-patient relationship is consensual in nature and as such a doctor may generally limit the scope of his professional involvement at the beginning of said relationship. However, he must inform the athlete of these limitations in advance unless the limitations are reasonably expected based upon common practices or past dealings. This truism is relevant for preparticipation and post-injury physical examinations, especially if the doctor is hired on a one time only basis for school preseason physicals. Even these physicians must be responsible both for conditions that are within the scope of the examination that they knew or should have known and for those conditions that are outside the scope of the examination but which the doctor know or had reason to know about as a result of the examination.

A standard of care for a team physician can be typically defined as performing to the level of expertise that conforms to a reasonably competent medical practitioner under similar circumstances taking into account all reasonable limitations that are placed on the scope of the doctor's undertaking. However, it appears that sports medicine has reached a specialty status for purposes of establishing a minimal standard of care. In the future, courts will probably elevate sports medicine doctors to a specialist's standard. This standard will be limited to the fundamentals of the sub-field of sports medicine which are known to all practitioners in the field based on the types of athletes with whom the doctor is primarily involved. Traditional specialists, such as orthopedic surgeons, who happen to concentrate in sports medicine, will still be expected to act to the standard of a reasonable orthopedist.

The types of legal relationships between a doctor and the school or professional team are myriad. In an attempt to establish the type of relationship, the preliminary inquiry goes to the contractual obligations between the parties and the degree of control the doctor retains in his management of the athlete. The duties and obligations of the physician to the team should be delineated by their contract. This is more true with professional teams. It is less the case in the amateur level where the duties are often less well-defined. The physician for an amateur team may be paid little or nothing for his participation, and his ties to the team may be limited solely to preparticipation physicals and treatment of specific injuries on a referral basis as opposed to the plethora of duties that a team physician to a professional sports enterprise will generally contract for (e.g., preparticipation, injury treatment, attending practices and games, referrals, rehabilitation, certification of fitness, etc.).

The next question is the degree to which the school or professional team controls the doctor's treatment of the athlete/patient. If the doctor maintains autonomy in his therapeutic decision-making, then he will usually be deemed to be an independent contractor. If that is the case, then the doctrine of respondeat superior will be inapplicable and the team or school as the employer will not be vicariously liable for any negligent acts of the physician.

A team physician is usually deemed to be an independent contractor; however, in some cases a professional sports franchise will be found vicariously liable for the physician's tortious conduct. In one such case, a team physician detailed a story that alleged that a particular player had a fatal disease and then released that story to the media. The physician was liable for the intentional infliction of emotional distress and the team was liable under the doctrine of respondeat superior. *Chuy v. Philadelphia Eagles Football Club* (1977). Also, a school district was held vicariously liable for the negligence of both the football coach and the team doctor who exhibited improper techniques in the removal from the playing field of an injured player who was suspected to have suffered a fractured neck; this improper removal technique exacerbated the existing injury. *Welch v. Dunsmuir Joint Union High School District* (1958).

5. Failure to Refer and Vicarious Liability

To establish vicarious liability the team must have the power to select, control and dismiss the doctor. Also, there must be responsibility by the team to supervise; the doctor's services must be part of the services rendered by the team; the services supplied by the doctor must assist the purposes of the team; and there must be at least a certain amount of control asserted by the team over the doctor in the carrying out of his or her work.

A physician may also be liable when she identifies the problem or potential problem; fails to warn the patient of the nature of that problem; and then fails to recommend further care or treatment pursuant to a solution that will ameliorate those medical problems. However, courts have distinguished between the liability of the doctor and the liability of the team for failure to refer. Whether a team can be liable has turned on the degree of control that the team has over the doctor and whether the doctor served the interests of the athlete or those of the team when he allowed the athlete to play without informing him of the conditions that warranted a referral.

C. PRODUCT'S LIABILITY

Actions in product's liability are associated with tort actions that involve defective items that are used in sports. These items would include football helmets, golf carts, lawn darts, etc. An equipment manufacturer must meet state regulated standards of safety and care in the product's design, manufacture, and use; the supplier and seller may likewise be liable for negligence if they fail to exercise reasonable care. A manufacturer must adhere to the standard of reasonable care in the manufacture and design of sports equipment. The manufacturer must assure that the product is reasonably safe when used for the intended purpose and in the intended matter.

When the product is dangerous, e.g., a golf cart, then even if properly used a manufacturer will still have a duty to warn of potential hazards. Sellers or retailers of sports equipment will be liable if they know that the equipment is dangerous and fail to warn an otherwise oblivious purchaser. A seller may also have a duty to inspect if she knows that the product may be dangerous. Similarly, advertisers may also have the duty to warn about the dangers associated with the product. Suppliers or wholesalers of equipment must also use reasonable care to make the product safe. However, warnings are not required when the danger is obvious or when the user already knows of the product's dangerous propensities.

Product warnings must be adequate to perform the intended function of risk reduction. A warning will be inadequate if it does not particularize the risk presented by the product, if it is inconsistent with how the product will be used, if it does not provide the reason for the warning, or if the warning was not designed so as to reach the foreseeable user.

D. STRICT LIABILITY

Strict liability is liability without fault. Athletic equipment suppliers will be liable if they sell an unreasonably dangerous piece of sporting equipment which is harmful as a result of a defective condition. The manufacturer will be liable to the ultimate consumer for injuries suffered provided that the seller is in the business of selling that product and the product has not been substantially changed or altered.

Plaintiff has the burden of proving that the defect existed when the product left defendant and that the defect caused injury to a reasonably foreseeable user. However, plaintiff does not have to prove the negligence of the manufacturer. To prove that the equipment is defective will require more than the mere showing that the product caused injury. Defects can be the result of the manufacturing process or it can be in the design.

Regarding design, factors that should be weighed to determine if a particular piece of equipment is reasonably safe include the gravity of the danger posed by the design defect, the likelihood that danger will occur, the mechanical feasibility of a safer design, the cost of an improved design and the adverse consequences to the product and to the consumer that might result from an alternative design. *Everett v. Bucky Warren, Inc.* (1978).

Strict liability is imposed by operation of law for public policy reasons and the protection of the public. A product is defective if it is not reasonably fit for the purposes for which it is sold. This is important in sports since each piece of protective equipment is specifically geared for a particular function. The seller may avoid liability by proper instructions and warnings which if followed properly would avoid injury. The seller can also assume that the athlete will read and follow these admonitions. With strict liability the defense of contributory negligence is generally unavailable although assumption of risk still applies.

E. WARRANTY LIABILITY

Breach of warranty is another theory of recovery under product's liability. Warranty liability is based on a breach of contract. A warranty is akin to a promise that concerns the quality and condition of the product. If the product fails to meet the expectations of the promise then the warranty is broken and the seller is liable under contract law for the resulting damage.

There are two types of warranties under the Uniform Commercial Code (UCC), express and implied. Express warranties are those warranties that are made by statements or conduct on the part of the manufacturer or seller; these warranties exist if a reasonable person would take the seller's actions or conduct to be a promise or representation of fact concerning the quality or condition of the product.

There is also an implied warranty of merchantability. Merchantability means fitness for ordinary use. There will be a breach of the implied warranty of merchantability when a specific piece of sporting equipment does not meet the representations that are made on its label; and therefore, it is not fit for the ordinary use for which it was sold.

Privity may be required to maintain an action for breach of warranty. Privity is the direct line that goes from the manufacturer to the buyer. It is a relation between parties that is sufficiently close and direct to support a legal claim on behalf of the plaintiff against the other person with whom this relationship exists. UCC § 2–318 waives the requirement of privity if a purchase is made by a member of the victim's immediate family.

F.   FACILITY LIABILITY

1.   Status of Injured Party

A large portion of sports negligence suits are against stadium owners and operators. The question in these suits is the status of the injured party who has entered the premises. Is that person an invitee, licensee or trespasser? With each category there is a different standard of care on the part of the facility owner or operator.

2. Invitees

Generally, participants and spectators are business invitees. The occupier is not an insurer of the invitee's safety. The duty to an invitee is one of ordinary and reasonable care including protection from negligence and reasonably discoverable hazards created by a third party and an obligation to inspect premises and make them safe for a visit. There is also a duty to warn of known, unsafe conditions.

For example, a health spa patron is a business invitee and the owner-operator owes a duty to keep the premises in a reasonably safe condition for his protection. This duty will include the detection of reasonably discoverable conditions on the premises which might be unreasonably dangerous and the correction of these conditions or warnings to the invitee of the danger. Examples would be the need to shut down a faulty stair master that might injure a shin and/or the need to post a warning that one should stop exercising when dizziness occurs.

The invitor/owner/operator also has the duty to furnish reasonable security and protection against the possibility of injury; and to refrain from negligent or careless acts which might make the premises hazardous to invitees. This duty to an invitee does have realistic boundaries and practical ramifications. For example, a ball park owner who screens in the home plate area where the danger of being struck by a foul ball is the greatest was deemed to have provided sufficient protection for as many invitees who could reasonably be expected to desire screened seating. In this situation, the proprietor fulfilled his duty of care and could not be held liable in negligence for injury to a spectator from a foul ball. *Akins v. Glens Falls City School District* (1981).

3. Minors

The standard of care will change with the type of invitee, e.g., if the invited person is a minor, invalid or senior citizen. Health spa operators have a duty to keep their premises in a reasonably safe condition for the protection of a patron. In negligence actions against spas the court will consider the type of person entering the establishment: for example, whether the customer was someone who joined the club for treatment of a physical infirmity.

Where minors are involved, one question is whether the minor is capable of appreciating the risk involved in either watching or participating in the sport. For an eight-year old who was struck by a foul ball, the factual question presented to the court was the boy's ability to appreciate the risk of occupying the place that he occupied and whether the design of the screening was negligent since it ignored the high risk area of a picnic grounds adjacent to the right field foul line. *Atlanta v. Merritt* (1984). The key is the foreseeability of the injury. However, even with children all the elements of negligence must be present.

4. Unreasonably Hazardous Conditions

An owner will be liable in negligence when he has prior knowledge of unreasonably hazardous conditions. The proprietor's duty of reasonable and ordinary care to an invitee includes the detection of reasonably discoverable conditions which may be unreasonably dangerous and the correction of them or at least a warning of their danger. When there is a question of whether the condition is unreasonably dangerous or not, the court may look at prior events. In a case where a high school student crashed through a glass panel located near a gymnasium, the court found negligence because a similar act had occurred several years earlier when a visiting coach walked into that panel. The school authorities should have known of the hazard that this situation created and then have taken steps to either ameliorate or warn of the potential of the danger. *Wilkinson v. Hartford Accident and Indemnity Company* (1982). However, recovery will not be allowed for obvious dangers.

5. Design, Construction, Maintenance and Repair

Owners of premises will be liable for the negligent design, construction, maintenance or repair of their sports facilities. The preeminent example is when the negligent design and construction of screening at a baseball stadium allegedly causes injury to a spectator from a foul ball.

Another typical case from baseball is when a player slides into an unprotected spike at a base and then alleges that the injury was a result of the negligent design, construction, maintenance or repair of the base. The question will be whether the alleged negligent design of the base and the spike was the cause of the runner's injury. Still, there must be an applicable duty. When a player fractured his ankle while sliding into third base and alleged that the field was negligently packed and the infield dirt too hard, the court found that plaintiff failed to state a claim from which relief would be granted since the player did not allege that the defendant had any duty to maintain the infield dirt in any particular manner or that there was any owed duty. *Blancher v. Metropolitan Dade County* (1983).

G.   PROFESSIONAL SPORTS

In professional sports, a participant can now sue another participant (see chapter seven, § D). The appropriate standard for the intentional striking of an opposing player during a professional football game is one of recklessness.

CHAPTER 7

PARTICIPANT INJURIES

A. GENERALLY

Historically, participants could not recover for injuries that occurred on the playing field. The defense of assumption of risk would block all attempts at recovery. Today, as a general rule, participants assume the risk of unintentional injuries but will not assume injuries that are intentionally inflicted or result from a disregard for safety.

The injured participant might also face the defenses of consent and contributory negligence. Also, an injured participant cannot recover from another participant if the latter did not breach a recognized duty of care.

Liability was found when a basketball player struck an unprovoked blow to an opponent whose back was turned. *Griggas v. Clauson* (1955). Liability was also found when a player violated a safety rule by kicking a soccer goal keeper in a penalty area. *Nabozny v. Barnhill* (1975). Another example of liability was when a base runner deliberately ran into a second baseman who was five feet from the bag. *Bourque v. Duplechin* (1976). Liability was found when a catcher deliberately and without warning struck a batter. *Averill v. Luttrell* (1957).

Recovery was denied when a second baseman was injured as an unintended consequence of an opposing player's slide into the base. *Tavernier v. Maes* (1966). Liability was likewise denied when a bat slipped out of the hands of a batter and struck another player. *Gaspard v. Grain Dealers Mut. Ins. Co.* (1961). Recovery was also denied when a basketball player was accidentally struck by an opposing player. *Thomas v. Barlow* (1927).

Recent cases illustrate the difficulty that participants have in recovering for athletic injuries inflicted through contact with another participant. In *Keller v. Mols* (1987), a minor was injured while playing goalie in a floor hockey game. Recovery was disallowed on the grounds that participation in contact sports precluded recovery in negligence if the players were organized and coached; the shooting of plastics pucks in an attempt to score was not viewed as either willful or wanton conduct. Similarly, in a 1986 Louisiana case which involved a softball player injured in a collision with a second softball player, the court found that defendant was neither reckless nor unsportsmanlike while running to first; therefore, the risk of collision between defendant and plaintiff/first baseman was a reasonable risk and one that the player assumed. *Novak v. Lamar Ins. Co.* (1986).

In *Niemczyk v. Burleson* (1976), an action was based on injuries sustained when defendant shortstop in a softball game ran across the infield and collided with plaintiff/base runner as she was running from first to second base. A sports participant accepts reasonable dangers that are inherent to the sport; but only to the point that they are obvious and a usual incident to that sport. Material factors that can be used in determining if a participant's conduct which causes injury to another constitutes actionable negligence include the specific game involved, ages and physical attributes of the participants, their respective skills at the game, their knowledge of its rules and customs, their status as amateurs or professionals, the type of risks which are inherent to the game and those which are outside the realm of reasonable anticipation, the presence or absence of protective uniforms or equipment and the degree of enthusiasm with which the game is played. In *Niemczyk,* the plaintiff sufficiently stated a claim on which relief could be granted on the grounds of negligence.

B. VIOLATION OF SAFETY RULES

A participant can avoid the defenses of assumption of risk and contributory negligence by basing his cause of action on defendant's violation of a safety rule. In *Nabozny v. Barnhill* (1975), plaintiff, a soccer goal keeper, was allowed recovery for being kicked in the head while holding the ball in the penalty area. It was a clear rule violation for the defendant to make contact with the goal keeper in this manner. Safety rules charge participants with a legal duty, breach of which produces actionable negligence. Each player is charged with a legal duty to every other player on the field to refrain from conduct proscribed by a safety rule.

In a 1980 Illinois case, *Nabozny* was interpreted to reflect that a violation of the rules of the National Federation of High School Associations was alone insufficient to establish negligence, since liability for injuries based on a breach of safety rules cannot be predicated on ordinary negligence. A rule violation only establishes a duty if the conduct was more than ordinary negligence; either deliberate or willful conduct or conduct with a reckless disregard for the safety of others. *Oswald v. Township High School District* (1980).

C.   UNSPORTSMANLIKE CONDUCT

Recovery may be allowed when a plaintiff was injured through defendant's unsportsmanlike conduct. In the case of *Bourque v. Duplechin* (1976), defendant base runner in a softball game charged the plaintiff who was five feet from second base, with the result that plaintiff suffered substantial damages. Defendant was under a duty to play softball in an ordinary fashion without unsportsmanlike conduct or attempting wanton injury to fellow participants. Defendant breached this duty. A player on the other hand, will most likely assume the risk of injuries from standing on a base and being spiked by someone sliding into that base, which is common in softball.

Participants assume all the ordinary and foreseeable risks incidental to that particular sport.

However, they do not assume the risk from fellow participants who act in an unexpected or unsportsmanlike manner with a reckless lack of concern for other players.

D. PROFESSIONAL SPORTS

At one time, recovery for participant injuries was extremely unusual in professional contact sports such as football, due to the defense of assumption of the risk. This ended with *Hackbart v. Cincinnati Bengals, Inc.* (1977). In *Hackbart,* one Booby Clark, a member of defendant's team, ran a pass pattern during which the ball was intercepted by the opposing team. Plaintiff Hackbart was a defensive back. After the interception, Hackbart and Clark both ended up on the ground near each other and were watching the progress of the play as it transpired up field. Clark, acting out of anger and frustration but without a specific intent to injure, struck a blow with his right forearm to the back of the kneeling Hackbart's head and neck. Neither player complained during the game. Clark testified that his frustration was brought about by the fact that his team was losing. Although there were no protests or any fouls called by the officials, the game film clearly showed that the incident had occurred. Plaintiff later suffered great pain which ultimately forced him out of the game. The injury was eventually diagnosed as a serious neck fracture.

The question was whether in a regular season professional football game an injury which is inflicted by one professional player on an opposing player could give rise to liability in tort when the injury was inflicted by the intentional striking of a blow during a game. The district court ruled in favor of defendant on the grounds that conventional standards of tort liability cannot apply to professional football, since it is a business which is violent by its very nature.

The Court of Appeals, however, reversed and brought professional football back into the standard orbit of recovery for negligent injuries. The Court of Appeals stated that principles of law governing the infliction of injuries must not be disregarded simply because an individual's injury occurred during a professional football game. The alternative would be to admit that the only available option left to the injured football player would be retaliation. The court determined that the instigating player acted impulsively and in the heat of combat in intentionally striking an opposing player in the back of the head during a professional football game. The appropriate standard was recklessness, since Clark intended to inflict serious injury.

E.   CONTACT SPORTS

Contact sports are different from other sports in regard to potential for recovery. In contact sports a certain amount of contact between participants is not only expected but even required.

In *Kabella v. Bouschelle* (1983), a minor sued another minor in an attempt to gain damages for injuries sustained in an informal game of tackle football. Plaintiff did not have a negligence cause of action. Voluntary participation in a sport like football constitutes an implied consent to the normal risks that attend permissible bodily contact. But, participation in football still does not constitute consent to contact prohibited by rules which are designed to protect participants and not merely to control the game's flow.

Keller v. Mols (1987), involved a minor who was injured while acting as a goalie in an informal game of floor hockey on a friend's patio. The court held that the inquiry should be whether floor hockey was a contact sport and not whether the participants were organized or coached. After they decided that floor hockey was a contact sport, the court established that the standard for contact sports is that mere negligence is insufficient to establish a cause of action. However, willful and wanton behavior will be sufficient to establish a participant negligence suit. Willful and wanton contact is an intentional or reckless disregard for the safety of others. The defendant's action in this case was neither willful nor wanton. Anything normal in the game will not rise to the level of willful or wanton conduct and thus will be insufficient to support an action in negligence.

F. THIRD PERSONS

Another aspect of participant injuries is the interaction of participants with non-participants: spectators or other third persons, such as, referees, coaches, camera men, facility operators, etc. There is also the phenomenon of spectator abuse. Spectator abuse may take various forms: from a bottle thrown at an outfielder to a mob scene involving an umpire. The key to any evaluation lies in deciding who is responsible for the injuries. A bottle thrower who is caught will obviously be responsible for the consequences of his acts. However, the more difficult situation is when there is no clear cut correlation between injury and the person allegedly responsible. In *Toone v. Adams* (1964), an umpire was injured after a call during a minor league baseball game. The umpire contended that fan reaction began and was inspired by the manager of the home team. The court dismissed this claim on the grounds that the injury was not contemporaneous with the manager's antics nor could the manager be held responsible for the acts of the fans.

Some participant injuries stem from the negligent acts of third persons. Many of these types of injuries are created by the conduct of coaches. Courts have imposed tort liability when an athlete was required to compete after sustaining a previous injury, when a coach or a team failed to render medical assistance, when a coach failed to provide proper equipment and when there was negligent instruction. Another third party, in this case, a wrestling referee, was liable for injuries suffered by a participant because of the referee's negligent supervision in not detecting an illegal hold. *Carabba v. Anacortes School District* (1967).

In a softball injury case, a player alleged that his fractured ankle which he suffered while sliding into third base, was due to the negligence of the owner of the field who was responsible for the negligent maintenance and packing of the infield dirt in a way that made it too hard. However, the court held that there was neither a duty to maintain the infield dirt in any particular manner nor was there a breach of an owed duty. *Blancher v. Metropolitan Dade County* (1983).

CHAPTER 8

SPECTATOR INJURIES

A. GENERALLY

Like participants, spectators run the risk of injury while observing a sport. These injuries can come from foul balls, errant pucks, out of control halfbacks, etc. Spectators, however, will not recover for injuries that result from ordinary and foreseeable risks that are inherent to that particular sport. This is true because they have legally assumed those risks. However, they will not assume the risk of intentional harm, nonforeseeable injury or the negligent acts of a participant. Spectators will also not assume the risk of an arena operator who fails to meet his duty of care.

Although filled with exceptions in most jurisdictions, the doctrine of assumption of risk remains a viable defense in the area of spectator injury, especially baseball spectators. The classic example of an unassumed risk is the outfielder who charges into the stands and assaults a heckler. Under certain circumstances, ordinary negligence is sufficient to establish a participant's liability for injuries to a spectator.

Also, spectators do not assume the risk of an arena operator's failure to meet his duty of care.

The owners or operators are business invitors and as a result are liable for conditions which cause harm to invitees, if they knew or should have known that a condition existed which posed an unreasonable risk to the spectators, the spectators could not have discovered and protected themselves against this risk, and the owners failed to exercise reasonable care for the spectator's protection. Arena operators have a duty to maintain the premises in a reasonably safe condition and to supervise the conduct of those on the premises so as to prevent injury. Therefore, spectators may assume that the operators exercised reasonable care to make the arena safe for the purposes of the invitation. The operator is not an insurer of the spectator's safety. The spectator must prove that the acts were a breach of the duty of care and that the breach was the proximate cause of the injury.

B. BASEBALL

Baseball has traditionally been America's number one pastime. Cases of foul ball injuries have received numerous judicial reviews throughout the years. However, the general rule is that a spectator cannot recover for ordinary risks inherent in the sport; and in baseball, foul balls are viewed as an ordinary risk. In *Schentzel v. Philadelphia National League Club* (1953), a female spectator was hit by a foul ball at Philadelphia's Shibe Park. Although she had watched televised broadcasts and had viewed foul balls that went into grandstands, this was her first visit to a ball park. She claimed that defendant had a legal duty to extend the screen protection to encompass all the women patrons, many of whom were both ignorant of the game and lured there by special invitations, such as free admissions. Although plaintiff did not expressly consent to the foul ball injury, the court found that stray balls were a matter of common everyday practical knowledge. As a matter of law the plaintiff had impliedly assumed the normal and ordinary risk incident to attendance at a baseball game. As long as the risks were ordinary, the mere fact of plaintiff's attendance signified that she had assumed those risks.

However, in *Jones v. Three Rivers Management Corporation* (1978), the court argued that the no-duty rule applies only to common, frequent and expected risks, and in no way affects the duty of a sports facility to protect patrons from foreseeably dangerous conditions not inherent in the amusement activity. *Jones* involved a patron who was injured when she was hit by a batting practice foul ball while standing in the interior walkway of a stadium concourse. One who attends a baseball game as a spectator cannot properly be charged with anticipating as inherent to baseball the risk of being struck by a baseball while properly using an interior walkway. The court held that concourse openings are simply not a part of the spectator sport of baseball. As a result, the no-duty rule did not apply and plaintiff was not barred from recovery.

An owner fulfills his duty of ordinary care when there is sufficient screening to provide adequate protection for as many spectators as may reasonably be expected to desire this type of seating. The stadium owner or operator does not have a duty to inform their patrons of the availability of protected seats because their existence is obvious. *Dent v. Texas Rangers* (1989). Assumption of risk to spectators has also been extended to include errant softballs. *Arnold v. City of Cedar Rapids* (1989). As in baseball, the court held that the owner discharged their duty to protect spectators when they supplied sufficient screened seats. The owner could not be held liable for those who chose to sit elsewhere.

In *Clark v. Goshen Sunday Morning Softball League* (1985), a father who brought his son to a pregame softball practice was struck by a warm-up pitch as he stood around the infield as a bystander. The court held that it was inconsequential that the injury occurred during warm up because the father was a spectator as a matter of law and neither the league nor the player who threw the pitch had a duty to warn him of that danger. Whether or not the umpire actually called "play ball" did not minimize the dangers to spectators who are present during warm up prior to the game. When a ball is thrown from point A to point B, its arrival at the last point is not guaranteed in the normal course of baseball. Even after reasonable care, there is some risk of being struck by a ball. The court averred that spectators at baseball games assume the risk of being struck and injured by thrown balls. Interestingly, the father was viewed as a spectator since he was not a casual passerby on the sidewalk. He elected to come specifically into the ballpark thereby placing himself in the zone of danger subject to all the known and inherent risks that are a part of attendance at a ballpark, including casually standing around the infield.

C. GOLF

Unlike baseball where there is some predictability to the flight of a foul ball; in golf there is far less predictability when one improperly strikes a golf ball. In order to avoid possible liability, golfing sponsors and owners must meet standard safety requirements. Golf spectators assume the inherent dangers and risks involved with the sport. However, golf courses and sponsors still must provide reasonably safe premises for the spectators. For example, in *Duffy v. Midlothian Country Club* (1985), a golfball struck a spectator's eye causing total blindness during a golf tournament; the incident occurred in a roped off concession area. The court held that the sponsors had a duty of reasonable care towards the spectators as business invitees. In a similar case, *Grisim v. TapeMark Charity Pro–Am Golf Tournament* (1986), plaintiff alleged that there was a negligent failure to provide adequate safety to spectators and cited the fact that she was forced to sit on the ground because of a lack of space in the stands. Even golf tournaments have minimal safety requirements as established by various golf associations; these standards usually include the use of barricades and marshals, neither of which were provided for during this particular tournament.

The landowner does not have to protect the invitee from known or obvious dangers unless the landowner anticipates the possibility of harm. Golf exhibitions, however, do carry a certain amount of risk. The key is whether the defendant has reason to expect harm to the plaintiff from an obvious risk in circumstances where the plaintiff's attention might be distracted from the risk, causing him to forget to protect himself against that harm. *Baker v. Mid Maine Medical Center* (1985).

D. HOCKEY, CAR RACES AND WRESTLING

Inherently dangerous sports tend to define the legal parameters that control spectator injuries. However, the crux is still whether a plaintiff clearly knows and understands the risk that has occurred and, if so, whether that choice is entirely free and voluntary.

A knowing and voluntary assumption of risk is especially important in ice hockey, automobile racing and professional wrestling. Spectators assume all risks that are matters of common knowledge. Spectators assume the risk of injury from these potential harms as a matter of law. However, what is common knowledge at one time may not have been common knowledge at an earlier time. In a 1952 Pennsylvania case, *Schwilm v. Pennsylvania Sports* (1952), a female hockey fan was deemed not to have the requisite knowledge to understand that the area behind the hockey net was dangerous. Defendants breached their duty to her by improperly screening the goal area; however, they did not breach their duty to her husband, who was a co-plaintiff and an experienced hockey buff who knew the danger and assumed the risk of sitting near the goal. Arguably this case might be decided differently now because of the widespread popularity that hockey currently enjoys.

It is the duty of management to exercise ordinary care for the safety of spectators at hockey games. Courts often contrast knowingly encountered danger with a negligently encountered risk. In the first example, plaintiff consents to the possibility of harm whereas in the second example plaintiff fails to accurately assess the possible results of his or her own actions. Hockey clubs are not insurers of the safety of their spectators. But they do have a duty to use reasonable care. The clubs should eliminate or warn of hazards which they ought to know of and which are not reasonably expected by patrons.

In professional wrestling and automobile racing, the operators must also exercise reasonable care for the safety of their patrons. But, like in all other sporting endeavors, they are not insurers and are likewise not liable unless they fail to act reasonably.

For example, in one professional wrestling match (which is by definition noisy and undignified), an unknown person threw a whiskey bottle into the crowd. The court held that the operator was not negligent because there was no showing that the facility breached its duty of care. *Whitfield v. Cox* (1949). But a spectator at a automobile racing event should expect the same type of screened protection that is required at a baseball park. For example, an operator would be negligent if he failed to provide sufficient protection in the form of fencing between the pit and the area where the spectator is seated near the edge of the track.

E. MINORS

The capability of a person to assume a risk is extremely important. This is especially true for minors. The nature of the risk that may be assumed is not conclusive as to whether it has been assumed. The plaintiff must know and understand the risk that he incurs. Also, the choice to incur that risk must be free and voluntary. With minor spectators, the question is whether they can assume the risks that are inherent in the activity. In *Brosko v. Hetherington* (1931), an eleven year-old caddy in the first day of service recovered damages when a defendant negligently struck a golf ball that injured him, without warning of the potential danger. The defendant had a duty to observe if anyone was in the area where the ball could possibly travel if sliced (i.e., hit to the side) and had a duty to warn anyone in that area in order that they might protect themselves. In golf it is customary to give a warning when driving a ball from the tee under certain circumstances.

It is not customary to give a warning in a baseball game for each ball that is either pitched or batted. When an eight year-old was struck in the face by a foul ball during a game in which he and his parents attended in an inadequately screened picnic area directly adjacent to the right field foul-line, the court observed that spectators at a baseball game are presumed to be aware of the dangers inherent in that sport. However, whether a child's assumption of that risk bans recovery is a question for the jury unless the facts are so plain that they demand a finding by the court as a matter of law. The court found nothing which demanded the conclusion that the eight year-old plaintiff understood the risk of occupying the place he occupied or that he assumed the inherent risks. Because of his age, the lack of evidence in the records concerning his ability to appreciate the risk and his actual understanding of the risk, the court held that the child did not as a matter of law assume the risk of the injury that he sustained. To recover, the child must not possess the ability to appreciate the risk of occupying the place that he occupies and must not understand the risk involved. *Atlanta v. Merritt* (1984).

However, in a similar Texas case where an eleven year-old baseball spectator was injured by a foul ball the court held that the stadium had no duty to

warn the spectator of the danger of being hit by a
foul ball while in the area behind the first base dug
out. *Friedman v. Houston Sports Association*
(1987). The operator met his duty by providing an
adequately screened area for those that desire it,
although the spectator chose to sit elsewhere. The
court concluded that it would have been absurd and
no doubt resented by many patrons if the ticket
seller had warned each person entering the park
that there was a danger of vagrant baseballs in
unscreened areas. The fact of the child's age did
not alter the fact that the stadium operator had
fulfilled his duty to provide adequately screened
seats for those who desire them. Under the circumstances, the operator met his duty to exercise
reasonable care to protect patrons against injury.

F. FACILITIES

Spectators will not assume the risk of an arena
operator who fails to meet his or her duty of care.
Operators are business invitors and will be liable
for conditions which cause harm to invitees, if 1)
the operators know or should have known that the
conditions existed, 2) the conditions imposed an
unreasonable risk to spectators which they could
not discover or protect themselves against, and 3) if
the operators failed to exercise reasonable care for
their protection. Operators have a duty to maintain premises in a reasonably safe condition and to
supervise the conduct of those on the premises so as
to prevent injury. Spectators can assume that op-

erators have exercised reasonable care to make arenas safe for the purposes of the invitation. But, operators are not insurers of the spectator's safety, therefore, the spectator must prove that the acts were a breach of the duty of care and that the breach was the proximate cause of the injury.

The proprietor's duty of reasonable and ordinary care to an invitee includes the duty to detect reasonably discoverable conditions which may be unreasonably dangerous. In deciding whether a condition is unreasonably hazardous a court may look at prior events. One significant question is what constitutes prior knowledge of a dangerous condition. Courts typically deny recovery for obvious dangers.

CHAPTER 9

SCHOOL LIABILITY

A. NEGLIGENCE

In the past, courts were reluctant to hold school systems liable in ordinary negligence because the courts felt that a teacher could not give personal attention to every student all of the time. There were also a number of powerful defenses at the service of the school districts and this helped to create a dearth of actions against schools; these defenses included sovereign immunity, assumption of the risk, etc. Today, there are many negligence actions against schools, school employees, school districts and school boards. A majority of these actions involve either participant injuries in interscholastic sports or injuries that occur while participating in mandatory physical education courses. These actions center on the following acts of alleged negligence on the part of various school officials: failure to warn, failure to instruct, failure to supervise, failure to hire and train competent coaches and staff, and the failure to provide adequate equipment and safe facilities.

The key for recovery against school districts is the determination of whether a duty exists. Along with the duty, there must be some causal connection or proximate cause between the alleged negligence and the injury, without which recovery will not be allowed. Generally, there are several factors that bear on a school's potential liability. For example, public schools are liable for tortious conduct when under the circumstances they owe a duty of ordinary care to participants and spectators in athletic events. The duty owed an athlete takes the form of adequate instruction, proper equipment, reasonable matching of participants, non-negligent supervision and proper post injury procedures. Also, there is a duty of the school to take reasonable protective precautions for spectators; this will extend to those injured by players, those injured because of rowdyism where it is reasonably anticipated and those who are injured as a result of inadequate grandstands. A basic issue is whether the school district fulfilled its duty of care owed to the injured person and more importantly whether recovery was barred by assumption of risk or contributory negligence.

The school district may be liable for negligent supervision by a person not an employee of the district where the school district encouraged the athletic activity and had a duty to provide non-negligent supervision. The school district is also liable when an injury to an invitee occurs in an athletic event as the result of a defect in the premises.

A school district can also be liable for injuries that occur during a non-sponsored athletic event if the event is conducted by the student body under school district auspices, is encouraged by the district and is held on school property. Questions of contributory negligence are always for the jury, whereas assumption of the risk has been disposed of as a matter of law in a number of cases.

B. VICARIOUS LIABILITY

Lawsuits against school districts are usually predicated on the negligence of the school district's employees. Schools, on the other hand, attempt to avoid negligence by claiming that they are not responsible for their actions or that the events are not school sponsored. However, an employer is vicariously liable for the wrongful acts of his servants and a principal for those of his agent, when the acts are performed within the scope of their employment. Vicarious liability is used to bring the liability of the coach, referee, trainer or groundskeeper under the school board's insurance coverage.

Typically, coaches, aides, teachers, janitors, principals, administrators, groundskeepers, referees, trainers, etc., are viewed as agents of the school district. Without specific statutory immunity the school board will be vicariously liable for their actions. The school board will be liable for the negligent actions of their employees if alleged negligence occurs during the course of employment.

There also is the question of individuals who are not actual employees, but act as quasi-employees, for example, volunteers. The school board may be liable for the actions of the quasi-employee under the principle of vicarious liability. The end result will depend on the amount and quality of the indices that connect the volunteer and his actions to the school board.

C. FAILURE TO WARN

One basis of liability under negligence is a failure to warn. Coaches have a duty to warn of both unforeseeable risks and those risks that although not completely unforeseeable are still not entirely and fully understood.

D. FAILURE TO INSTRUCT

Another basis for liability is the failure to properly instruct. In these cases it must be shown that the coaches' or teachers' failure to instruct the student in a proper manner, or no way at all, is the proximate cause of the student's injuries.

E. FAILURE TO HIRE COMPETENT COACHES

Schools may also be liable for the negligent hiring of employees if that negligence is the proximate cause of the athlete's injuries. The school has a duty to hire a coach of reasonable ability whose competence, experience and training is comparable to other similarly situated coaches.

F. FAILURE TO PROPERLY SUPERVISE

The most important duty of a coach or instructor is the supervision of students. School officials cannot be absent from their appointed places at the appointed times if students injure themselves during that period. In those cases, plaintiff will only have to show that the injury was reasonably foreseeable and that proper supervision would have prevented the harm. However, the lack of supervision must be the proximate cause of the injury. Liability would not lie if the injury would have occurred notwithstanding the presence of the school official. Where the gravity of harm increases, then the degree of supervision must also correspondingly increase. In certain activities, continuous and constant supervision is demanded by the nature of the activity. An example would be *Carabba v. Anacortes School District* (1967), where a high school wrestler was severely injured when the referee looked away while an illegal hold was applied to the plaintiff. Negligence was found on the failure to adequately supervise the match due to his attention being diverted. The failure to break the hold was the proximate cause of the injury.

However, supervisors do not have the duty to supervise every student every second in every possible area. For example, when a student was injured by rocks thrown in a playground, it was held that there was no liability on the part of the school district. See *Fagan v. Summers* (1972); and

Hampton v. Orleans Parish School Board (1982). Even though there is a requirement that there must be reasonable supervision by school officials at a playground; there is no requirement that supervisors have every child under direct, constant and continual supervision.

A school district's duty to supervise is best served when supervision is constant and consistent. The lack of direct supervision of activities that are foreseeably dangerous and failure to continually supervise potentially harmful activities are unwise procedures as regards the range of possible personal injury suits that might develop from any injury.

G. FAILURE TO MAINTAIN EQUIPMENT AND FACILITIES

Schools have a duty to provide proper and safe equipment and facilities. To their students, they owe a duty to use reasonable care to inspect and maintain equipment and to protect the students from an unreasonable risk of harm. Schools must maintain reasonably safe facilities for both participants and spectators. A breach of the school's duties to provide and maintain equipment or to provide and maintain reasonably safe facilities will be actionable if it is the proximate cause of plaintiff's injuries.

Certain sports demand a very particular type of protective equipment, for example, football and hockey. It will be a breach of duty if the schools do not provide and maintain appropriate protective equipment. Schools also have a duty to inspect and maintain the equipment that they already possess. In fact, there is a duty of reasonable care to protect students from unreasonable risks even when that harm was a prevailing custom if that custom fell below the reasonable care standard. (*Tiemann v. Independent School District* (1983); student injured during physical education gymnastics instruction on a pommel horse with exposed holes.)

Owners and operators are required to show ordinary care and diligence in maintaining both premises and equipment in a reasonably safe manner. Included in this duty is the establishment of a cleaning, inspection and maintenance schedule. The frequency of inspection will depend on the potential harm anticipated, e.g., scuba diving equipment by its very nature demands almost constant inspection. Owners and operators do not have to possess actual knowledge of a dangerous condition, only that they either knew or should have known of its existence. School employees have a duty of reasonable care to inspect the premises for hidden and lurking dangers. School districts will be liable for harm caused by dangers that coaches discovered or should have detected and failed to warn. However, they are not liable for unconcealed dangers that are known or should be obvious to participants.

CHAPTER 10

COACH LIABILITY

A. GENERALLY

Coaches must use reasonable care to avoid the creation of foreseeable risks to the athlete under their supervision. The standard of reasonableness will change from sport to sport. That degree of care will increase if the activity involves a contact sport. Generally, coaches have a duty to exercise reasonable care for the safety of their players.

Coaches may also be liable for the breach of certain duties. Coaches have a duty to instruct their athletes regarding safety procedures and methods to minimize injuries. Coaches have a duty to provide safe and effective protective equipment. Also, they cannot force their athletes to participate when those athletes have already sustained injuries, if there is a risk that further participation will only aggravate the original injury. Coaches must also take reasonable steps to provide medical assistance when and if it is necessary. Liability has been found when a coach failed to summon medical aid in a timely fashion when a player showed symptoms of heat stroke. *Mogabgab v. Orleans Parish School Board* (1970).

Negligence will not lie if the coach has fulfilled his duty to exercise reasonable care for athletes under his supervision. This duty will be satisfied by providing proper instructions and explaining to the athlete how to play the game and also by showing due concern that the athlete is in proper physical condition. This duty of care will be satisfied if the coach takes all reasonable steps to minimize the possibility of injury. Although the player must have proper and sufficient instruction, the coach will only be liable if he fails to exercise reasonable care for the protection of his players and that the injury was a result of that failure.

In a recent New Jersey trial decision, a novice player, a track star who was recruited for football solely for his speed as a receiver, was severely injured while tackling an opposing player on an interception. The player contended that his injury was a result of the negligence of the coaching staff who failed to provide sufficient training, conditioning, equipment and supervision. Specifically, he only had one practice session on tackling. Expert testimony averred that tackling is an extremely dangerous aspect of the sport and that the correct technique and manner, including keeping the head elevated which plaintiff did not do, must be reinforced by repeated practice. The experts agreed that one practice session was insufficient. Plaintiff also contended that he was not provided with sufficient preseason training, including weight training, to strengthen neck muscles which experts contended was essential and the absence of which contributed to the incident. The jury found the head coach 40% negligent and the interior line coach 60% negligent; they then awarded 6.5 million dollars. The jury was presented with an array of coaching techniques which could be viewed as an indifference to the player's health. The jury emphasized that the plaintiff was a senior who was trained in track and did not receive extensive training in his first year of football; this lack of training only reinforced their view that this was a coaching staff who stressed victory over safety. This inference was reinforced by the deposition testimony of the interior line coach who indicated that the plaintiff was only a name to him. *Woodson v. Irvington Board of Education* (1987); Coburn, J. 3 *Natl. Jury Verdict Rev. & Anal.* 10 (No. 8, 1988).

To determine negligence, some states apply the so-called locality rule which is comparable to the one used to establish applicable standards in medical malpractice cases: this requires that the coach will be held to the standard of other coaches in that specific geographical area. For example, coaches in rural areas might not be expected to possess the expertise that their big city colleagues undoubtedly possess.

Coaches are judged by regional rather than a state or national standard. The locality rule was originated at a time when new coaching techniques were not expected to travel to the more obscure rural areas in America. However, in these days, in an era of coaching clinics, videos, consumer education, instructional pamphlets and coaching magazines, the rationale for a locality rule may no longer be legitimate.

B. QUALIFICATIONS

There is a movement in amateur sports that would demand a basic minimum in education and experience before one could become certified as a coach. Also, coaches would be obliged to take a certain amount of continuing education to maintain certification. In *Everett v. Bucky Warren, Inc.* (1978), an injured school hockey player sued his coach and a helmet manufacturer for injuries received when a puck struck him in the head causing severe injuries. The helmet in question was a three-piece helmet which allowed for gaps that under the wrong circumstances allowed enough space for a puck to squeeze through and cause injury. At the time there was another type of helmet available which was a single piece and would have prevented the injury. This single piece design was known to all parties and was available at the time of the accident but at a slightly higher price than the three-piece helmet. The coach was negligent in supplying the helmet: he should have known that the three-piece design was faulty and that another more safely designed helmet was also readily available. The coach who had substantial experience in hockey, could be held to a higher standard of care and knowledge than the average person as it relates to the ordering of the unsafe hockey helmet.

Coaches are expected to possess a minimum of education and experience that is thought to be generally prevalent within the industry as a whole. The coach in *Everett* went below that standard.

Coach certification is the key. Approximately half of the physical education departments in institutions of higher learning provide professional training in coaching. As an example, the American Alliance for Health, Physical Education, Recreation and Dance recommends that a minor in coaching should include the following courses: Medical Aspects of Coaching, Problems of Coaching, Theory and Techniques and Kinesiological and Physiological foundations. By the 1980s, eight states had minimum requirements for coaches in addition to teacher certification; this trend seems certain to continue.

However, the majority of the states still require only teacher certification, regardless of the subject area, as a prerequisite for coaching. If you are certified to teach you are also qualified to coach. In *Stehn v. Bernard McFadden Foundations* (1959), a student was injured during a wrestling program supervised by a faculty member who had only a small amount of wrestling or coaching experience. This so-called coach was supervising two matches at once. The hold that allegedly caused plaintiff's injury was one that the coach had learned while in the service. However, the coach failed to explain a method of escape and a defense to that hold. The plaintiff's case was built on the failure of the coach to supervise and his lack of qualifications in coaching wrestling.

Since one has to be certified to teach, arguably the school districts should require additional training and education as a prerequisite for coaching. This would be a logical step since coaching does provide extra monetary income. This extra preparation should require courses in physical conditioning, the learning and performance of physical skills, first aid, theory and techniques of coaching, and the legal aspects of coaching. Additionally, a minimum of three to five years experience in coaching should be a prerequisite to a head coaching position. School boards should support this trend since they are the ones who will usually be responsible for the acts and omissions of their coaching staffs.

Another aspect of the qualification issue is the training and preparation of assistants and assistant coaches. Under the doctrine of respondeat superior, it is possible that coaches will be responsible for the actions of their assistants whether paid or voluntary, whether student or non-student, and whether or not they were student teaching. Generally, coaches have a duty to warn their athletes of any hidden dangers known to them and then instruct them in methods to avoid these hazards. If the instruction is negligent because of the lack of training of the assistants then the coach would be responsible.

In *Brahatcek v. Millard School District* (1979), plaintiff's decedent was a fourteen year-old junior high school student who was injured during mandatory golf instruction when he walked into the back swing of a fellow student who he had asked for instruction. The deceased had never had a golf lesson prior to the accident. His actual instructor was busy instructing another student and thus unable to supervise the decedent. This instructor was actually a student teacher, who only had five weeks experience; the regular teacher was absent that day. Although he had helped with golf instruction in four to six classes on the previous two days, this was his first class as an instructor. In this case the inexperience of the student teacher was found to be the proximate cause of the injury.

C. PREPARATION OF PARTICIPANTS

It is obvious that every athlete must be prepared before he enters the playing field. It is the responsibility of the coach to make sure that the athletes under his charge are ready and prepared to participate. This preparation should consist of the following specific duties: instruction, physical preparation, providing proper equipment, maintenance of equipment and issuance of warnings. Coaches have a duty to prepare; a failure of which could lead to liability based on negligence.

A coach has the responsibility to minimize serious injuries. One way of accomplishing this goal is to provide competent and thorough instruction in the sport's technical aspects and their corresponding safety rules. In *Vendrell v. School District* (1962), no negligence was found when football coaches provided adequate, standard instruction and practice without negligently omitting any detail. The program in *Vendrell* contained a daily calisthenic "bullneck" exercise which was designed to strengthen the neck muscles and thus help to prevent neck injuries. The *Vendrell* court averred that the player had a duty to ask questions on matters to which he was unclear. Since there were no questions, the coaches could have assumed that he was aware of the possibility of injury that could have occurred from using his head as a battering ram.

Another aspect of preparation is the physical preparation of the athlete. This of course includes weight training, calisthenics, coordination drills, stretching exercises, etc. The requirement here is to prove that this lack of training was the proximate cause of the injury.

It is also expected that the athlete will be furnished with the proper protective and safety equipment which is appropriate for the sport especially if it is a contact sport. Added to that, the athlete must be properly instructed as to the appropriate use of this equipment; also, the equipment must be properly maintained so that its effectiveness is maximized. In *Hemphill v. Sayers* (1982), the coaches were potentially liable for the negligent failure to warn the football player of the danger inherent in the use of a football helmet.

When one defends against these types of charges, the school can protect themselves by having enough equipment brochures and equipment specifications available so as to show a conscious effort to choose the best available equipment. Equipment manufacturers will generally provide fitting and maintenance instructions with their equipment at the time of purchase and will usually supply additional copies upon request. Coaches should read, understand and file these instructions; distribute copies to players and make sure they comprehend the instructions; and retain extra copies so they can maintain a permanent library of information. Coaches should also follow the manufacturer's recommended instructions for periodic inspection and maintenance. These programs of inspection, maintenance and proper repair must be documented. For example, there must be a maintenance history for each helmet.

Coaches can never be totally free from the fear of potential liability. However, one way to decrease potential liability is to check the equipment before the contest and to develop enough expertise in the field so that the equipment that is available is state of the art.

In *Thomas v. Chicago Board of Education* (1979), a coach was protected from suit on basis of sovereign immunity since his conduct was neither willful nor wanton. The conduct in *Thomas* was furnishing but failing to inspect defective football equipment. This conduct was held to be ordinary negligence as it related to injuries that resulted from defective equipment.

In many jurisdictions a coach's act of ordinary negligence is protected by sovereign immunity. However, wanton or gross negligence in the supplying of faulty equipment will still usually expose the coach to liability.

The preparation of the athlete by the coach also includes appropriate warnings about certain types of dangers, potential injuries, conduct, and techniques before the athlete actually participates. Failure to warn exists if the coach fails to specifically warn the student about the potential dangers of using one's head as a battering ram in football; moreover, the student should also be warned that using the head in this way could cause permanent paralysis. In football, each helmet has a written warning explaining the dangers of using a helmet as a ram. However, it would be beneficial to the coach to reinforce this warning orally: if possible, prior to each game or practice.

The duty to warn is the last defense that the coach should use in his preparation of the athlete before participation; however, it relates only to dangers that are non-obvious to the coaches. This applies to all potential dangers including equipment use, proper techniques, and the quality and consistency of the playing field.

The preparation of the participants may appear to be harsh on coaches, but they are usually in the position to give the last piece of advice and check the athlete one more time immediately prior to the athlete's entering onto the playing field. Also, many coaches are in a semi-paternal position to their athletes: the students trust their coaches and rely on their expertise.

D. SUPERVISION

Coaches also have a responsibility to properly supervise the athletes under their charge. This duty is not an absolute but varies with the danger of the activity and the age and maturity of the participant. Coaches are not insurers of the actions of the students under their supervision. An instructor, was not negligent when a student in a physical education class was injured when she and her classmates decided to run a race in the foyer of the gymnasium. The plaintiff, while running at full speed, crashed into a glass wall; the coach was not negligent since he had exercised proper supervision over the class. *Wilkinson v. Hartford Accident and Indemnity Co.* (1982).

In *Nydegger v. Don Bosco Preparatory High School* (1985), a high school soccer player was injured and brought an action against the opposing coach for failure to supervise his players and for teaching them to compete in an aggressive and intense way and to believe that victory was all important. The court held that in the absence of instruction by the coach to one of his players to specifically commit a wrongful act or his instructing the player in procedures that would increase the risk of harm to opposing players, the coach would not be responsible to the injured player. There was no proximate cause, and the aggressive athlete was not an agent of his coach.

Ignoring a potentially dangerous activity might be sufficient to act as a breach of that coach's duty to supervise. This rationale would apply to supervising a spectator's contact with players, leaving children unattended at a swimming pool or not correcting an athlete's faulty maneuver during play. A coach has to use reasonable care in the supervision of athletes under his control so as to avoid the unreasonable risk of harm to the athletes and those associated with the activity.

CHAPTER 11

REFEREE LIABILITY

Many referees and officials are now finding themselves named as defendants in personal injury suits for alleged acts of negligence. Although they are usually not found personally liable, these suits are still an inconvenience.

To counteract what is viewed as an alarming trend, some states have promulgated laws that eliminate suits against referees and umpires unless they are grossly negligent. For example, New Jersey passed a law that provides partial immunity for volunteer referees from civil suits for damages that result from acts or omissions during the ordinary course of their supervision. N.J.Stat.Ann. 2A:62 A–6.

It is a referee's duty to properly supervise an athletic contest. For example, a wrestling referee was held to be negligent for not properly supervising a match; while the referee's attention was diverted one wrestler used an illegal hold to the other wrestler which resulted in permanent paralysis below the neck. The referee was negligent in that he breached his duty to non-negligently supervise conduct. The referee's standard is one of an ordinarily prudent referee under similar circumstances. The injured athlete will not assume that risk since one cannot assume another's negligence or incompetence. *Carabba v. Anacortes School District* (1967).

When the standard of care is met, recovery will not be allowed. In *Pape v. State* (1982), personal injuries were sustained during a college intramural floor hockey game when plaintiff attacked an opponent. Plaintiff alleged that the injuries were attributable to a lack of proper supervision and training by the referee. The referee's alleged inexperience was argued to be the proximate cause of plaintiff's cervical spine fracture. The court held that the duty owed by the referee to plaintiff was the duty to exercise reasonable care under the circumstances to prevent injuries. The court concluded that the duty had been met.

A. DUTY TO ENFORCE RULES

The referee has a duty to enforce the rules of the sport and to prevent illegal holds or actions. The standard is one of an ordinarily prudent referee. Id. Although referees have a duty to enforce the rules of the game, there is no separate referee malpractice for bad calls. Referees cannot prevent all rule violations, and they only have a duty to use reasonable care to see that the rules of the game, including safety rules, are followed. Reasonable care consists of advising the participants of adverse conditions and illegal maneuvers, showing due diligence in detecting rule violations, penalizing the rule breakers, etc.

B. DUTY TO PROTECT PARTICIPANTS

As a part of a referee's duty to provide non-negligent supervision there is also an implied duty to protect and warn participants. However, like coaches, referees are not insurers of the safety of participants. In *Pape v. State* (1982), where plaintiff was injured in a floor hockey game, the court found that there was no connection or proximate cause between the referee's alleged negligence and the injuries. The referee cannot guarantee the safety of each participant; moreover, the court found that the plaintiff's injury occurred while using his own initiative to attack his opponent. Therefore, the injury could not be attributed to a lack of supervision or training on the part of the referee. The duty owed to the plaintiff only required that the referee exercise reasonable care under the circumstances to prevent injury; the referee did not have a duty to protect the plaintiff from the danger that was inherent in a maneuver that was initiated and controlled by the plaintiff himself.

C. DUTY TO WARN

There is an implied duty on the part of the referee to warn participants of possible dangers. For example, it is the duty of a wrestling referee to warn participants of the consequences and dangers of an illegal maneuver. *Carabba v. Anacortes School District* (1967). This duty can arguably be expanded to include the referee's responsibility of controlling the game as regards hazardous conditions and inclement weather. For example, ceasing play during the following circumstances: a lightning storm or an overly oiled basketball court or inadequate lighting for a baseball game. It also includes protecting participants from more aggressive players by penalizing or warning athletes of their inappropriate conduct.

D. ANTICIPATING REASONABLY FORESEEABLE DANGERS

Comparable to the duty of the referee to protect and warn participants is his duty to anticipate reasonably foreseeable dangers. Before the contest and while the game is in progress, it is the responsibility of the referee to determine that the playing conditions are safe. This could reasonably include checking for the following: glass on the running track, holes on the field in football, metal stakes protruding from the dirt in a baseball diamond, loosely secured bases in softball, etc. Officials have an obligation to inspect field conditions. In basketball, the safety rules provide that a referee must ascertain whether there are loose basketballs in the vicinity of the court, whether the padding at the basket supports is secure and continuous around the entire pole, and whether the area surrounding the court is clear for the players.

Another group of reasonably foreseeable dangers that the referee ought to anticipate are adverse weather and overall unsafe playing conditions. Before the game, it is the referee's responsibility to decide whether the game should start. His first duty is to inspect the overall playability of the playing surface. It is conceivable that a referee could be held liable for allowing play to continue if a football field is overly muddy and correspondingly unsafe. The crux of this issue is the referee's reasonable judgment: the responsibility to call a game will rest solely on the shoulders of the referee.

E. FAILURE TO CONTROL GAME

One other potential area for referee liability is the failure to control and properly supervise the flow of the game. *Carabba v. Anacortes School District* (1967). It is the duty of the official to detect and control the use of illegal and dangerous maneuvers. The standard of care is one of an ordinarily prudent referee.

However, the duty to supervise and control only requires that the referee exercises reasonable care under the circumstances to prevent injury. It is clear that the referee has the duty to stop the match if it appears that an opponent is in serious danger of injury. This is especially true in the dangerous contact sports of boxing and wrestling.

Most of the cases to date have revolved around actions against referees for personal injuries to participants. There are many other conceivable tort cases that could be brought against referees. The most probable would be actions based on "blown calls". However, absent corruption or bad faith, no independent tort exists for "referee malpractice". There has been no court yet that has recognized a viable cause of action against an official for either an honest error in judgment or a misapplication of a game rule. The rulings of an umpire or referee are presumptively correct.

CHAPTER 12

DEFAMATION

Sports is an established part of the American existence, and because of that sports figures and people involved in the sports industry are constantly commented on in various ways. The business of sports journalism is to create controversy through opinions and accusations about the problems of different athletes. Therefore, there is a great possibility that sports figures will be defamed by journalists or newscasters. The question is whether journalistic tirades are defamatory and, if so, are they also actionable. Statements will be defamatory if they are published, false and cause damage to one's reputation. Defamation is the taking from one's reputation: it is defamatory if it tends to diminish the esteem, respect, goodwill or confidence in which the plaintiff was held or, if the remarks excite adverse, derogatory or unpleasant opinions.

A. SPORTSWRITERS

The source of defamation cases is the sportswriter, sports journalist or radio sports personality. These people are paid to create as much controversy as possible concerning sports heroes. It is their job and they do it well. They are also protected in a majority of the cases by the privilege of fair comment: their analyses are deemed opinions and are thus protected by the First Amendment. But, a "mixed opinion" that is capable of implying an underlying defamatory fact is actionable. *Milkovich v. Lorain Journal Co.* (1990).

In one instance a television sports commentator called a soccer player a quitter and then at the end of the broadcast took a photograph of the athlete and drew a mustache and a beard on it, spat on the photograph, laid it on the floor and jumped on it, and then threw it off the set. The question is whether these antics are defamatory. The Colorado Court of Appeals said they were not and that the commentator's comments were merely opinions and thus constitutionally protected. These comments were not deliberate or reckless falsehoods, since the athlete did decide not to play for the team in question during playoffs. Therefore, these comments were not capable of defamatory meaning. *Brooks v. Paige* (1988).

B. PER SE

There are two forms of defamatory publication, libel and slander. Publication is a necessary element of the tort and is the means of communication of the defamatory statement to a third party. The tort of libel originally referred to the written or printed work whereas slander was oral. The distinction is that libel must have some embodiment or some permanent physical form. The slandered plaintiff must prove actual damages as opposed to libel where the damages are assumed to be greater because the language is in a more permanent form.

There are four exceptions to a plaintiff's requirement of proof in a slander action. A statement that imputes one of the four exceptions is slander per se or slander which is actionable per se. These instances are so egregious that no actual proof of damages is necessary to support an actionable slander claim. Slander per se occurs when one imputes a crime, imputes a loathsome disease, adversely affects the plaintiff in his trade, business or profession, or imputes unchastity to a woman. Therefore, if one accuses an athlete of suffering from AIDS or states that a coach lacks good sportsmanship and is a rowdy drunk, then these comments may be per se defamatory.

Many courts apply this rule: a libelous statement that imputes one of the exceptions is libel per se and any other libel is libel per quod. Under libel per quod the plaintiff must prove damages. Some decisions, however, accept the proposition that any libel is actionable because it is more permanent than the spoken word and is accordingly more circulated.

Other courts use the term "defamation per se," that is, defamation on its face, which is thereby actionable. In *Fawcett Publications, Inc. v. Morris* (1962), the plaintiff was a member of the 1956 Oklahoma University football team and was allegedly defamed in a 1958 *True Magazine* article entitled

"The Pill that can Kill Sports" in which that Oklahoma team was alleged to have used amphetamines. The court found that the article was defamatory on its face and was libel per se, in that it exposed the entire football team to a public hatred and contempt and tended to deprive the team and its members of any public confidence they might have earned. The reader was unequivocally informed that members of the team had illegally used drugs.

This case also stood for another principle: that as a member of the team, plaintiff could sue even though he was not specifically named in the libelous article. The court's view was that since it was libelous per se and since the suggestion of drug use is both criminal and adverse to plaintiff's professional and business standing, it libeled every member of the team including plaintiff even though he was not specifically named. Moreover, the court felt that the average reader would identify the player as a subject to these accusations since he was a starting player and thus not a changing element within the defamed group.

C. PUBLIC FIGURES

Certain people must meet a heightened burden of proof of actual malice before they can maintain a successful libel suit. These certain individuals would include public officials and public figures. Public figures are people who by reason of their notoriety or success or their achievements or the manner in which they seek the public's attention are categorized as public personalities.

The first remedy of a defamatory victim is self-help, that is, using available opportunities to offset the lie or correct the error and thereby minimize its adverse impact on his or her reputation. Public officials and public figures enjoy significantly greater access to channels of communications and, therefore, have a much more realistic opportunity to counter false statements than a private individual would enjoy. Private individuals are more vulnerable to injury and the state's interest is correspondingly greater. More important is the likelihood that private individuals will lack the opportunity to rebut. Consequently, the press is allowed more room for error with public figures since the stars have greater access to the press for rebuttals than a truly private person.

Usually public figures want to be one, that is, they obtain that status and purposely assume roles of special prominence in the affairs of society. Some occupy a position of such pervasive power and influence that they are public figures for all purposes; more commonly, however, public figures have thrust themselves to the forefront of a particular public controversy in order to influence the resolution of the issues involved. In either event, they invite attention and comment. Thus, not only can one be a public figure if he thrusts himself to the forefront of a public controversy but he also can be a public figure for a limited purpose.

The media is entitled to act on the assumption that public people have voluntarily exposed themselves to an increased risk of defamatory falsehood. Courts have focused on whether the libel plaintiff has voluntarily sought media attention in determining whether he or she is a public figure. Several courts have even held that individuals by entering certain lines of work have voluntarily exposed themselves to media attention. Entertainers and professional athletes in major sports are considered to be public figures. This presumption of a public figure is also applicable to coaches who share the limelight with their athletes. Player disagreements, coaching philosophy or just plain personality problems will always be given great attention by the media. Therefore, an individual who manages a professional sports team or who is involved with the management has voluntarily stepped into the public eye. Since the organization that he works for attracts and courts media attention, he is a public figure at least for the limited purpose of stories that relate to his job.

Athletes are usually deemed to be limited public figures. In sports, there are many personal factors in an athlete's life which may affect his career but which may not be the proper subject of unlimited publication.

It may be hypothetically possible for someone to become a public figure through no purposeful action of his own, but the instances of truly involuntary public figure status are exceedingly rare. One can be a public figure if one thrusts himself into the forefront of a public controversy like Bucky Woy, the sports agent who during a contract dispute with one of his athletes used the media (through press conferences) to help make his point. *Woy v. Turner* (1983).

But in *Time, Inc. v. Firestone* (1976), the court held that the spouse of a millionaire was not transformed into a public figure by filing for divorce. She had no less of a public forum than filing to assert her rights; she did not freely choose to publicize issues as to the propriety of her married life. She was compelled to seek the court by the state in order to obtain release from the bonds of matrimony.

In a 1980 case the court found that a football player and his wife, an ex-movie star, were limited public figures. *Brewer v. Memphis Pub. Co.* (1980); see also *Chuy v. Philadelphia Eagles Football Club* (1979).

Every story that is related to a public career is controlled by the *New York Times* standard. *New York Times Co. v. Sullivan* (1964). That standard is that public officials and public figures must demonstrate that the statements were made with actual malice. In *Nussbaumer v. Time, Inc.* (1986), the plaintiff was in a high profile job with an organization, the Cleveland Browns, that sought and thrived on media and public attention. Nussbaumer, an official with the team, was viewed as a public figure in a controversy where an article five years after the event characterized him as "spying" on a team meeting. A professional football team is a business whose product is sold by having people purchase tickets or watch the games on television. Media attention is a critical tool to attract and keep the public's interest. During the football season the local daily paper carried at least one story on that team every day; in fact, part of Nussbaumer's job was to help this coverage by informing the media about things that affected the club's performance. The managing of a professional club attracts intense media coverage. Decisions that control what a player will do on the field, coaching, and general management philosophy are all publicized and much discussed by the public. News conferences are frequently held to announce changes that affect the team. When Nussbaumer accepted a front office job with the Cleveland Browns, he stepped into the public eye. He was in charge of player selection, and he helped arrange player trades with other clubs, select possible choices in the college player draft, and negotiated contracts with players on the team. All of these chores directly affected who would be playing for the team; hence, these activities attracted continuing media coverage. Since the article in *Nussbaumer* dealt solely with the management of his team, Nussbaumer was required to demonstrate actual malice on the part of the defendant even though the article stated that he was spying on the head coach for the front office.

D. RULE OF REPOSE

Hypothetically, after one attains public status, he might possibly slip back into the veil of privacy. This is called the rule of repose. But this is difficult in sports since sports heroes are in many ways larger than life and therefore, their public image will last. A sports personality will usually always be a sports personality. However, there can be exceptions. One case in this area involved Jack Dempsey, the great heavyweight boxing champion. The champion was defamed 45 years after the alleged event occurred when in a *Sports Illustrated* article his manager claimed that he had loaded the champion's boxing gloves with plaster-of-paris. This was too much for even a sports icon, that is, to reach back almost 50 years to discuss non-noteworthy tactics. The court averred that reaching back that far is not within the purview of the *New York Times* standard; therefore, the glove loading was not cloaked with the veil of privilege. *Dempsey v. Time Inc.* (1964).

However, *Johnston v. Time, Inc.* (1970), a former professional basketball player sued a sports magazine for publishing an allegedly defamatory article by a professional basketball coach who described him as being "destroyed" by another player. This article was published 12 years after the event and nine years after plaintiff's retirement. At the time of publication, plaintiff was an assistant basketball coach at a university. There is no question that plaintiff was a public figure in his days as a basketball player, but this article was 12 years later. The lower court acknowledged that the rule of repose could apply. At the time of the publication of the article, the plaintiff did not command a continuing public interest nor did he have access to the means of a counter argument. The Court of Appeals, however, held that plaintiff was still a public figure since he remained in basketball.

Public officials will also usually continue their role as a public person after retirement. In Ohio, the retirement of a public school superintendent did not diminish his status as a public official concerning his alleged perjury at a high school athletic association hearing regarding a fracas which had occurred at a wrestling match and was related to his former position. In short, he was still a public figure for purposes of a defamation action. *Scott v. News–Herald* (1986).

E.　INVASION OF PRIVACY

Related to defamation is the right to protect one's privacy. The right to privacy will compensate the athlete for the distress created by the public exposure to accurate but private facts. Privacy is the right to be left alone and to live one's own life as one may choose, free from assault, intrusion or invasion except what can be justified by the clear needs of the community living under governmental law. However, to the extent the athlete is a public figure, the actual malice standard of *New York*

Times Co. v. Sullivan (1964), will still apply, since to recover one must prove that the defendant published the report with the knowledge of its falseness or in reckless disregard of the truth. In the absence of malice, invasion of privacy suits must deal with an athlete's private life as opposed to his athletic pursuits.

The test for determining whether information on the star's private life is newsworthy and thus privileged under the first amendment, or non-privileged and an invasion of privacy, is to discover if the information is the type that the public is entitled to or just a morbid and sensational delving into the private lives of people for some prurient machination.

In *Spahn v. Julian Messner, Inc.* (1966), a publication of a fictitious biography of the Hall of Fame pitcher, Warren Spahn, was found to constitute an unauthorized exploitation of his personality for purposes of trade. Although Spahn gave away his rights to his public privacy, he still maintained the right to secure his privacy in his personal, non-public life.

Comparable to the right of privacy is the athlete's right to his commercial representation. The right of publicity recognizes the commercial value of a non-newsworthy pictorial representation and protects the propriety interests in the profitability of his public image. In *Ali v. Playgirl, Inc.* (1978), an unauthorized pictorial representation of Muhammed Ali was used for commercial purposes.

The portrait depicted a nude black man sitting in a corner of a boxing ring and was claimed to be unmistakably recognizable as Muhammed Ali. The court upheld his right to the commercial value of this photograph. In *Zacchini v. Scripps–Howard Broadcasting Co.* (1977), the court gave the entertainer, in this case, the "human cannonball," the power to protect his publicity rights in that it did not immunize the television station from liability for televising Zacchini's entire act.

F.   DEFENSES

Even though certain statements about athletes can certainly appear to be defamatory in their content, they may still be non-actionable if there are defenses that are available to the defendant, for example, truth, fair comment or privilege. Truth is a defense to any civil action for libel or slander; also, it is a defense that the comment was substantially true. For example, in *Nussbaumer v. Time, Inc.* (1986), defendant claimed that plaintiff spied on a team meeting after a lost to the Los Angeles Rams, but instead it occurred after a loss to the San Diego Chargers. The defendant's claim was substantially true.

Another way for a sportswriter to avoid defamation is the doctrine of fair comment. Everyone has a right to comment on matters of public interest if it is done fairly and with an honest purpose. Public individuals, especially those who engage in sports, must expect critical reviews, but they may not complain unless they are in fact falsely accused of wrong-doing. The *New York Times* standard requires that false comments about public figures must be knowing and in reckless disregard of the truth to be actionable. Reckless disregard means that the defendant entertained serious doubts as to the statement's truth before publication.

The corollary to fair comment is the first amendment right to express an opinion. Sports columns are usually opinions and thus protected. An Ohio Supreme Court case discussed the parameters of a sports columnist's right to express opinions. The key here was the determination of whether an alleged defamatory statement was an opinion or an assertion of fact; this determination is a question of law. *Scott v. News–Herald* (1986). The standard to be applied is totality of the circumstances which will include specific language, whether the statement is verifiable, the general context of the statement, and the broader context in which the statement appears. Sports columns are traditionally the home of hyperbole and invective. Columns can be protected when the headlines of these captions show in some way that the statements are protected opinions (e.g., "in my opinion," etc.). When a column is prefaced with an opinion-like statement, then it is highly suggestive that it is indeed the opinion of the author; however, such language is not always dispositive, particularly in view of the potential for abuse.

In *Stepien v. Franklin* (1988), the former owner of the NBA Cleveland Cavaliers was verbally attacked by a radio sports talk show host. He was described as stupid, dumb, buffoon, nincompoop, scum, a cancer, an obscenity, guttless liar, unmitigated liar, pathological liar, egomaniac, nut, crazy, irrational and suicidal. Nevertheless, these attacks were viewed as opinions and thus constitutionally protected. The first amendment protects unrestricted debate on issues of concern to the public including what may well be viewed as vehement, caustic and unpleasant attacks. Public figures like the owner of this basketball team have thrust themselves in the public eye, and because of that they cannot later prevent others from criticizing their actions. Opinions are not capable of defamatory content; assertions of fact on the other hand are unprotected and thus capable of a defamatory meaning.

Sportswriters can also sue for defamation. In *Falls v. Sporting News Publ. Co.* (1987), a long time columnist was terminated by his employer, who issued uncomplimentary remarks that categorized the writer as less energetic than other sportswriters and out of touch with the current sports scene and implied that plaintiff was on a "down swing." The court observed that certain opinions of public concern could qualify as forms of privileged criticism which are protected in the name of fair comment. There are three kinds of expressions of opinion. First, simple expression of opinion which occurs when the comment maker states the facts on which he bases his opinion and then expresses a comment as to the plaintiff's conduct, qualifications or character. The statement of facts and the expression of opinion are treated separately at common law in the sense that either or both could be defamatory. Secondly, a pure type of opinion may occur when the maker of the comment does not express the facts on which he bases an opinion but both parties of the communication know the facts or assume their existence and the comment is clearly based on those facts and does not imply the existence of other facts in order to justify that comment. The privilege of fair comment is said to apply to the pure type of opinion. Thirdly, the mixed type of opinion, while an opinion in form, is apparently based on facts regarding the plaintiff that have not been stated by the defendant or assumed to exist by the parties to the communication. The expression of the opinion gives rise to the inference that there are undisclosed facts which justify the forming of the opinion.

The Supreme Court, in *Gertz v. Robert Welch, Inc.* (1974), determined that the common law rule that an opinion of the pure type may be a basis of an action for defamation offends the first amendment guarantee of freedom of speech. However, the mixed type of expression of opinion may still be the basis of defamation since it could imply undisclosed defamatory facts as the basis of the opinion. It is the court's responsibility to determine whether opinion can reasonably imply the assertion of undisclosed facts, and it is the responsibility of the jury to determine if this meaning was attributed by the recipient of the communication.

In *Falls,* the defendant's "on the down swing" comment, was held to be capable of a defamatory meaning since the jury could reasonably find that the defendant knew of undisclosed facts that could justify such an opinion. For example, the plaintiff's writing and reasoning ability might have deteriorated or the quality of his work might have declined to the point that other people had to rewrite or cover for him. Similarly, defendant's implication that plaintiff was inferior to his replacements could create a reasonable inference that the comment was also justified by the existence of other undisclosed facts, for example, the plaintiff did not work hard, etc.

CHAPTER 13

TORT DEFENSES

A. GENERALLY

There are many defenses that the stadium owner or team owner or school district can use in their attempts to avoid liability. The preeminent defenses are assumption of risk, contributory negligence and comparative negligence.

B. ASSUMPTION OF RISK

Assumption of risk can be defined as a voluntary assumption, expressed or implied, of a known and appreciated risk. A participant or a spectator who assumes the risk created by the conduct of another cannot recover when harm in fact occurs.

In sports or recreational activities, the plaintiff will assume the ordinary risks of the game; however, he does not assume the risk of injury from a violation of a duty owed him by the promoter or stadium operator and thus is not precluded from recovery for injury that results from their negligence. This duty will include reasonable care in the construction, maintenance and management of the facility and reasonable care with regards to the character of the exhibition and the customary con-

156

duct of invited patrons. But the operator is not an insurer of the safety of the plaintiff. For recovery for injuries sustained in a sports facility, the participant or spectator must prove both that specific acts or omissions constituted a breach of defendant's duty of care and that the breach was the proximate cause of the injury.

Professional baseball park operators are required to provide seats protected by screens for as large a number of patrons as may reasonably be expected to call for such seats on an ordinary day of attendance. A breach of this duty may constitute negligence which would make the operator liable to injured spectators. It is generally held that a spectator who has knowledge of the game and takes an unprotected seat will assume the risk of injuries from thrown or batted balls and thus cannot recover for those injuries when they occur.

Assumption of risk was once an impenetrable and monolithic defense. This, however, has markedly changed in recent years. Recovery is now allowed for injuries which result from safety violations. *Nabozny v. Barnhill* (1975). Plaintiff can also recover for the intentional misconduct of another participant. *Bourque v. Duplechin* (1976). Participants also might recover when the injury was caused by the negligent acts of third persons, usually coaches or referees. *Nabozny* and *Bourque* both involved participants, as opposed to spectators. Voluntary participants usually are viewed to assume all risks that are incident to the contest which are also obvious and foreseeable.

Spectators assume the risk of hazards incident to the game. Spectators assume the risks that are a matter of common knowledge. Courts have allowed recovery where the risk of the sport was not considered common knowledge. Spectators will assume only the ordinary and inherent risks of attending sports activities. For example, a swinging gate at a baseball game and a baseball flying into an interior corridor are not ordinary risks and thus will not preclude recovery.

Spectators will also not assume the risk of unreasonable conduct by participants, e.g., a ball player who intentionally throws his bat into the stands. Assumption of risk will not apply as a complete bar when there is either a direct dereliction of a duty by the defendant or a lack of knowledge of the risk on the part of the plaintiff.

There may be a question of whether plaintiff had actual knowledge of the specific danger involved. This knowledge must include not only a general knowledge of the danger but also knowledge of the particular danger and the magnitude of the risk involved. Actual knowledge of the risk may be inferred from the circumstances.

For plaintiff to assume risk, he must knowingly and voluntarily encounter those risks which cause harm: he must also understand and appreciate the risks involved and accept the risk as well as the inherent possibility of the danger which can result from that risk.

The necessary ingredient for plaintiff to assume risk is knowledge: there must be a knowing assumption of risk which means that the plaintiff has actual knowledge of the risk involved or that knowledge is imputed because of certain observations and from that he should have reasonably known that the risk was involved.

For example, coaches can assume that a football player knows he may get hurt if he uses his head as a battering ram. The high school football player has a duty to ask his football coach questions concerning any matter on which he is not clear; and coaches have a right to assume that their players possess the intelligence and stock of information of a normal young man interested in sports. Therefore, it has been held that coaches can assume that a player knew of the possibility of injury that comes to the player who uses his head as a battering ram.

It has been held that voluntary participation in football games constitutes an implied consent to the normal risks that go with the bodily contact that is permitted by the rules of football. However, participants involved in contact sports do not automatically consent to contacts which are prohibited by the rules or customs of that sport, if those rules are designed for protection rather than the control of the mode of play.

1. Expressed

The injured spectator or participant may expressly assume the risk and waive his right to be free from those bodily contacts inherent in the sport, that is, he takes his chances and is therefore barred from recovery. The doctrine of expressed assumption of risk includes expressed covenants not to sue and situations of actual consent (such as voluntary participation in contact sports) which will create a complete bar to plaintiff's recovery against the negligent defendant.

In the determination of whether a plaintiff who is injured in a contact sport subjectively appreciates the risk giving rise to the injury, it is within the power of the jury to review all evidence as to what plaintiff really expected while participating in that sport. If plaintiff is found to have recognized the risk and continued participation in the face of danger, then the defendant can raise the defense of expressed assumption of risk.

2. Implied

An injured spectator or plaintiff may also impliedly assume the risk of injury. This situation will arise when the plaintiff is aware of the risk created by defendant's negligence but continues to voluntarily proceed. Plaintiff's consent is implied from the continuation of the activity in that he goes forward although aware of the risk. Plaintiff's actions in assuming the risk may be unreasonable or reasonable, however, if the conduct is unreasonable then it is no different from contributory negligence.

Some states have abolished the doctrine of implied assumption of risk by statute. In other states the defense is still applicable.

3. Jockeys and Car Racers

Assumption of risk is more intransigent as a doctrine in the ultra-hazardous sports of horse racing and race car driving. Where a horse racing jockey is injured in an accident and sues a fellow jockey to recover for injuries sustained as a result of the other jockey's alleged negligence; barring a specific intent to injure on the part of the fellow jockey there can be no recovery for injuries which the jockey sustained as a result of jockey error or careless riding.

In a case where a jockey was thrown and injured during a race as a result of the closing of two other horses, it was held that reasonable implied assumption of risk remained a viable defense in the absence of comparative fault since the jockey assumed the risk of injury as a result of the negligence of another jockey even though the second jockey was in violation of the rules as long as that jockey's conduct was not reckless. *Ordway v. Superior Court* (1988).

Thoroughbred horse racing by its very nature is a sport that poses great peril to its participants. It is a situation where up to a dozen horses each weighing up to 1200 pounds break from a starting point and attempt to gain a preferred position at the rail as the first turn approaches. On these charging horses moving at full speed are persons weighing approximately 100 pounds; these jockeys also drive for position.

In this attempt to acquire the best position, due to both jockey error and the difficulties in controlling a sensitive thoroughbred horse, contacts and collisions are common place which occasionally result in spills that create injuries. These dangers are inherent to the sport of horse racing and are well known to the jockeys especially those who have significant experience in riding professionally.

Although a participant in a horse race does relieve his fellow participants of the duty of care in respect to those dangers that are normally associated with the sport, he does not relieve them of the duty to refrain from reckless, wanton or intentionally injurious conduct. A jockey also does not have to assume the risk brought about by the negligence of others.

A jockey was injured when his horse veered across the track towards a negligently placed exit gap; he then brought a negligence action against the race track alleging that the accident resulted from the negligent placing of the exit gap. The jockey was deemed not to have assumed the risk of the negligent placement of the gap in the race track which was also determined to be the proximate cause of his injuries. *Ashcroft v. Calder Race Course, Inc.* (1986).

Even more obvious is the application of assumption of risk to the race car driver. When a race car driver has actual knowledge of the presence of a disabled automobile off the drag strip and several hundred feet beyond the finish line, he will be held to know the conditions of the track. Since he knew of the inherent danger, he actually and subjectively comprehended the risk of undertaking the trial run under the existing conditions including proceeding in the face of a known danger by voluntarily racing his car and knowingly assuming the risk of injuring himself. *Robillard v. P & R Racetracks, Inc.* (1981).

A race car driver, whether he signs a release or not, assumes the risks of known, inherent dangers by simply entering the race. When an oil slick developed on the surface of a race track during the course of a race, it constituted a development over which the defendant had no control. Yet when an accident occurred as a natural result of the slick, it was held to be among the type of risks which were assumed by the plaintiff in taking part in the race. *Seymour v. New Bremen Speedway, Inc.* (1971).

4. Skiing, Golf and Baseball

Assumption of risk is also applicable to skiing, golf and baseball spectator injuries. Skiers are business invitees. The operators owe the skiers the duty to exercise reasonable care to keep the premises in a safe condition so that skiers are not unnecessarily or unreasonably exposed to danger. A skiing operator not only owes the duty to protect the skier from known dangers but is also required to exercise reasonable care in locating unknown dangers which pose a potential threat to skiers. Whether the duty to exercise reasonable care has been discharged is the key issue in ski injury litigation.

Often the issue of reasonable care is not reached in a ski injury suit, because the skier assumes the risk inherent in that sport. For a skier to assume the risk, the defendant must show that plaintiff knew the risk, appreciated the extent of those risks and accepted those risks voluntarily. Thus, where ski areas have changed the nature of the sport by improving slope grooving and maintenance, one can argue that these improvements make it questionable that the hazards encountered by skiers are currently obvious and necessary to the sport and therefore, they might be viewed as no longer inherent to that sport.

Since skiing may be a large part of a particular local or state economy, many state legislatures have enacted statutes protecting resorts. Some statutes have created presumptions that skiers, rather than resorts, are responsible for collisions occurring between skiers and other individuals and for injuries not incurred on improved trails or slopes.

Generally, courts have held that skiers assume the risk of dangers that are obvious, necessary or inherent in skiing. Courts have held that the hazards presented by the presence of a tree stump or a metal pole used for ski lift supports, snow making or other utilities are obvious, necessary or inherent to the sport and thus assumed by participants. A skier who collides with a pole subsequent to a collision with another skier is required to demonstrate that the pole constituted a hazard capable of producing liability on the part of the resort independent of the initial collision.

Courts generally reject plaintiff's argument that skiing is an activity to which a standard greater than reasonable ordinary care applies. Ski resorts will also protect themselves through releases on the back of lift tickets which waive the skier's right to bring an action against the resort.

Ski resorts must use at least reasonable care in the marking of trails and taking other precautions to assure that skiers do not stray from the designated trails. Liability, may be imposed on a ski area for selling its service in such a manner that allows persons on toboggans access to the same hill used by beginning skiers. Likewise, the variation of the terrain of a slope, a loose bush and an unmarked rock outcropping have been found to be hazards for which ski areas may be held liable.

In golf, golfers assume only some of the risks of the game. It is negligent for a golfer to drive another ball without warning when his prior drive is already on the fairway: he has a duty to warn under those circumstances. Also, when a golfer allows another party to play through and is struck by a golf ball, assumption of the risk will bar recovery even though the defendant did not yell "fore" since plaintiff voluntarily placed himself in the orbit of the shot of the person behind him. Plaintiff purposely requested the defendant to shoot; therefore, he certainly had notice that defendant would indeed shoot. This notice obviated defendant's duty to warn.

As regards to baseball spectators, the spectator assumes the foreseeable and known risks of a baseball game. For example, he would assume the risk of a foul ball at a evening baseball game. However, spectators do not assume injuries from baseballs that are projected into the stands by non-normal means. Also, a spectator does not assume the risk of a foul ball while she was walking in the inner corridor of a baseball stadium. *Jones v. Three Rivers Management Corp.* (1978).

5. Minors

Assumption of risk takes a slightly different variation when the injured person is a minor. A young child need not conform to the behavioral standard which is reasonable as an adult, that is, his conduct is to be judged by the standards that are expected from a child of a like age, intelligence and experience. However, when a minor was injured when a baseball bat flew from the hands of another minor, evidence failed to establish defendant's negligence. The minor plaintiff voluntarily participated in the game and thus assumed the risk of injury. *Gaspard v. Grain Dealers Mut. Ins. Co.* (1961).

C. CONTRIBUTORY NEGLIGENCE

If an athlete or spectator with knowledge of conditions goes into danger then he or she assumes the consequences of that danger even though there might be negligence on the part of another; if his or her negligence is the proximate cause of the injury then he or she is barred from recovery. This is contributory negligence.

In a health spa slip and fall case, a spa member who allegedly slipped and fell on a foreign substance in the shower was contributorily negligent where she had used the spa facilities on several occasions and had heard that the showers were slippery, filthy and dirty. She exposed herself to the risk without ever protesting the danger and without ascertaining the condition of the showers on that day.

Contributory negligence is a question for determination by the jury, but when the evidence admits but to one reasonable inference then it becomes a matter of law for determination by the court. There will be no recovery for negligently inflicted injuries if the injured person proximately contributed to his own injury.

Contributory negligence is conduct that falls below the standards which a plaintiff should meet for his own protection and which is a contributing cause of his injuries. It frequently involves plaintiff's inadequate failure to notice and appreciate danger; however, absent notice to the contrary, a spectator can usually assume that the premises are reasonably safe. Plaintiff's contributory negligence is a complete bar to recovery even if the plaintiff was only slightly negligent and defendant was primarily so.

At common law, a plaintiff who had negligently contributed to his own injury was barred from recovering damages. This situation imposes a duty for his acts or omissions towards others with a similar obligation existing as regards his own safety. Therefore, if a plaintiff does not use reasonable care for his own safety and his lack of care is a substantial factor in causing her own injury, a defendant may raise plaintiff's contribution in defense of his own acts. Under this theory, the existence of contributory negligence on the part of the plaintiff is sufficient to preclude recovery.

For minors, contributory negligence involves three distinct issues: the existence of capacity on the part of the child, the standard of care to be applied and conformance by that child to the applicable standard of care. Courts have recognized the general rule that the ultimate determination of a child's capacity to be contributorily negligent is a question of fact, and some courts have specifically held that children within a certain age group as a matter of law may not be contributorily negligent. Generally, children over five may or may not be contributorily negligent depending upon the circumstances.

Where a young golfer was struck by the ball hit by a mature golfer, the older golfer must be aware that young children possess limited judgment and are likely at times to forget the dangers and behave in a thoughtless manner. The negligence of a child golfer in standing on the fairway or raising his head from safety into danger when the mature golfer drove a golf ball at his general direction was not contributory negligence which would bar recovery for injuries. A nine-year old may be capable of contributory negligence but like a 12–year old, he is not held to the adult standards of comprehending danger and the duty of self care. *Outlaw v. Bituminous Ins. Co.* (1978).

D. COMPARATIVE NEGLIGENCE

Many states have responded to the onerous effects of assumption of risk and contributory negligence by creating comparative negligence as an alternative. Comparative negligence compares the fault of defendant to that of plaintiff. Although each state may have a different version of comparative negligence, the essential principle is that plaintiff will be allowed to recover at least a proportion of the damages sustained if plaintiff's negligence was proportionally less than the negligence of defendant.

Also, assumption of risk is not necessarily merged into the defense of contributory negligence under principles of comparative negligence. For example, an experienced skater who intentionally and voluntarily chose to perform an unsupervised traverse on a ramp while holding a ski pole in either hand will assume the risk of injury. *Gary v. Party Time Co.* (1983).

E. WARNINGS

Courts favor warnings. Warnings explain the inherent dangers that are involved in a certain activity as opposed to a release which by means of an agreement releases the defendant from all potential liability that might accrue from injuries to participants.

Participants must be warned about inherent risks in a sport. The more dangerous the sport, the more important the warnings. It is preferable to place warnings in writing and to read through the written warnings with players and parents, if the sport is a particularly hazardous one and the players are minors. A signed, written warning, dated and understood by players and parents, will assist the coach in his attempt to defend himself against liability.

Certain types of sports equipment, e.g., football helmets or trampolines should also contain general warnings that explain the hazards that are associated with that product. Each warning should contain a description of the demands and stresses that the sport places on the human body. It is especially important that the description include any potential cardiac stress so that the players can appreciate the physiological demands that are a part of the sport.

On the other hand, it has been held that a stadium owner did not have the duty to warn an injured spectator of the danger of the possibility of being hit by a foul ball while in the area behind the first base dugout; the stadium owner met his duty to provide adequately screened seats for those desiring them even though spectators chose to sit elsewhere. *Friedman v. Houston Sports Association* (1987).

An owner or occupier of premises owes a duty to invitees to exercise reasonable care such as inspecting the premises for any latent defects and making safe any defects or providing an adequate warning about those defects.

In practice, warning sometimes merge with waivers. There are usually both warnings and waivers on the back of a baseball ticket. There are also statements on the back of season passes that acknowledge the hazards that exist in skiing and that specifically waive injury from the carelessness or negligence of fellow skiers. However, in a suit against a ski area for injuries when plaintiff collided with a metal pole after a collision with another skier, the court analyzed that type of warning and waiver, and since the document was ambiguous, the court decided against the drawer of that document. *Rosen v. LTV Recreational Development, Inc.* (1978).

F. WAIVERS

The main feature of all exculpatory agreements is to relieve one party of all or part of his responsibility to another. A waiver is simply one form of an exculpatory agreement. A waiver is a contract and presents a conflict between two fundamental legal axioms: one in contracts where all persons are free to contract as they desire, and one in negligence where one is responsible for negligent acts which cause injury to others. Although exculpatory clauses are valid in certain circumstances, they are not favored in the law. Any clause which exonerates a party from liability will be strictly construed against the party that benefits. If the clause is ambiguous in scope or purports to release the benefiting party from liability for intentional, willful or wanton acts, it will not be enforced. Waivers, to be valid, must be nonambiguous, particular as to the wording regarding liability, not against public policy, not intimate condemnation of gross negligence, and not allow results that would indicate a large disparity in bargaining power.

The most significant aspect of a release is the particular words that are used. For example, when the injured plaintiff is an expert in a particular sport, the failure of the release to include the word "negligence" does not preclude other language which may have the same effect. The release will be enforceable as long as the release agreement is sufficiently clear to show the party's intent that defendant is to be held harmless for any injury that is caused by his own negligence.

A waiver will be valid if it does not contravene any policy of law and does not involve a quasi-public entity that supports or supplies essential services, but rather relates to the private affairs of individuals.

If there is no ambiguity and the contract is not one of adhesion, the exculpatory clause will not violate public policy. Ambiguity will not be an issue if the clause simply purports to exonerate a facility owner from liability for acts of negligence and for negligence only. However, where a contract is drafted unilaterally by a business enterprise and forced on an unwilling and often unknowing public for services that cannot readily be obtained elsewhere then that contract is an "adhesion contract", that is, a contract that is generally not bargained for but one that is imposed on the other party on a take it or leave it basis.

However, this view will not apply to health club memberships when there is no disparity in bargaining power and no evidence that the services were necessary or that the services could not be obtained elsewhere. Since the services were not essential, suitable for public regulation or of such great importance as to be clearly a necessity for some members of the public, then the waiver clause did not violate public policy.

However, it is universally held that a waiver will not bar a claim for gross negligence. This is correct even though the same exculpatory clause would bar an action for simple negligence. Similarly, a disclaimer is against public policy if it is inconspicuous.

Where a release was obtained only from racing participants and those choosing to be in the pit area of a race track, the exculpatory clause was held unenforceable as regards protecting the race track owner against possible dram shop liability. The exculpatory agreement did not release the defendant from dram shop liability, because if it did it would be against public policy. *Scheff v. Homestretch, Inc.* (1978).

Waivers that public school students are required to sign as a prerequisite for participation in high school sports which release the school district from the consequences of all future school district negligence are invalid because they are a violation of public policy. *Wagenblast v. Odessa School District* (1988).

The factors that are essential in a determination of whether a release will violate public policy include the following: whether the agreement concerns the type of business that is generally thought suitable for public regulation; whether the party seeking the waiver is engaged in performing services of great importance to the public; whether the party holds itself out as willing to perform these services for any member of the public; whether the party invoking exculpation possesses the decisive advantage and bargaining strength; whether the party thus invoking confronts the public with a standardized adhesion contract; and whether as a result of this contract the purchaser is placed under the control of the seller and, therefore, subject to the risk of carelessness by the seller.

1. Foot Races

An integral part of any jogger's routine is to scrutinize the ubiquitous waiver on the form for road race participation. A waiver of this sort will not release the defendant from all types of liability. The question is when and under what circumstances this release will be applicable.

The leading case in this area involves a young law student who was gravely injured while participating in a 10,000 meter event in Atlanta, Georgia, in July. The young man accused the organizer of being negligent by failing to adequately warn that he could suffer serious injuries from participation in the extreme heat and humidity. Also, that defendant failed to provide liquids and medical facilities along the race and failed to ascertain whether all entrants were physically capable of completing the race. However, the plaintiff not only signed but understood the waiver agreement.

Each participant was required to pay a fee and sign a very specific and particular application form that described the race and the physical conditioning necessary in a very specific manner, along with a particular description of the type of heat and humidity that would be expected. The application form added that all of this made it "a grueling ten thousand meter race." *Williams v. Cox Enterprises, Inc.* (1981).

Regardless of the explicit warning, the law student, as a result of extreme exertion in the exact conditions that were described in the waiver, succumbed to heat prostration which resulted in a permanent impairment of some motor functions. It was decided that this waiver was not against public

policy. There was no disparity in bargaining position. Plaintiff alleged that road racing had become
so popular and this race in particular was one of a
kind that he and other participants were under
enormous pressure to enter it under whatever
terms were offered to them. The court made short
account of this argument. The court also determined that recovery was precluded under assumption of risk because the waiver was described in
extremely particular terms and the plaintiff agreed
that he read the waiver and was already aware of
the danger. Because of this, any injury that resulted from over heating and dehydration could not
reasonably be construed to have emanated from any
breach of duty on the part of the defendant.

2. Car Races

Releases also will usually be allowed in ultra-
hazardous sporting activities such as race car driving, especially when the signed waiver is voluntary
and a product of knowledgeable agreement. Waivers for participation in a vehicular racing event will
especially be upheld where there is valuable consideration as an exchange for a signed released. The
valuable consideration deemed important in law is
the right to participate in the event with the hope
of winning prize money. In this situation, the
waiver constitutes a full defense to any claim for
damages except those due to wanton or willful
negligence. Willful negligence does not occur, for
example, when an oil slick develops on the surface
of the race track during the course of the race and

as a result creates an accident which causes injury to plaintiff. *Seymour v. New Bremen Speedway, Inc.* (1971).

Even a race car driving release, however, will not waive liability for defendant's gross negligence. Similarly, it will not always act as a bar to an action by decedent's spouse on the grounds of loss of consortium (the courts are split). Nor will a waiver release a defendant for liability under the state's dram shop act, since that type of waiver even under the conditions of a car race would violate public policy. Another question is, who is included under a waiver which stipulated that both "participants" and "advertisers" were released from liability; it was held that the tire distributor and tire manufacturer respectively, were included in those descriptions. *Kircos v. Goodyear Tire and Rubber Co.* (1981).

3. Minors

Generally when a minor is involved with a release, the law will not bind him to it. This is correct whether he signs it or whether it's signed by his parents or any combination thereof. A minor who was injured while attending an ice hockey clinic was not bound by the fact that his father had signed a release on behalf of his son which purported to exempt the city and the hockey league for injuries. Also, since the father's cause of action was derivative to his child, the father's waiver was not barred by the waiver that involved his child. The father's cause of action was derivative to his son's and drew its life from the existence of the cause of action which inured to the benefit of the infant. A parent cannot release a child's cause of action. *Doyle v. Bowdoin College* (1979).

A minor's waiver is unenforceable because a child does not have the capacity to contract; the traditional rule for minors is that they can disaffirm a contract unless it involves life's necessities. Since recreation is not a necessity then an exculpatory contract signed by a minor is usually voidable. This is true even when a minor misrepresents his age.

G. SOVEREIGN IMMUNITY

Another way for tortfeasors to avoid liability for sports-related injuries is to plead immunity based on the fact that the particular activity was protected from liability. These immunities are designated as either sovereign or charitable. Recently, however, courts and legislatures have made broad-based attacks against these doctrines so that in many jurisdictions, public, private and charitable institutions receive the same status as most other tortfeasors, that is, they must compensate those who are injured by their wrongful acts.

Broadly, sovereign immunity provides that a state or its instrumentalities shall not be subject to suit without its consent. This immunity relies on several policy considerations including that as a sovereign entity the state can do no wrong, that public agencies have limited funds and can expend them only for public purposes, that public bodies cannot be responsible for the torts of their employees, and that public bodies do not possess the authority to commit torts. Immunity in its purest form will protect actions of all public bodies, including school districts, their employees, school boards, racing commissions, board members of a state university, etc., in as much as they are agents or instrumentalities of the state itself.

Although sovereign immunity once provided a broad umbrella of protection to state and state-related agencies, consent to suit has been provided by the legislatures in many states in a variety of ways. Where such consent is not allowed, courts in several jurisdictions have responded to the criticism of sovereign immunity by abrogating it through judicial action.

When trying to understand sovereign immunity, it is important to distinguish between state and municipal entities. Municipal corporations have a duality which have influenced their tort liabilities. These corporations are entities that perform both governmental functions and subdivisions with special local interests which are comparable to those of a private corporation and not shared by the state. The doctrine of sovereign immunity has attempted to respond to this duality. Immunities are provided for the acts of the municipal corporation while in its governmental posture, but not when its in a corporate posture. Political or governmental functions can be described as those which are necessary to the well-being of the community. Therefore, public education and protecting public health are governmental functions while mere amusement or entertainment is not.

An example of the governmental-private duality is provided by cases that turned on the status of the party which is utilizing a public owned stadium for sporting events. When a public school is using the stadium, courts have generally found that the contests are a part of the state's educational responsibility and thus are governmental functions to which sovereign immunity would apply. However, if a public school leases its stadium, courts have held that through that process the school has conducted a proprietary activity and will be liable for injuries sustained as a result of negligent facility maintenance. One convenient standard in determining whether an event is governmental or private is the charging of a fee; but usually that is viewed as only one factor in reaching a determination.

In a Michigan case, when an injured football player brought suit against both his football coach and a helmet manufacturer for damages which left him a quadriplegic, the court held that football coaches were entitled to governmental immunity. The court stated that a public school in the operation of its athletic program will include the administration and supervision of football and, thus, is entitled to governmental immunity. Teachers and their supervisors are entitled to immunity when their duties are performed within the scope of their employment. The argument is that a physical education program, as either part of a general curriculum or as an extracurricular activity, is in furtherance of and an integral part of the total public education provided to students. Football is a part of these day-to-day operations and is therefore immune. *Churilla v. School District* (1981).

Similarly, in Illinois, a high school varsity football player brought an action against the board of education and his coach for injuries sustained in football. The court held that the coaches were immune under the school code from liability for ordinary negligence as it relates to a player's injuries due to allegedly defective equipment. Absent willful and wanton conduct in the course of their supervision, which encompasses inspecting and supplying students with appropriate equipment, coaches will be immune from liability for alleged negligence under the Illinois school code.

1. Discretionary Acts

The doctrine of discretionary immunity allows state officials and their employees to receive partial immunity but usually only for discretionary duties as opposed to ministerial duties. Under the doctrine of discretionary immunity, state officials are not absolutely immune from suit, but ordinarily will be liable only in the performance of ministerial duties. The question is what type of activities are properly construed as ministerial as opposed to discretionary. Discretionary duties are those which call for the exercise of the public official's judgment or discretion; for these types of activities, he will not be personally liable to an individual for damages unless he is guilty of a willful or malicious wrong. A ministerial duty is one in which nothing is left to discretion, that is, a simple, definite duty arising under and because of stated conditions as imposed by law. An official duty is ministerial when it is absolute, certain and imperative, involving only the execution of a specific duty arising from fixed and designated facts.

The determination of what is discretionary as opposed to ministerial is often a difficult one. The distinction is nebulous and abstruse because almost any act involves some aspects of both freedom of choice and perfunctory execution. Generally, the answer will be decided after evaluating the nature, quality and the complexity of the decision-making process involved in that particular responsibility. The question is deciding whether a teacher's performance in a physical education course is a discretionary or ministerial function. If it is discretionary then defendant is protected by the doctrine of discretionary immunity. Applicability of this doctrine is not dependent upon whether a person's duty requires some degree of judgment and discretion. The crucial analysis centers on the nature of the act undertaken. Decisions intended to be protected by discretionary immunity are those made on the planning level of conduct.

The doctrine of discretionary immunity is intended to protect public officials or employees whose policy making duties include choosing between various alternatives even if one of the options is to do nothing. If a teacher never engages in the type of decision making that is relevant to developing and administering a physical education curriculum, then his negligence will not involve decision-making on the planning level. Therefore, the teacher's activities would be construed as ministerial rather than discretionary.

2. Policy Considerations

Traditionally the crown could do no wrong and hence suit against the crown was not allowed. The primary policy consideration behind this view was that for governmental officials to do their job they must be free from the fear of suit.

At direct conflict with this idea is the equitable principle that every plaintiff must have his day to plead his case when an alleged negligent action produces injury. This is especially true in sports where robust activity is coupled with the possibility of catastrophic injury. Although the strength of the immunity doctrine has been decreased by both the governmental/proprietary distinction and the ministerial/discretionary question, this relic still survives. Therefore, it is imperative that the first step for plaintiff's attorney is to evaluate the status of the immunity doctrine in the relevant jurisdiction before evaluating a sports injury case that involves a governmental or charitable institution.

H.   CHARITABLE IMMUNITY

Like sovereign immunity, charitable immunity, if applicable, will provide an umbrella from suits against charitable institutions that is comparable to that provided governmental institutions. Like governmental immunity, the bases of charitable immunity are large and diverse. The most prevalent is the concept of a trust fund in which charitable funds are held in trust for charitable purposes and may not be diverted for other uses. Another theory is that charities are immune from the doctrine of respondeat superior and therefore are not responsible for the injury-causing actions of their employees since no profit is derived from their work. Under this theory liability can result only from the acts of the charity itself.

However, even where this doctrine is still applicable it has exceptions and distinctions which neutralize it to a great extent. One distinction is that charities may be liable to strangers but cannot be liable to their beneficiaries, that is, to the recipients of their charity. Another distinction has been drawn between employees and non-employees, with only employees allowed to recover from that charitable organization. Finally, charities have been held liable for activities which involve non-charitable aspects: e.g., when admission fees are charged or for those activities that constitute a nuisance.

I. RECREATIONAL USE STATUTES

A recent addition to the immunity umbrella is the so-called Recreational Use Statutes (R.U.S.). Although they vary from state to state, the basic principle is that landowners who allow free recreational use of their property, owe no duty of care to keep their premises in safe condition or warn of dangerous or hazardous conditions. However, if a fee is paid for use, then the statute will not apply. As with sovereign immunity, these statutes offer some protection from suit for those entities (either public or private) that perform a "state-like" function, namely, providing the means and opportunities for the masses to satiate their recreational and sporting needs.

CHAPTER 14

WORKERS' COMPENSATION

Usually, the first step in recovering for an injured athlete is to sue in tort. However, there is a parallel universe created by state statutes that provides for employees to secure compensation for employment-related injuries. This alternate form of recovery is workers' compensation. The relevant statutes will differ from state to state. Even though a singular description does not exist, the following is an overview of the basic attributes of the various state laws.

A. PROFESSIONAL SPORTS

Professional athletes and other employees of professional teams will usually come under the protection of their particular state's workers' compensation statutes. However, there are certain states that specifically exclude professional athletes from coverage.

As a general caveat, the basic requirements for any workers' compensation statutes is usually that the person must be an employee who was injured by an accident while involved in a job-related function. Workers' compensation will also generally be the exclusive remedy against the employer for that injury if the injury is covered under the statute; if that is true then the employee will not have the option to bring a judicial action against either his employer or his co-workers for injuries that result from the same accident.

For injuries to professional athletes, it must be determined whether the injured person is an employee. For an injury to a horse jockey it was held that because he was employed and paid by the job as a independent contractor, he did not come under the control of the owner or trainer and thus was not an employee. Since he was not an employee he was not covered under workers' compensation. *Munday v. Churchill Downs, Inc.* (1980).

Another obstacle for the professional athlete is whether the event that created the injury was an accident. This can be an interesting question in physical sports such as football. Where the injury occurred to an offensive guard while blocking, that event could not be construed to be an accident under the applicable workers' compensation statutes. That was because the relevant statute only protected against injuries that were the result of an accident, that is, trauma from unexpected or unforeseen events in the usual course of the employee's occupation. This statute did not contemplate that the deliberate collision between human beings during a professional football game was an accident, or that the injury, in the usual course of his occupation was caused by an unexpected event. *Palmer v. Kansas City Chiefs Football Club* (1981).

In *Bayless v. Philadelphia National League Club* (1979), a former pitcher brought an action against a professional baseball team seeking damages for mental illness allegedly caused by the team's administration of drugs following complaints of severe back pain. Plaintiff based his claims on a breach of defendant's contractual duty to provide him with sound medical care in the event that his skills were impaired by injury. The court held that the pitcher's exclusive remedy was workers' compensation. In the athlete's complaint, he averred that his injury was caused by the club's failure to provide medical care thus placing himself within the ambit of the Pennsylvania Workmen's Compensation Act (the Act).

The pitcher then attempted to skirt coverage of the Act by placing his injury in the same category as an exception for exposure to diseases whose gradual progression would not constitute an accident. However, the court disagreed on the grounds that the pitcher's complaint established that the onset of mental illness was directly traceable to treatment received from the club and not a gradual progression of a disease that preexisted the club's administration of the drugs. The court also held that the Act applies equally to high paid professional athletes as well as lower paid athletes; it applies to all athletes regardless of their earnings.

B. COLLEGIATE SPORTS

In professional sports the injured athlete is an employee of the team. A more ambiguous situation occurs when the injured athlete is a member of a college sports team. The question then is whether the injured athlete is an employee for purposes of workers' compensation. If the athlete was a walk-on and had no financial relationship with the school, the courts will not view that person as an employee for workers' compensation purposes. However, some courts will view the athlete as an employee if the athlete is paid in anyway whatsoever for his participation. For scholarship athletes, the general view is that if there is a contract to pay for the athlete's participation, then there is a relationship on which to base compensation coverage. If there is a continued receipt of a job, free meals or money, and it is contingent upon the athlete's continued participation in a sport, then a contract to play that sport has been created. Since there is a contract of employment, then compensation coverage will exist for student-athletes who are injured in accidents during the course of their employment as an "athlete."

C. EMPLOYER–BASED SPORTS

Another frequently used category of sports compensation plaintiffs covers those that are injured in employment-related sports, such as team softball or bowling leagues. Employment-related sporting activities that have been brought under the coverage of workers' compensation include those which occur on the jobsite during job hours, those which are controlled by the employer who furnishes uniforms, league fees, equipment and encourages participation, and those that the employer will receive direct benefit from, such as advertisement, public relations or improved customer relations.

The key to coverage is whether the employer has brought this sporting activity within the course of employment. If there are few or no indices that bring the activity under the course of employment, workers' compensation will not be applicable. This includes those sports-related activities that are significantly employee-generated, have little contact with the employer and are basically an ad hoc employee recreational activity. However, the opposite is true in those situations when the employer actively encourages and provides for participation in the sporting enterprise.

The more indices that show that the activity is within the course of employment then there is more of a chance that the court will find that coverage applies. Indices can include that the team was entered in an industrial league and played against teams of other employers who were involved in a similar occupation as defendant employer; that a championship trophy is displayed on the employer's premises; that the employer paid the entrance fee to the league; that the employer required bats, balls, and other equipment to be kept on the company's premises; that equipment is paid for by the employer and that the name of the company was displayed on the uniforms of the athletes; and that the uniforms were paid for by the employer and/or that the employer paid towards the costs of each uniform. Other indices would be that the umpires of each game were paid for by the employer; that a raffle was allowed to be held in cooperation with the employer and the members of the team on the employer's premises during working hours in order to help gain more financial support for the team; that schedules were passed out at the plant, copies of which were given to the employer; and that when the employer withdrew support from the team, it resulted in the disbanding of the team for lack of support. All these factors are the type which will be used in the determination of whether the activity falls within the course of employment. *Scott v. Workmen's Compensation Appeal Board* (1988).

D. NON–PARTICIPANTS

There is always the possibility that coaches, physical education teachers, team managers, stadium attendants, trainers, umpires, referees, and similar athletic personnel will also be employees and because of that fall under the coverage of workers' compensation statutes for job-related injuries. Because of their proximity to the field of action, trainers, referees and coaches are the most likely non-athletic personnel to be injured and thus apply for coverage.

Trainers and referees are usually not viewed as employees but instead as independent contractors who are not covered under the applicable workers' compensation statute. The question is who has the right to control the details of another's performance. If there is control of the details of the performance of the referee or the trainer, then that could be used to show the necessary indices to prove employee-status.

Coaches, on the other hand, are usually employees of the school district or team. However, in those situations where the coach is not a salaried employee per se, it must be determined what type of relationship exists between the coach and the supervising authority.

CHAPTER 15

CRIMINAL LIABILITY

A. VIOLENCE IN SPORTS

There is no question that some degree of violence is a part of sports. This is especially true in contact sports. This is even more true in the extreme contact sports, like football and hockey. There is some degree of violent contact that is unavoidable in any contact sport. However, arguably there is an unnecessary amount of violence in today's professional sports. This excessive violence has spilled over to amateur sports.

One attempt to deter unnecessary violence is through league and disciplinary rules in professional sports. Each team and league through their SPK and their collective bargaining agreement (c.b.a.) have established rules and procedures to penalize and control violence that is deemed to be unnecessary and not an inherent part of the sport. These procedures include an independent arbitrator to decide if there is a conflict between the player and league as regards disciplinary disputes. But, these documents contain ambiguous terminology which does not precisely reflect the degree that violent behavior cannot exceed. For example, the standard language is "contrary to the best interests of the game." Subjective language of this type does not clearly define the parameters of acceptable behavior.

Another way to curb violence is civil actions for injuries that occur through participant contact. These tort cases are few and far between, and they usually revolve around principles of negligence and/or assault and battery. They have not effectively decreased the amount of unnecessary violence that is evident today in professional sports.

A third way to deter violence is to punish the offenders criminally. Criminal sanctions might be useful in this endeavor if one accepts that the rationale behind criminal punishment is deterrence. As an example, other athletes would be on notice that incidents of that type will no longer be tolerated or unpunished. The trial of a professional athlete would be a highly publicized media event which would be both embarrassing to all parties and expensive. The time lost through litigation and possibly a jail sentence would be irretrievable. The end result is that the athlete's career might be significantly altered or even destroyed.

The threshold question that arises when one contemplates criminal sanctions for violent conduct is to determine if the facts require the imposition of criminal sanctions, i.e., if the particular penal laws in question are intended to be applied to conduct in sporting events. Next, one needs to concentrate on the elements of the particular crime, for example, assault and battery, or manslaughter, and then to ascertain if these elements were present at the time of the incident. It must be determined if the accused had a defense. The standard defense is that the injured person consented to the injury by voluntary engagement in that sport. Also, if the conduct was provoked, a self-defense argument might arise.

B. CRIMINAL ACTION GENERALLY

The philosophy behind criminal law is based on society's need to be free from harmful conduct. Criminal law defines criminal contact and prescribes the punishment to be imposed on persons convicted of that proscribed conduct. Violence and possibly criminal conduct, however, is looked on differently when that violence occurs in a sporting or recreational event. That is because the harm and violence are confined to the participants who obviously know and assume the risks that are inherent to the game. Also the innocent public is not subjected to that risk of physical harm. The question becomes whether the violent conduct is accidental or within the rules of the particular sport or criminal conduct. The crux is that certain sports are extremely physical and violent physical conduct is part of the sport. For battery to be a crime, there must be illegality. Yet, that element is to some extent negated in conventional sports. However, arguably the most onerous and heinous acts that occur in contact sports such as football, hockey and basketball extend beyond any possible justification that is built within the scope of the game.

The criminal defendant will use consent and self-defense as defenses in a criminal prosecution that accrues from sports violence. Consent usually is not a defense to a criminal act since one cannot consent to be a victim. In the crime of battery, consent of the victim is not an element, but in certain battery cases, the unlawful force application element is not present because of consent. Consent to application of force per se is not unlawful. The difficult problem with the consent defense is establishing a demarcation between reasonably foreseeable hazards that one can consent to and unreasonably foreseeable hazards to which one cannot consent. One can knowingly consent to the normal violence associated with a sport, whereas, one cannot knowingly consent to non-normal physical contact. To use the consent defense in this context, one must ascertain for each particular sport the type of violence that is foreseeable and thus capable of consent.

C. INHERENTLY VIOLENT SPORTS

In inherently violent sports, the question is to what type of violent conduct is consent a defense. Consent is arguably a defense to criminal charges that arise from injury so long as it is a reasonably foreseeable hazard of that sport and not a result of intentional conduct that is not reasonably related to that particular sport. Although there is no direct American authority on point, the situation where consent would not be a defense is arguably the type of unforeseeable and unexpected punching incident that occurs every once in a while in professional basketball. An athlete would arguably be criminally responsible for an intentional and reckless act. As regards the consent defense, an athlete would not be deemed to consent to intentional or reckless acts that are not reasonably related to the conduct of the particular sport.

A certain degree of consent to violent behavior and contact is expected in professional contact sports. Consent is an effective defense to conduct that does not threaten or cause serious injury or to reasonably foreseeable conduct that results in reasonably foreseeable harm. Therefore, in the attempt to prove that plaintiff did not consent to defendant's violent conduct, one must prove that defendant's behavior was not or could not have been reasonably foreseeable by the plaintiff. There is a difficulty in distinguishing between reasonably foreseeable conduct and injurious non-foreseeable harmful conduct; this difficulty as a rule will discourage athletes from seeking criminal charges against fellow participants and has added to the dearth of criminal prosecutions in sports cases. If criminal prosecutions are going to be regularly pursued in sports that have an inherently violent nature drawn into their very existence, like football and hockey, it is essential to define and ascertain the acts that will incur criminal penalty. Currently, there are no neat and predictable lines as to when a certain act will go beyond the parameters of the game and the rules and be eligible for criminal sanctions.

D. BATTERY

Battery is the criminal offense that is most usually applicable in cases of sports violence. A battery is an unlawful application of force to the person of another that results in bodily injury. Battery possesses an element of unlawfulness and that is the key to the question of whether battery is relevant or not in the sports arena. Society and the criminal codes have made sports violence an exception from criminal laws by treating it as lawful. The type of activity that is unlawful on a city street might be entirely lawful when used in a professional football game. The elements of battery are a guilty state of mind, an act, a physical touching of a victim and causation. Battery's state of mind does not require actual intent. Criminal negligence or a conscious disregard of known and serious risks will be sufficient. Both states of mind allow for aggravated battery and will punish battery as a felony when the use of a deadly weapon or the causing of serious bodily injury is a part of the criminal act. Deadly objects can be ordinary objects if they are used in a way that may cause death. For example, hockey sticks or baseball bats, under certain circumstances, could easily qualify as deadly objects.

E. THE CANADIAN APPROACH

American courts have been very hesitant to cross the line between physical contact that is a part of violent sports and that type of contact that is deemed to be criminal behavior. However, in Canada, criminal prosecutors have used criminal laws much more frequently against athletes accused of violent contact towards fellow players. This is especially true because of the popularity of hockey and the dangerousness that is inherent in the use of ice skates and hockey sticks. There have been numerous criminal convictions for offenses that involve player to player violence in Canada, as opposed to a near absolute dearth of reported cases in the United States.

As in the United States, the major problem that Canadian courts have faced is the status of the consent defense. The statutory definition of assault in Canada specifies that the intentional application of force to the person of another must be without that person's consent; a finding that there was consent will negate a necessary element of this offense. Three issues have evolved in the consent defense in reported Canadian cases: consent implied by participation, consent implied by specific acts and a public policy limitation on ones' ability to consent.

Self-defense is also a tool that is commonly used by defendants in Canadian criminal prosecutions for assault and battery. A defendant may use whatever force is reasonably necessary to repel an attack; this is especially logical in the sport of hockey where one is attacking with a hockey stick while his opponent is using his stick to parry blows and thrusts.

In the case of *Regina v. Maki* (1970) and *Regina v. Green* (1970), defendants were able to successfully assert the defense of self-defense in hockey injury prosecutions. In *Green,* the court found that plaintiff did indeed consent to being hit with a glove during a hockey match. An incident of this type was found to be a common occurrence in that sport. The court, however, brushed over the consent defense and justified defendant's action by the use of a self-defense explanation which ended with the court's conclusion that defendant did nothing "more in the circumstances than protecting himself."

For a successful assertion of self-defense, defendant must show that he was not the aggressor. This creates a problem in sports injury cases since the athlete will often fail to qualify as a non-aggressor. Therefore, self-defense will be unavailable in the majority of sports violence cases.

CHAPTER 16

AMATEUR SPORTS

A. GENERALLY

The term, "amateur athlete," is a true oxymoron. Amateurism was at one time a pure recreational outlet for the upper class. Today, all amateur sports are tinged with some shadings of professionalism. The distinction between amateur and professional athletes is ambiguous and uncertain. Amateur athletes of the past did not expect remuneration in any form for their athletic endeavors. However, this is certainly different today: for example, most college athletes are supported by scholarships. Also, many college athletic programs are a grooming ground for professional sports. The student athlete is subject to rigid rules, requirements and restrictions.

B. ADMINISTRATION

Amateur sports can be divided into two basic forms: restricted competition and unrestricted competition.

Restricted competition includes high school and collegiate competition. It means that competition is restricted to essentially the same groups at different levels. Administratively, competition is controlled and organized by athletic conferences or associations or leagues which encompass high schools and colleges. These entities establish rules of competition and organize the means of scheduling competition within these groups. Part of their function is to ascertain and establish participant eligibility. These entities are established to insure that their members comply with the pertinent rules and regulations; they will determine if inappropriate conduct has occurred. They will also impose sanctions if applicable to either the individual athlete or the school.

Unrestricted competition, on the other hand, is open to all athletes. An example would be Olympic competition, which in the United States is controlled by the United States Olympic Committee (USOC). This type of competition allows competition among all types of people and groups and is not restricted by age or college or other restrictive criterion.

C. STATUS OF ATHLETE

What is amateur sports turns on the status of the amateur athlete. If one is an amateur then one cannot by definition also be a professional. But the applicable categorizations are ambivalent, especially in the context of collegiate sports where a well known amateur athlete can also be a quasi-professional since he is under scholarship and perhaps creating revenue in other ways. The definition of an amateur is defined by the governing body of that particular sport and for that particular athlete. The definition of an amateur athlete may change from one organization to another. For example, it is possible that an individual can be viewed as an amateur under the rules of the USOC but not be an amateur under the NCAA rules.

D. RULE-MAKING

The courts are generally reluctant to overrule the rules, regulations and restrictions of the athletic associations as regards eligibility, participation and discipline of their members. Generally, courts will not interfere with the internal affairs of voluntary associations. Unless there is mistake, fraud, collusion or arbitrariness, the decisions and the rules of the governing body will be accepted by the courts as conclusive.

Voluntary associations may adopt reasonable by-laws, rules and regulations which will be valid and binding on their members unless their rules violate law or public policy. Courts eschew the responsibility of inquiring into the expediency, practicability or wisdom of these rules and regulations. Courts will not substitute their interpretation of an association's rules and regulations for those interpretations that are placed on these rules by the association itself, so long as the association's interpretations are fair and reasonable.

E.　NCAA

The NCAA is only one of a very large number of groups of governing bodies that control athletic participation in amateur sports; however, regarding college sports, it is easily the most important one and perhaps it is the most important governing body in sports of any type at any level. The NCAA is controversial in that many critics view it as paternalistic. There has been much debate, for example, on the various propositions (e.g., proposition 42, proposition 48 and proposition 16) which limit academic eligibility based on achievement on standardized tests and high school grade point averages in core courses.

The NCAA was found in the early 1900's and throughout the years has offered championships in a variety of sports. During this time, it obtained football television contracts, and accordingly greatly increased its financial and regulatory powers. It is a voluntary, unincorporated association of colleges of which approximately 50 percent are state supported. At the present, the NCAA is composed of more than 1200 member schools; all schools that are accredited by a recognized academic accrediting agency will meet NCAA standards and may become a member. Not only does it sponsor national championships but it also possesses the authority to make and enforce rules and regulations. The purpose of the NCAA is to formulate policy and regulations that in essence govern almost all aspects of intercollegiate athletic participation.

The NCAA is governed by a large and detailed compendium of rules and regulations. This compendium, or manual, contains the constitution and bylaws, as established at the annual convention of its members; it also contains interpretations and executive actions that emanate from these conventions. In between the annual conventions, NCAA affairs are controlled by a council, its executive committee and a paid staff. The interpretation and enforcement of the large body of NCAA rules, regulations and precedents are interpreted, enforced, and reviewed by legislative assistants and enforcement personnel; attorneys are involved when and if litigation occurs.

The NCAA general policies were formally promulgated at their annual convention. However, it is no longer one school, one vote. The governing structure is changed so that policy is now implemented through a series of levels (see enclosed chart for the procedures that make up the new process for approving legislation). It has a professional staff with headquarters in Indianapolis (formerly in Overland Park, Kansas). When the convention is not taking place, policy is established, controlled, and directed by the NCAA council which is elected by the entire membership at the annual meeting.

NCAA Division I Legislative Process

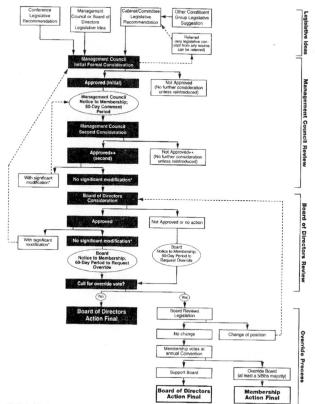

*Significant modification = a greater modification from the current rule than the original proposal.
++On a topic for which the Management Council has been delegated final authority by the Board of Directors; the override process begins at this point.
Note: During the Management Council's first and third meetings of each calendar year (e.g., January and July meetings), the Management Council shall be authorized to adopt only emergency, noncontroversial legislation, subject to approval by the Division I Board of Directors.

CHAPTER 17

ELIGIBILITY

A. GENERALLY

The key to amateur sports is the question of eligibility. Eligibility is the decision by the athletic governing body of whether a particular athlete or team is eligible to participate in a specific sport or a specific event. Establishing eligibility under a particular rule or bylaw is the province of the applicable governing association. The question is whether a denial of eligibility is a violation of that participant's constitutional or civil rights. An athlete's right to participate may be protected by the constitutional guarantees of due process and equal protection.

B. SCOPE OF ELIGIBILITY RULES

Eligibility rules cover all of the possible requirements and rules that might control a potential athlete including age, years of participation and academic standards. They range from grade point average to length of hair, transfer rules, red shirting rules, the number of semesters enrolled in school and married status. All these elements are used as a means to restrict an athlete's eligibility to participate. Whatever the regulation, it still has the same common objectives: the protection of the athlete, the promotion of education and the continuation of amateurism. A further objective is the control and regulation of a system of fair competition between the various schools and their athletes.

C.　PARTICIPATION AS A RIGHT OR PRIVILEGE

The threshold question in an analysis of the eligibility of the student athlete to participate is whether that individual has a right or privilege to participate. When there is a right, then the relationship between the athlete and the governing body which administers the competition will be on a much different legal status than if the participation is viewed as a mere privilege. The question becomes whether an athlete in a public institution has a sufficiently important interest in participation so as to require due process safeguards. If the questioned interest is a right, then due process will apply. To receive due process protection, the constitutionally guaranteed right must be either a liberty or property interest.

There is a great difference in the way that high school and intercollegiate sports can be analyzed. For example, a high school athlete will receive no present economic benefit from participation; his only benefit is the possibility of the receipt of an offer of a college scholarship. This possibility is too speculative to be recognized as a property right. However, a college athlete can receive a scholarship of substantial monetary value. Scholarships often cover the complete cost of attending a school; therefore, for a college athlete the right to participate is not a mere speculative interest but a property right of some present economic value. *Gulf South Conference v. Boyd* (1979).

One federal district court case has also recognized an athlete's limited property interest in being allowed to participate in intercollegiate sports. *Hall v. University of Minnesota* (1982). In this case, procedural due process was ignored when a basketball player (who had the requisite g.p.a. to continue in school but did not have sufficient credits for a particular program) was disallowed the opportunity to participate further in intercollegiate basketball. The court held that he had a sufficient property interest in the continuation of his basketball career to warrant constitutional protection since it was a distinct possibility that this lack of playing time would affect his ability to be drafted by a professional basketball league and earn a livelihood as a basketball player.

Yet, in a Court of Appeals case, the court found that the interest of student athletes including scholarship athletes to participate in intercollegiate hockey did not rise to the level of any right that would earn due process protection in connection with the NCAA's imposition of sanctions against the school for failure to declare several of its players ineligible. *Colorado Seminary v. NCAA* (1978). The court found no difference between high school and collegiate athletes. The court did concede that though other courts may aver that scholarships create a distinction between high school and collegiate sports, that type of distinction is more of a difference in degree. The court observed that the fundamental positions of these athletes are the same and the goals and issues are the same. Since the same relations exist between the primary academic functions of both colleges and high schools, it was held that the degree of difference does not lead to a different result.

In high school sports, the courts rarely find that a right to participate exists. In the Texas no pass, no play case, for example, the court held that fundamental rights are born in the express and implied protection of personal liberties as recognized in federal and state constitutions. Therefore, a student's so-called right to participate in extracurricular activities does not rise to the same level as the right to free speech or religion both of which have long been recognized as fundamental rights. *Spring Branch I.S.D. v. Stamos* (1985).

Although the opportunity to participate in extracurricular activities is not by itself a property interest, under certain circumstances a high school student can establish an entitlement to due process in connection with his suspension and exclusion from high school athletics. *Tiffany v. Arizona Interscholastic Association, Inc.* (1986); and *Boyd v. Board of Directors of McGehee School District* (1985).

D.　STATE ACTORS

In a determination of the eligibility of an athlete, it is essential that one ascertains if the association's regulation is deemed to be state action. Generally, the protections of the 14th Amendment, due process and equal protection, will not extend to private conduct that abridges only individual rights. The question is whether the actions of the governing body are state action or fall under the color of state action. This question is extremely important as regards the actions of the NCAA. At one time, this was a fairly close question. However, a 1988 Supreme Court case suggests that NCAA eligibility regulations may no longer be viewed as state action. *NCAA v. Tarkanian* (1988).

Tarkanian is a narrowly drawn opinion that establishes that the NCAA did not assume the role of the state when it directed a state university to initiate certain particular actions against one of its employees. This case, however, does not definitively settle the question of whether the NCAA can *ever* be a state actor. The court observed that the action of removing a coach from a state institution is a state action. However, in *Tarkanian* the NCAA did not take part in that particular action.

Even after *Tarkanian,* state action nonetheless might lie if a university by embracing the NCAA's rules transforms them into state rules and thereby arguably transforms the NCAA into a state actor. Some states, e.g., Texas, have passed legislation that provides for liability for violation of an NCAA rule. With legislation of this type the NCAA's regulations will arguably be deemed to represent state action.

On the other hand, all actions by a state high school athletic association will usually be viewed as state action for constitutional purposes. An example is the action of a state high school association that declares a high school must forfeit football games when an ineligible player suited up; this action is construed to be state action for constitutional purposes. *Florida High School Activities Association, Inc. v. Bradshaw* (1979). Also, a state athletic association, which is a purely voluntary group with a membership made up of 85% public schools, has sufficient public character to confer state action status on the activities of the association. *Griffin High School v. Illinois High School Association* (1987).

The state action question has been reviewed in the context of evaluating the legality of a mandatory drug testing program for high school athletes. In that case, a public school district, as opposed to a state athletic association, established the requirement that all varsity athletes must consent to submit to random urine analysis drug testing as a prerequisite to interscholastic athletic participation. This regulation was viewed as an action that was initiated under the color of state law. *Schaill v. Tippecanoe County School Corporation* (1988).

E. DUE PROCESS AND EQUAL PROTECTION

After determining whether a regulation is state action, one must review it for purposes of equal protection. Although it is acceptable to classify per se, it is not acceptable to differentiate among classes when the purposes behind classification are not constitutionally permissible. Permissibility is determined by applying either the permissive or strict standard of review. If the standard is the permissive one, all that is required is that there must be a reasonable relation to the stated purpose. The strict standard, however, requires that classifications be precise and substantially justified. The strict standard will be applied whenever a classification touches on a fundamental interest, e.g., freedom of religion, or is based on a suspect criteria, e.g., race or national origin. When a suspect criteria is involved, constitutional permissibility will be determined by whether the classification promotes a compelling interest of the governing body. Usually, participation in sports is not a fundamental right; and therefore, eligibility is not entitled to a strict standard of review. However, a strict standard of review might still be applied if the classification is based upon suspect criteria.

Equal protection will only require a rational relation to a legitimate state interest if the regulation does not infringe upon fundamental rights and does not burden an inherently suspect class. In a Texas

Appeals case it was held that a regulation that prohibits married high school students from participation in sports was a violation of the equal protection clause. There was no logical basis for the married student rule since the right to marry is a basic and fundamental right; therefore, the no marriage rule established a classification of individuals that was treated differently than other students without promoting a compelling state interest. *Bell v. Lone Oak Independent School District* (1974).

However, in another Texas case, a summer camp rule was found to be constitutional. This rule did not allow students to participate in interscholastic sports if they attended a same sport summer camp. The compelling state interest was that the rule sought to achieve a balance in interscholastic athletics. This interest outweighed a parent's freedom of choice in family matters as regards the student's participation in summer activities. *Kite v. Marshall* (1981).

In a 1981 Texas Supreme Court case, a state's sports association's non-transfer rule which declared all non-seniors ineligible for varsity football and basketball competition for one year following their transfer to a new school was held to be unconstitutional on equal protection grounds. The court stressed the over-inclusiveness of the rule in light of its intended purpose of discouraging the recruitment of student athletes and the irrebuttable presumption created by that rule. In light of these two factors, the court declared the rule not rationally related to its intended purpose. *Sullivan v. University Interscholastic League* (1981).

However, in the Texas no pass, no play case, the rule provided a strong incentive to participate in extracurricular activities and to maintain a minimal level of performance. In view of the rule's objective to promote and improve scholastic performance, the court found that the rule was rationally related to a legitimate state interest of creating quality education. *Spring Branch I.S.D. v. Stamos* (1985).

The next basic area of review is whether due process exists. Due process is used to eliminate regulations which are overbroad in application or those that overlook more reasonable alternatives, which are less restrictive of protected liberties. Procedural due process will only apply where a state or federal action is involved, the aggrieved party is a person, and an interest in life, liberty or property is threatened.

Due process as a whole is flexible and calls for such procedural protections as the particular situation might demand. Where a student asked for a hardship waiver from an athletic association's rule that limited eligibility to those 19 years old or younger, the courts recognized that the student did not have a constitutional right to participate in high school sports, but concluded that the executive board of the association was unreasonable, capricious and arbitrary when it failed to exercise its discretion in even considering the student's request for a hardship waiver from this rule. *Tiffany v. Arizona Interscholastic Association, Inc.* (1986).

F. TYPES OF RULES

There are many rules, but they all possess the same theme of attempting to control the way in which an individual will be deemed to be eligible to participate in high school sports. Usually these rules involve around such broad concepts as the "no transfer" rule, the anti-marriage rule, rules that relate eligibility to grade point average, no-agent rules and anti-red shirting rules.

1. Red Shirting

The concept of "red shirting" is a tendency of some schools to hold students back academically so they can develop their bodies and playing abilities in the hope of increasing their potential for athletic success. In an attempt to stop this practice, some associations have devised eligibility rules to prevent red shirting. These rules can be classified as four year rules, eight semester rules or age rules. All these regulations have in common the goal of restricting eligibility to a certain time period and thus thwarting attempts to red shirt. With these so-called anti-red shirting regulations, plaintiffs will usually lose. When an athlete challenges an anti-red shirting rule, he will usually argue that the rule violates the 14th Amendment due process right. He will also argue that he has a constitutional right to participate in interscholastic sports. However, the courts will generally hold that a student does not have a constitutionally protected right to participate. The courts will not interfere with these regulations unless the action complained of is fraudulent, an invasion of a property right, capricious or an arbitrary instance of discrimination.

The rationale for supporting a regulation of this type is that the classification made by the athletic association rule (for example, that beginning with sixth grade a student that repeats any grade which he has passed shall lose his fourth year of eligibility in high school), is neither inherently suspect nor an encroachment on a fundamental right but rather is reasonably related to the legitimate state interest of defeating the anti-academic tendency of red shirting. However, due process will usually require that the association at least allow the student a chance to argue hardship as a means to circumvent the eligibility rule.

2. No Transfer Rules

The "no transfer rule" was created to thwart the negative effect of recruiting athletes from one district or one school to another as a means to enhance the athletic ability of the team to which the athlete was recruited. This rule is usually viewed as rationally related to a legitimate state purpose of preventing school shopping by athletes and the prevention of their recruitment by coaches. This type of regulation will usually not violate equal protection.

However, in one case, a transfer rule did not pass constitutional analysis. *Sullivan v. University Interscholastic League* (1981). This particular rule provided that a student who represented any high school other than his present school in either football or basketball was ineligible for a calendar year after moving to another district to participate in the same sport in the new school. This rule was not rationally related to the purpose of thwarting recruitment of high school athletes and, therefore, was violative of equal protection. It was not rationally related to the purpose of stopping such recruitment because it was overly broad and punished those students, for example, who moved with their parents from one state to another because of economic hardship.

3. Anti-marriage

While transfer rules and red shirting rules usually will pass analysis under constitutional standards, eligibility rules that infringe on a fundamental right will not pass constitutional analysis. The classic example of such a rule is the no-marriage rule, which prohibits married high school students from participating in high school sports. This rule is violative of equal protection since the school board has the burden of proving that the regulation that prohibits married students from participation promotes a compelling state interest. Since there is no compelling state interest and since the rule treats two classes in a different way, the discrimination is unconstitutional. *Bell v. Lone Oak Independent School District* (1974).

4. "No-agent" Rule

Another cluster of restrictions to eligibility are those created by the NCAA. Most of their rules tend to restrict eligibility either for incoming freshmen or continuing students. However, the so-called "no-agent" rules are designed to terminate eligibility when an athlete instigates any step towards a professional career.

These two rules are contained in a section of the NCAA rules entitled "Amateurism." The first rule (no. 12.2.4) states that an athlete will lose his eligibility to participate in a particular sport once the athlete requests to be included in the pool of players that are eligible to be chosen in the annual professional draft of collegiate athletes. The second rule (no. 12.3) renders an athlete ineligible once that athlete agrees to be represented by an agent.

The combination of these two rules will clarify the line of demarcation between professional and amateur athletes. An example of how these rules tend to operate and their affect on a student-athlete's attempts to maintain his eligibility can be shown in the case of Braxston Lee Banks. *Banks v. NCAA* (1990). Mr. Banks filed a class action suit against the NCAA alleging that these two rules were violative of the antitrust laws. Banks was a talented Notre Dame football player who had been injured throughout his collegiate career; at the end of the 1989 football season, he had a year of eligibility remaining. Banks originally wanted to use this remaining year of eligibility; however, he changed his mind between the conclusion of the 1989 season and the 1990 NFL college draft. His plan was to test the waters as regards his marketability. Accordingly, he petitioned the NFL for eligibility and retained an attorney to advise and represent him. The NFL approved his petition and invited him to a league-wide scouting combine. His plans failed in that a bad knee reduced interest in him, and as a result he was neither drafted nor offered a free agent contract. At that time, Banks decided to return to college, complete his eligibility, and prove to the NFL scouts that his knee was rehabilitated; however, his college refused to reinstate him.

To test the waters, Banks had to petition the NFL; the NFL will only invite players to their combine that have either exhausted their eligibility or renounced their remaining eligibility by requesting to be included in the draft. However, this process of petitioning and obtaining legal counsel violated the NCAA's so-called no-agent rules and thus automatically eliminated his remaining year of eligibility. It made no difference that Banks did not receive an offer to contract with any team or that he received any monies from his agent.

Banks filed suit. He was denied a preliminary injunction to enjoin Notre Dame from enforcing the rules that prevented him from playing football during the 1990 season. In the court's ruling on a subsequent motion to dismiss, it held that the NCAA's rules produced significant pro-competitive effects and that Banks failed to show that the rules produced an adverse market impact on either college players or NCAA member schools. Banks alleged that the rules created a group boycott by restricting the football labor market; however, the court held that the rules did not have a non-competitive impact on any identifiable market.

G. PROPOSITION 48 AND PROGENY

Proposition 48 and other proposed NCAA propositions create academic requirements as a barrier for incoming freshmen who desire to participate in interscholastic athletics. These requirements relate to the prospective athlete's academic performance in high school and in certain standardized tests. An earlier rule, the 1.600 rule, required that NCAA schools grant athletic scholarships only to prospective athletes with whom they could predict through high school grades, class rank or scores in standardized tests, a minimum of a 1.6 g.p.a. during the freshmen year. This rule passed constitutional analysis since the classification was reasonably related to the purposes for which the rule was created, that is, the maintenance of academic excellence. *Associated Students, Inc. of California State University—Sacramento v. NCAA* (1974). The 1.600 rule was rationally related to a legitimate state purpose and the privilege of participation was deemed outside the protection of the law.

Proposition 48 strengthened the old rules by requiring a combination of required high school g.p.a. and a minimum score on standardized tests as a prerequisite to freshman eligibility. When Proposition 48 was promulgated, the effect was immediate; a great deal of major college football and basketball recruits were ineligible in the first year of the rule. During 1989, a great furor was created when the NCAA discussed the possibility of Proposition 42. Proposition 42 called for tighter restrictions on borderline students. Proposition 42 would have eliminated the possibility that a partial qualifier, either a 2.0 or a passing score on a standardized test, of the Proposition 48 standards, could still receive an athletic scholarship in his freshman year. To qualify, both were required.

Proposition 48 has been viewed by many experts as arguably racist in that a disproportionate percentage of minorities are affected by the results of the rule. In the final analysis, the NCAA's propositions will probably pass constitutional muster. Since the NCAA's bylaws will not be construed as state action, it appears that most NCAA regulations and propositions will also be construed as not state action; and because of that, due process protection will be inapplicable. Replacing Proposition 48, Proposition 16 requires a minimum g.p.a. in 13 core courses with a corresponding minimum score on one of the standardized tests. This was declared invalid as a violation of Title VI of the Civil Rights Act by a federal district judge *Cureton v. NCAA* (1999). However, the NCAA was granted a stay on

March 30, 1999, re-establishing the Proposition 16 standards.

H. NO PASS, NO PLAY STATUTES

An integral part of many states' attempts to improve the educational potentiality of their students is the enactment of legislation that keys eligibility to play high school sports to the participant's ability to achieve certain academic grades. This type of legislation is generally called, "no pass, no play." The basic format of this legislation will demand that no student can participate in an extracurricular activity for a certain period if he fails any course during the preceding period other than the last grading period before the summer break. There are variations to these statutes in that some grant the power to specify the criteria to counties while some grant the power to a state's athletic association. Also, in Texas, for example, this statute applies to all extracurricular activities, however, in West Virginia it applies only to "non-academic" extracurricular activities (sports and cheerleading). But all have one thing in common: they tie high school athletic eligibility directly to the student's previous academic achievement.

An equal protection analysis is the first question that arises as regard to the constitutionality of no pass statutes. One can argue that the state illegally discriminates against those who participate in extracurricular activities as opposed to those who do not. However, it is well established that participation in activities is not usually a fundamental right. Because no pass neither infringes fundamental rights nor burdens any inherently suspect class, it is not subject to strict or heightened scrutiny. Usually, when the state's regulatory classification scheme neither infringes on fundamental rights nor burdens an inherently suspect class, then the equal protection analysis requires only that the classification be rationally related to a legitimate state interest. For example, since providing a quality education to Texas public school students is a legitimate state interest, then the no pass rule has only to be rationally related to that interest. *Spring Branch I.S.D. v. Stamos* (1985).

Other states have analyzed similar no pass statutes in similar ways. In *State ex rel. Bartmess v. Board of Trustees of School Dist. No. 1* (1986), the Montana Supreme Court was forced to deal with a school district rule that required a student to maintain a 2.0 (or "C") grade average for the preceding 9–week period as a prerequisite to participation in any extracurricular activities in the following 9–week period. This school district rule was even more stringent than the requirements of the Montana High School Association which required only a 1.0 (or "D") average for participation. However, the court held that this rule had a rational relationship to the state's legitimate goal in that the rule was an incentive for those students who wished to enjoy extracurricular activities and would also promote adequate time to study for those students who have not maintained a 2.0 g.p.a. In a strong dissent, Justice Sheehy opined that there was no rational relation between the rule and the goal and that the rule was overbroad.

It appears that all judicial reviews of comparable no pass statutes will conclude that a rational relation to a legitimate state purpose exists. In *Bailey v. Truby* (1984), the West Virginia Supreme Court reviewed a rule that required students to maintain a "C" g.p.a. in order to participate in extracurricular activities. The court held that this rule was a legitimate exercise of the State Board of Education's general supervision power over the educational goal of academic excellence. The rule did not violate the student's rights to procedural due process, substantive due process or equal protection. The rule in *Bailey,* however, differentiated between academic extracurricular (theater, debate, school newspaper, 4–H, band, etc.) and nonacademic extracurricular activities on the basis that the academic extracurricular activities were too closely related to identifiable academic courses and served to complement those courses. In dissent, Justice Harshberger recommended that if a student satisfies the State Board's academic and attendance requirements for graduation with his class, then all programs should be open to that student. He also viewed the rule as violating a common sense penumbra to equal protection in that it placed a higher duty to achieve academically on those students who participated in extracurricular activities than is required of those students that loiter at malls. He further noted as to the distinction between academic and non-academic extracurriculars: "My brothers would let a flutist flunk without forfeiting his or her flute. But pity the poor punter who did not pass."

CHAPTER 18

THE DISABLED ATHLETE

A. GENERALLY

There are many ways in which eligibility to participate can be restricted; one way is through a person's alleged disability whether it is physical or emotional. Eligibility is restricted by rules that are based on paternalism and disallow individuals who are viewed as disabled from participation in interscholastic sports. Many schools, colleges, athletic associations and school districts have such rules.

Guidelines that bar students from participation are often based on rules provided by the American Medical Association (AMA), which recommend that students with particular types of disabilities be disqualified from participation in certain recreational activities. When a student challenges a disqualification to participate based on these rules, courts will usually defer to the judgment of the school and uphold the disqualification unless the school's actions are arbitrary or capricious.

However, in recent years disabled students have used § 504 of the Rehabilitation Act to establish a right for disabled athletes to participate in interscholastic sports, if they are otherwise qualified. 29 U.S.C.A. § 794. The act provides in pertinent part that no otherwise "qualified handicapped individual * * * shall, solely by reason of his handicap, be excluded from the participation in * * * or be subjected to discrimination under any program * * * receiving federal financial assistance." A handicapped individual is described as any person who "has a physical or mental impairment which substantially limits one or more of such person's major life activities, * * * has a record of * * * impairment or * * * is regarded as having * * * an impairment." 29 U.S.C.A. § 706. This law is further refined in 45 CFR § 84.37(C)(1), in which disabled students are specifically given the right to participate in organized sports: "in providing physical education courses * * * a recipient * * * may not discriminate on the basis of handicap. A recipient that offers physical education courses or that operates * * * interscholastic, club or intramural athletics, shall provide to qualified handicapped students an equal opportunity for participation * * *."

For example, an outstanding high school athlete was precluded from playing his last year of football because he possessed only one kidney; he then won an injunction on the ground that he was discriminated against in violation of § 504 of the Rehabilitation Act of 1973. *Grube v. Bethlehem Area School District* (1982).

B. ELIGIBILITY TO PARTICIPATE

As mentioned above, disabled athletes were regularly restricted under a paternalistic attitude. Even after medical assurance that athletic participation would not harm the individual, school boards would still restrict participation. Courts usually supported the school board's decision that the athlete was not qualified to participate. For example, an individual who was blind in one eye was precluded from participation in contact sports because of medical testimony that indicated that continuation in that sport would result in a high risk of injury to his good eye. *Kampmeier v. Nyquist* (1977).

Courts progressed to a point where a person who is otherwise qualified would not be excluded from participation in a federally funded program solely by reason of disability. The mere possession of a disability is insufficient to assume that there is a corresponding inability to function in an appropriate manner in a particular sport. Otherwise qualified individuals are people who are able to meet all the program requirements in spite of their handicap. *Southeastern Community College v. Davis* (1979). A disabled athlete must have the opportunity to participate for inclusion in a sports team. An example is the person who only has one kidney but still wants to participate in a contact sport such as interscholastic wrestling. In *Poole v. South Plainfield Board of Education* (1980), plaintiff and his parents were well aware of the risk involved in his participation and were prepared to sign a waiver that would release the school from all liability. The court held that the school's only duty was to advise the family of the risk and not to impose a paternalistic view of the proper course of action for the family.

The courts are now beginning to recognize that under the legal definition of a disabled individual the more subtly handicapped such as the emotionally disturbed or the learning disabled have the same rights as other more overtly disabled students. A disabled student who was learning disabled, sought an injunction against the high school athletic association to preclude it from enforcing their transfer rule that would prohibit him from participation for a year after transferring from a private religious school to a public school.

This individual was a certified disabled student under the Education of the Handicapped Act, 20 U.S.C.A. § 1400 et seq.; the association discriminated against the student by prohibiting participation by failing to grant a special hardship exception to the transfer rule. The student was granted a preliminary injunction of the athletic association's rule; the association was similarly precluded from punishing the high school by forcing them to forfeit games in which the student participated pursuant to a federal court order. *Crocker v. Tennessee Secondary School Athletic Association* (1990). See also *Crocker v. Tennessee Secondary School Athletic Association* (1989).

C. SECTION 504 OF THE REHABILITATION ACT

In § 504 of the Rehabilitation Act, the prohibition of discrimination against otherwise qualified handicapped individuals in a federally funded program creates a private course of action for monetary as well as injunctive relief. Typically, where the school board is aware of the parents' knowledge of the dangers involved in their handicapped son's continued athletic participation and the school board knows of the parents' encouragement then the school board will have neither the duty nor the right under § 504 to deny the student's right to participate. See *Poole v. South Plainfield Board of Education* (1980). See also *Neeld v. National Hockey League* (1979).

Under § 504, a high school student with one kidney must be allowed to play football if his parents sign a waiver. *Grube v. Bethlehem Area School District* (1982). In a case where a college student with vision in one eye wanted to play football, the university claimed that § 504 was not applicable to the football program because the program itself did not receive federal funds. However, the court noted that under the regulations, a recipient of funds was defined as "any public or private agency * * * to which federal financial assistance is extended directly or through another recipient * * *" 45 CFR § 84.3(F). The court then concluded that federal funds need not go to the football program specifically to bring that program within the protection of § 504. The court averred that, even if the football program was not a recipient per se, the decision to prohibit the athlete from participation was ultimately made by the school itself and not the program. Therefore, the school was a direct recipient of funds. *Wright v. Columbia University* (1981).

As regards § 504, school districts must now consider the needs of each handicapped student and devise a program which will enable each individual handicapped student to receive an appropriate and free public education. A part of this education is the right for all otherwise qualified individuals to participate in the complete array of extracurricular activities. This right will pertain to a facially constitutional regulation (e.g., a rule that prohibits students from transferring to different schools in an attempt to stop the development of super-teams) when the impact of the rule would disallow a handicapped student the chance to participate if the basis of the decision involves his handicap.

For example, an emotionally disturbed student moved in with his grandparents and was urged by his therapist to play football at the school in which his grandparents were located as opposed to the school district in which his parents lived. The therapist felt that it was necessary for the student's emotional health. However, this transfer was a violation of the league's non-transfer rule. The rule stated that a student who changes schools to a school district in which his parents do not reside will be ineligible for varsity contests. Also, a student living with a guardian is ineligible if the guardianship is of a one-year duration and both parents are still alive. The league generally did not acknowledge the existence of legal guardianships. This was to prevent athletes from shopping around for a school or a coach. However, the result of this rule still violated § 504. The court concluded that if the student was denied the opportunity to participate in football, there would be a corresponding devastating effect on his emotional stability. *Doe v. Marshall* (1978).

D. AMERICANS WITH DISABILITIES ACT

To improve the conditions of the disabled, the massive Americans with Disabilities Act was enacted. This act, the ADA, is § 504 of the Rehabilitation Act with teeth (42 U.S.C.A. § 12101 et seq.). The ADA extends its coverage to most employers other than the smallest and thus covers professional athletic teams and probably college teams (in that most scholarship athletes are usually deemed to be employees). The act prohibits employment discrimination against individuals with real or perceived disabilities; it also prohibits discrimination in employment against associates of the disabled. This includes an employer who might refuse to hire a relative of an individual suffering with an illness such as AIDS based on the fear that this relative might contact the illness or that he or she might miss too much work due to the illness of the other person.

The ADA, like § 504 of the Rehabilitation Act, requires employers to make reasonable accommodations for otherwise qualified disabled individuals. An accommodation would not be reasonable under the ADA if it would impose an undue hardship on the employer's business. Undue hardship can be defined to be an action that requires significant difficulty or expense.

In *Martin v. PGA Tour, Inc.* (1998), a disabled golfer, unable to walk a course due to significant leg atrophy as a result of Klippel–Trenaunay–Weber Syndrome, challenged the PGA's "no cart" rule which precludes players from using carts during the third stage of the PGA qualifying tour and the tour itself. By not providing a cart, the PGA violated the ADA by failing to make the tournaments accessible to the disabled.

Under the ADA, a qualified individual with a disability is one, with or without reasonable accommodation, who can perform the essential functions of the particular job. However, the ADA provides that a disabled person is not qualified if he poses a direct threat to the health or safety of other individuals in the work area. But, absent an actual threat, an employer cannot refuse to hire a disabled person based on fears relating to safety; for example, an athlete with AIDS, a disease which is not transmitted by casual contact will not fall within the safety exception and thus will be protected from employment discrimination under the ADA.

Under the ADA, the term "qualified disabled person" will not include those currently using illegal drugs so long as their employer acts on the basis of such use. However, rehabilitated drug users are protected from employment discrimination under the ADA; although the act allows employers to adopt policies, including drug testing, to ensure that their employees no longer use illegal drugs. This is applicable to the professional athlete.

In a strengthening of § 504 of the Rehabilitation Act, Title III of the ADA also prohibits discrimination against the disabled in all places of public accommodation, including privately operated stadiums, auditoriums, convention centers and places of exercise or recreation (e.g., gymnasiums, health spas, bowling alleys, golf courses, aerobic facilities, etc.). Unlike the definition of the term employer under the ADA, the definition of the term places of public accommodation is not limited to entities of a certain size or having a certain number of employees. All places of public accommodation are now forced to comply with Title III accessibility requirements.

Owners and operators of places of public accommodation must allow the disabled to participate in an equal way or to benefit in an equal manner from the goods, services and accommodations provided by the establishment. These owners and operators must make reasonable modifications in their practices or policies. Likewise, the owners and operators must remove structural and architectural barriers where such removal is readily achievable.

CHAPTER 19

COLLEGE SCHOLARSHIPS

A. THE NATURE OF SCHOLARSHIPS

A major problem inherent in most cases that pertain to collegiate athletics is the phenomenon of the scholarship athlete. Scholarships are ways for colleges to get athletes into their schools to play sports. The problem is that a scholarship really is not defined in any neat or comprehensible manner. The question is whether the scholarship is a contract or just some sort of informal arrangement which does not require duties, responsibilities or obligations on each party.

By accepting a scholarship, an athlete enters into a relationship with the university which grants the award to the athlete. A relationship of this sort will typically require the athlete to maintain certain grade levels and to perform as an athlete for the school in return for tuition, books and certain other educational expenses. The question is whether a scholarship athlete is an employee of that school. This is important for ascertaining whether the athlete will be covered under workers' compensation laws if he is injured, and whether that scholarship is taxable as income.

Arguably, the better policy might be to accept college athletes as entertainers and treat athletes as employees. This makes sense since the big college football powerhouses recruit quasi-professionals to play in collegiate athletics. Yet, schools have been reluctant to acknowledge that the relationship between universities and their athletes is one that can be characterized as a business relationship. This in turn leads to a reluctance to recognize scholarships as contracts and the athletes as the college's employees. To do this would be to legally recognize the rights and responsibilities that are owed to the athlete as part of the contractual relationship in which the athlete must perform for that particular sports team. These institutions have benefited from the talents of their athletes: sometimes financially, sometimes to the detriment of the student-athlete. If there is a bargained-for exchange that is legally universally recognized between the institution and the athlete, then there will be significant consequences for both the student-athlete and the school in terms of the athlete's status as an amateur, as an employee, or as one who receives taxable income in the form of a scholarship.

When and if the schools admit that their athletes are indeed employees and the scholarship is an employment contract, then it may be necessary to compensate the athletes beyond the value of the scholarship; and with those students who genuinely desire to earn a degree, part of their compensation package might include tuition, room and board and other fees (approximately ⅛ of the big sports schools graduate less than 20% of their basketball players and ½ graduate less than 40% of their football players).

B.   SCHOLARSHIPS AS CONTRACTS

Some courts have viewed the relationship between the scholarship athlete and the university as contractual.   The university requires the student to meet certain requirements, e.g., maintain academic eligibility, attend practices, compete in games and follow the rules and regulations of the institution, the conference and the NCAA.   In return the athlete receives the benefits of the scholarship.   If an integral part of an agreement is not fulfilled or if one or both parties are unable to comply with the agreement, then the courts have allowed the college to rescind or revoke the scholarship.

A contract is enforceable because of the interplay among offer, acceptance and consideration.   When a college extends a scholarship offer to an athlete, the athlete who chooses to attend that college accepts the offer.   The receipt of the scholarship is the athlete's consideration, and it is in exchange for his participation in sports which is the college's consideration.   With the presence of offer, acceptance and consideration an enforceable contract is deemed to exist.

The NCAA requires that before the student signs a letter of intent that will form a relationship between the student and the college, the college must provide him with a statement that will list the terms and conditions, including amount and duration, of the student's financial aid packet. When the student signs this financial aid agreement, both parties have consented to be bound by the amount of the grant. Although each college will draft its own financial aid statement, some clauses are uniform, e.g., the athlete agrees to abide by the school's rules and regulations, the rules and regulations of the conference, and the rules of the team and the coaching staff. This type of clause is standard. The athlete also agrees to maintain athletic eligibility.

If the student does not meet any of the obligations as outlined in the agreement, the college often will reserve the right to revoke the student's athletic scholarship. The national letter of intent and the financial agreement combine to impose a series of obligations that the athlete will owe to the institution, obligations that exceed those imposed upon the average college student.

In *Taylor v. Wake Forest University* (1972), the university terminated an athlete's scholarship when that athlete refused to continue in football practice. Because of the contractual nature of the obligations between the athlete and the school, the court decided that the student was obliged to participate in the football program as an agreed upon exchange for his scholarship.

A federal trial court in *Begley v. Corporation of Mercer University* (1973), also used contract law to determine the rights of both the athlete and the school. In *Begley,* the school sought to terminate an agreement for an athlete's scholarship when it discovered that the entering student did not have the required high school grade point average. The court found that because the student did not meet one of the conditions of the contractual agreement, he could not expect the university to perform its part of the contract by allowing him to keep the athletic scholarship.

The contractual nature of the scholarship was further explored in dictum in a 1979 Alabama case where the court noted that the relationship between a college athlete who accepts a scholarship and the school which awards that scholarship is contractual in nature: the athlete agrees to participate and the school in return agrees to give assistance to that athlete. *Gulf South Conference v. Boyd* (1979).

However, a different result was reached by the Indiana Supreme Court. The court had to decide whether a scholarship athlete who injured himself playing football was eligible for workers' compensation. The Indiana Court of Appeals found that the athlete was an employee and noted that the University had conceded that some form of contract did indeed exist between the school and the athlete. The Court of Appeals then found that there was a contract between the athlete and the school to play football.

This decision, however, was unanimously reversed by the Indiana Supreme Court. Although it agreed that the determination of whether an employee/employer relationship existed between the athlete and the school was indeed complex and involved many factors, the court held that as regards whether a contract of employment, either expressed or implied existed, the primary consideration must be intent. The court found that there was no intent to enter into an employee/employer relationship at the time the parties entered into the agreement. The court found the financial aid that was received was not considered by the parties to be payable income; it was not given to the athlete in return for playing football anymore than academic scholarships are given to other students for their high scores in standardized tests.

The court found that in both cases, whether academic or athletic scholarships, the students will receive benefits based on their past demonstrated ability in various areas which will enable them to pursue opportunities for higher education as well as to progress further in their own field of endeavor. Scholarship recipients then are students that seek advance education opportunities and are not professional athletes, musicians or artists that are employed by the school for their skills in their respective areas. *Rensing v. Indiana State University Board of Trustees* (1982).

After *Rensing*, there is a real possibility that the scholarship agreements will not be viewed as an employment contract. Accordingly, it should follow that there is no contractual obligation between the athlete and the school. However, it is obvious that athletes are obligated to perform under the tenets of at least a quasi-contractual relationship. These schools may later deny that a contract existed in order to avoid extending the protection and the benefits of a contractual relationship to athletes. This will give the school an advantage, however, the issues as presented in *Rensing* are still far from being completely settled.

C. WORKERS' COMPENSATION

The status of amateur athletes and the evaluation of college scholarships has mainly occurred in workers' compensation cases. Typically an injured collegiate athlete on an athletic scholarship seeks workers' compensation coverage for that injury. The crux of the problem usually is whether that athlete is or is not an employee for purposes of the particular workers' compensation statute. If that individual is viewed as an independent contractor or a person of some other status, rather than an employee, then that person would not be included under workers' compensation coverage. These cases that interpret the eligibility of workers' compensation coverage for athletes on scholarships are important because they ascertain whether and under what circumstances collegiate athletes on scholarships will be viewed as employees.

Although there are numerous cases that hold that a scholarship athlete is eligible as an employee for workers' compensation purposes, the case of *Rensing v. Indiana State University Board of Trustees*

(1983) (discussed supra), arguably is currently the standard. In that case, the Indiana Supreme Court denied workers' compensation benefits and held that an individual on an athletic scholarship is not an employee of the particular school.

It must be noted, however, that pre-*Rensing* cases have indeed decided that a scholarship athlete is an employee of the school; that a contractual relationship exists between the scholarship athlete and the school; and that the athlete who is injured during competition should be awarded workers' compensation. See *Van Horn v. Industrial Accident Commission* (1963); *University of Denver v. Nemeth* (1953); *Taylor v. Wake Forest University* (1972); and *Begley v. Corporation of Mercer University* (1973). The more indices of employment that are present the more of a chance that the athlete will be deemed an employee for workers' compensation purposes. The Colorado Supreme Court has stated that simply performing for the school's athletic team does not confer the status of an employee upon the athlete for purposes of workers' compensation. However, if the athlete receives a financial benefit in exchange for and conditioned upon participation in that university's athletic program, then the athlete will be construed as an employee of that school for purposes of workers' compensation coverage. *State Compensation Insurance Fund v. Industrial Commission* (1957).

In *Rensing* where the Indiana Supreme Court reviewed the issue of whether the requisite employer/employee relationship existed between plaintiff and the school, the court found that the claimant failed to establish that a contract of employment existed between the parties. Plaintiff's failure to demonstrate the existence of this essential element precluded the possibility of the court finding him to be an employee for workers' compensation purposes. However, *Rensing* did not specifically disagree with the earlier decisions that found that a scholarship athlete is an employee for workers' compensation purposes; rather, *Rensing* turned on the question of whether sufficient proof was proffered as regards the existence of a contract of employment. *Rensing v. Indiana State University Board of Trustees* (1982).

D. TAXATION

Courts have also reviewed whether athletic scholarships are contracts and whether the athletes are employees in the context of the taxability of scholarships. The question is whether scholarship athletes are university employees and, if they are, should they be taxed on their scholarship income. Usually the scholarship is not includable within a person's taxable gross income. The athlete will not be taxed for all services, accommodations, and amounts that cover expenses for travel and equipment, as long as they are incident to the scholarship and expended for that purpose. However, this exclusion from taxation will not apply to amounts received by a student athlete which represents payment for the rendering of services for part-time employment as a condition of the receipt of the award. To qualify as non-taxable, the scholarship must be in the nature of a disinterested educational grant without the requirement of any substantial quid pro quo from the student athlete.

If the factual circumstances indicate that the athlete received the scholarship in consideration for his athletic participation, then the award will not be within the exclusion from taxability for scholarships because of the quid pro quo arrangement. The scholarship grant will be taxable. *Taylor v. Wake Forest University* (1972).

If the relationship is a "pay for play" arrangement between the athlete and the school, the scholarship income will be taxable. The IRS will use certain tests to determine the taxability of an athletic scholarship. Some courts have used a primary purpose test. The court will inquire whether the amount was given to benefit the grantor or the grantee; if the scholarship primarily benefits the grantor, then it is not an excludable scholarship. This test requires a scrutiny of the grantor's motives since they relate to the purpose of the grant itself. This test has generally given way to the *quid pro quo* analysis.

The *quid pro quo* analysis involves an appraisal of whether the grant results from a bargained for relationship as opposed to an endowment or no strings grant. Only those grants which lack a *quid pro quo* will be tax free. However, athletic scholarships usually involve a *quid pro quo*. Accordingly, it is important to go to the language of the scholarship grant itself. Also applicable to the *quid pro quo* inquiry is the type and nature of the negotiations that led to the awarding of the scholarship. If the grant is a result of a bargained for arrangement, then the scholarship will not withstand § 117 scrutiny. Recruiting is very elaborate and coaches visit high schools and bring prospective athletes to their colleges. This tends to imply the existence of negotiation: the give and take of trying to recruit a scholarship athlete and trying to sign scholarship athletes indicate a bargained for arrangement to receive the scholarship. This is further proven by the National Letter of Intent Program in which a student certifies that he intends to attend a particular school.

The last factor in the determination of the *quid pro quo* is the evidence of a present contractual obligation. The finding of consideration to support a contract will parallel to some extent the finding of a *quid pro quo* to establish taxation. Therefore, if one ascertains that a contract does indeed exist, this fact will support the existence of a *quid pro quo*. As a caveat, a *quid pro quo* will be established when an athlete loses a scholarship if he withdraws for any reason other than a physical injury.

E. EMPLOYEE STATUS

The discussion of taxation, workers' compensation, and contractual position all relate to the question of the status of the scholarship athlete as a possible employee. If a scholarship athlete is deemed to be an employee, then he will be covered under workers' compensation; however, his income will also be taxable.

In the *Rensing* case, the Indiana Supreme Court concluded that plaintiff did not receive pay for playing football within the meaning of the applicable act. Because of that, an essential element of the employer/employee relationship was lacking. *Rensing v. Indiana State University Board of Trustees* (1983).

However, in *University of Denver v. Nemeth* (1953), the court found that the college athlete was an employee of the school. The consideration received by plaintiff was actually an exchange for his participation in football even though the consideration was directed to him through his salary for cleaning the tennis courts. His financial gain was an exchange for playing football. Since the compensation was conditioned upon football participation, the court decided that he was an employee of the school and his participation was the form of his employment.

CHAPTER 20

INTERNATIONAL SPORTS

Sports is no longer a purely domestic activity. It is now international in scope, not only with the Olympics, but also with international leagues in different sports. American sports are becoming more and more international in their own outreach. All the major leagues now have some teams with foreign venues and some sports, for example, football and basketball, are actively courting foreign markets. Under international law, a Court of Arbitration (CAS) for sport and specialized tribunals help resolve sports-related disputes that transcend national boundaries.

A. OLYMPICS

International competition generally involves open competition among amateur and professional athletes. The United States Olympic Committee (USOC) has governed American participation in the Olympic and Pan American games and has operated under a federal charter since 1950. 64 Stat. 902, 36 U.S.C.A. §§ 371–383. The United States Olympics Committee is the sole organization in the United States that is recognized by the international governing board of the Olympics, the International

Olympics Committee (IOC). The USOC contains more than 200 amateur groups, but under the IOC rules its voting control lies in the groups which are recognized by the international sports federation for those particular sports which are a part of Olympic competition. The USOC has a constitution and bylaws which govern its administrative functions. For example, pursuant to the Amateur Sports Act of 1978, 36 U.S.C.A. § 391, the Athletic Congress (TAC) was designated as the national governing body for track and field athletes in the United States. TAC established a trust program that enables its member athletes to receive athletic participation funds and sponsorship payments without losing their Olympic and international eligibility.

Under public international law, the IOC is registered under Swiss laws as a non-profit, private society with legal status under both national and international law. Switzerland has also given it special status under tax and labor laws because of its international character. Under its own charter, the IOC has a legal status under international law and a perpetual succession. The Olympic Charter serves as the best evidence of international custom in governing international competition and related disputes. The Charter forms the basis of international sports law.

B. AMATEUR SPORTS ACT OF 1978

As a response to the report of the President's Commission on Olympic sports, the Amateur Sports

Act of 1978 was created. 36 U.S.C.A. §§ 371–396 et seq. The Act was established to coordinate amateur athletic activity; to recognize certain rights that belong to amateur athletes; and to provide for the resolution of disputes involving national governing bodies. The Act amends the statutory provisions that relate to the United States Olympic Committee. It also established that the USOC is authorized (for any sport which is included in the Olympic or Pan–Am games) to recognize as a National Governing Body (NGB) any amateur sport group, which files an application and is eligible for recognition. However, only one NGB is recognized for each sport for which an application is approved. Prior to recognition, the USOC holds a hearing on the application which is open to the public. It also must publish notice as regards the hearing. An amateur sports organization will be eligible to be recognized as an NGB only if it, *inter alia,* is incorporated as a domestic, non-profit corporation with the purpose of advancing "amateur" athletic competition (the distinction between "amateur" and professional is no longer a sharp one); submits an application for recognition; agrees to submit to binding arbitration; demonstrates that it is autonomous in its governance of the sport; demonstrates open membership; provides equal opportunity to amateur athletes and coaches without discrimination; is governed by a Board of Directors who are selected without regard to race, color, religion, national origin or sex except in sports where there are separate male and female programs; demonstrates that the Board of Directors includes among its voters individuals who are actively engaged in amateur athletic competition in that sport; provides for reasonable direct representation of the sport for any amateur sports organization for which recognition is sought; conducts national programs; demonstrates that none of its officers have conflicts of interest with other national governing bodies; provides procedures for prompt equitable resolution of grievances; does not have eligibility criteria relating to amateur status which would be more restrictive than those of the appropriate international sports group; and demonstrates that it is prepared to meet the obligations imposed on an NGB. 36 U.S.C.A. § 391(A). The USOC will recommend and support an NGB to the appropriate international sports group as a representative of the United States for that sport.

The Amateur Sports Act of 1978 is very detailed regarding specification of the duties of an NGB and establishes a guide which relates to the competition of amateur athletes and events sponsored by other organizations. 36 U.S.C.A. § 392(B). The Act also provides that any amateur sports group which is eligible to belong to an NGB may seek to require the NGB to comply with its responsibilities under the act, by filing a written complaint with the USOC; but only after exhausting all remedies within the appropriate NGB for correcting the problems (unless it can be proven that those remedies would have resulted in unnecessary delay). 36 U.S.C.A. § 395(A). The Act also provides that amateur sports groups may seek to replace an NGB under certain circumstances. 36 U.S.C.A. § 395(B). Disputes may be arbitrated by the American Arbitration Association or under rules of international sports federations, by the CAS or other special tribunals. 36 U.S.C.A. § 395(c). Also, there are provisions which are designed to protect the opportunity of amateur athletes to compete. 36 U.S.C.A. §§ 374(8), 382(B).

C. BOYCOTTS

Boycotts of Olympic sports occasionally occur by countries, who attempt to make political gains through not participating. An example is the boycott of the United States from the 1980 Olympics as a protest to the activities of the USSR in Afghanistan. The 1980 games were set to occur in Moscow, and the Soviet Union then correspondingly boycotted the 1984 games in Los Angeles. Usually these boycotts are based on political motivation (e.g., a protest in the 1980s against South Africa's apartheid). Boycotts are clearly illegal when their purpose is to induce conflict or to engage in measures of coercion that would violate the United Nations Charter. Similarly, they are also illegal when their purpose is to confirm diplomatic non-recognition in violation of governing international rules. Under some circumstances, boycotts can fall within a protected range of retaliatory sanctions. To be within this range the boycott must not violate provisions of the United Nations Charter or other binding instruments, it must conform to state practice, and it must not violate general principles of law. Also, otherwise illegal boycotts may be acceptable in some circumstances, if they are a reprisal measure against an illegal act of another state.

As regards the American boycott of the 1980 Moscow Olympics, a federal district court held that the USOC has the authority to decide not to send a team to the summer Olympics even if that plan was based on reasons not directly related to sports considerations, e.g., political considerations. While reaching this decision, the court rejected an argument that the provisions of the Amateur Sports Act of 1978 which relate to athletes' rights supersede the USOC's authority. Also, it held that there was no private cause of action under this act to enforce a right to compete in the Olympics in the face of a ruling by the USOC not to compete. *DeFrantz v. United States Olympic Committee* (1980).

D. DRUG TESTING

In the Olympic Charter and the constitutions and bylaws of international sports federations, it is made clear that the use of drugs contravenes the spirit of fair play in sports. The use of drugs is forbidden in all Olympic competitions, and the competitors will be liable to medical control and examination that are carried out in conformity with the rules of the IOC medical commission. There are a long list of procedures for more than 300 banned substances. Individual violators and teams that benefit from the use of drugs will be subjected to disqualification and exclusion under the Olympic rules.

To enforce the ban on certain drugs, the International Olympic Committee requires that each competition site have adequate testing facilities and that each competitor also agree to submit to a possible medical examination at the risk of exclusion. Any competitor who refuses to submit to an examination or is found using a drug must be excluded from competition. If this athlete is also a team member, the competition in which the infringement occurred will be forfeited by that team. Penalties will vary according to whether use was deliberate or accidental or whether the use constituted a first or a second offense. Any offense during competition would lead minimally to suspension from the games and forfeiture of all medals won during that competition.

Although not related to drug testing per se, another similar problem is the practice of blood doping. This is a technique in which an athlete's blood is drawn from his body during training and then returned to his body just before competition. This technique is starting to be used in sports that require endurance such as cycling or cross-country skiing. These transfusions are banned by international rules.

In addition to IOC regulations against drug usage, there also are individual agreements between the various Olympic committees of the various

countries that are established to ensure drug testing procedures. For example, the now dated United
States Olympic Committee (USOC) Olympic Committee of the Soviet Union (SOC) doping control
agreement which committed their organizations to
work together to eliminate blood doping and the use
of performance enhancing drugs (steroids) in athletes under their control. The CAS has, however,
upheld more drastic decisions of sports bodies including exclusion of athletes from competition for
life.

CHAPTER 21

DISCIPLINE AND PENALTIES

A. POWER TO DISCIPLINE AND PENALIZE GENERALLY

A major attribute of any amateur sports association is its power to discipline and penalize its members. The power to discipline and penalize is an essential and important aspect of the ability to determine if a particular athlete is eligible to participate. Rule enforcement by athletic organizations can include investigations, prosecutions and adjudication. If there is a potential problem, the organization will investigate the institution and, if applicable, the individual player. Usually, the athletic regulatory group must provide enforcement through fair, reasonable and constitutional procedures.

Enforcement must adhere to procedural due process. Due process will be determined by a judicial evaluation of the particular circumstances of each case. Due process comes to play when the act in question is a state action and infringes on a property right, i.e., when the plaintiff can show a legitimate claim of entitlement to the benefit which is sought to be protected.

If the incident is subject to due process, then it must be determined what type of process is due.

The courts will balance the interest of parties including the importance of the interest, the type of proceeding in which the interest is reviewed, the appropriateness of the procedure required to prevent any deprivation of the protected interest and the cost of the procedure. Another consideration is the seriousness of the possible sanction that may be imposed. Due process requires that before an action is taken the person who is to be affected must be given a fair hearing which will include notice and a hearing.

B.　NCAA

1.　Power to Sanction

The National Collegiate Athletic Association (NCAA) is the regulatory board in collegiate athletics. Their preeminent function is to penalize and discipline. After *NCAA v. Tarkanian* (1988), their disciplinary measures will not be deemed to be state action. The NCAA was not required to protect Tarkanian's constitutional rights because the NCAA is a private organization which acted independently of the state supported University of Nevada, Las Vegas (UNLV), when that school sought to discipline its coach. Tarkanian argued that UNLV had delegated its disciplinary power to the NCAA, and, because of that, the NCAA acted under the color of state law. However, the Supreme Court did not agree. The Supreme Court held that the NCAA is in actuality an agent of its member institutions, which as competitors of UNLV, have an interest in the even-handed enforcement of the NCAA's recruitment and disciplinary standards.

There is no question that the NCAA has significant power to invoke sanctions against a university's athletic program, but a few states have added power legislatively to enhance preexisting sanctions for any NCAA-imposed violations. Texas, for example, enacted legislation that stipulates that anyone that is shown to have violated the NCAA rules can be liable for monetary damages resulting from the sanctions that were enforced against the school. These damages can include ticket or television revenue that were lost because of probation or suspension by the NCAA against that university.

2. Death Penalty

The most onerous sanction that the NCAA can empower against a school is the "death penalty". The death penalty, basically, will not allow a school to participate in a particular sport for up to two years. The only school to be assessed this penalty is Southern Methodist University. After the imposition of the death penalty, it was disclosed that boosters and officials had been implicated in numerous violations. As a response, Texas enacted legislation that made it a civil offense to violate NCAA rules.

The death penalty is only for repeated violations, that is, if after a major violation another major violation is found within the five-year period following the starting date of the first violation. Basically, the penalty prohibits the coaching staff and the team from being involved in that sport, either directly or indirectly, for a two-year period and includes the elimination of all scholarship and recruiting activities. The price is severe and its effect can last for more than a one year period; with SMU, the end result was that the football team was disbanded for two years. The death penalty is specifically reserved for repeat offenders, with the goal of having a chilling effect on the prospect of future offenses and assisting in the self-policing by member universities.

C.   HIGH SCHOOL SPORTS

Penalties and discipline in high school sports usually take the form of a denial of eligibility to participate in a particular sport. Courts usually will not interfere with eligibility determinations made by a voluntary state high school athletic association. Unless there is fraud or the defendant acted in an unreasonable manner, the athletic association will usually be permitted to enforce its rules without interference by the judicial system.

Although high school students are not completely denied their constitutional protections, determinations of these rights is different in public schools than in other environments. Courts will not substitute their interpretation of the bylaws of a voluntary athletic association for an association's interpretation of those rules, so long as the association's interpretation is fair and reasonable. If high school associations do not act arbitrarily in applying a law which punishes, disciplines or permits the eligibility of an athlete, then there is no improper influence. An example would be an association's rule that limits eligibility for those who transfer without a change in the residence of their parents; this rule is not based on any suspect classification and does not represent an improper discrimination against a particular group. Therefore, it is constitutionally correct. Participation in high school sports is not a constitutionally protected right, even though the athlete may loose the opportunity to play in tournaments or to compete for scholarships at the collegiate level.

D.   PROFESSIONAL SPORTS

In professional sports, the athlete-employer relationship is based on consent and defined by agreements such as the SPK and the c.b.a. These agreements along with some principles of antitrust law define the boundaries that the employer must adhere to as regards disciplining or penalizing athletes for various infractions, e.g., gambling, referee arguments or drugs. Those who punish are the club and the league, and those who receive the punishment are the athletes. The power to discipline emanates from the consent of the player himself.

The basic foundation of this power emanates from the SPK which is an agreement between the ...er and the athlete. The SPK, however, is ...ly broad and simply secures a player's agreement to abide by the rules which the team or league may ultimately develop. A typical SPK will only outline that the club has the power to establish rules that will govern the conduct of the player, and in return, will require the player's express agreement that he will abide by those rules and regulations. Penalties can be in the form of fines, suspensions, expulsion or a termination of the contract. The SPK will stipulate the procedural rights that the player will be protected under; usually they will be in the form of notice and review by the league's commissioner. The SPK will also establish that the commissioner will have independent disciplinary authority. The question is whether the player has consented to be bound by the particular disciplinary rules. The answer will depend on the interpretation of the penalty clause in the SPK and an analysis of the breadth of the discretion which the league has to define and punish what they have determined to be inappropriate behavior.

Since it is controlled by both contract and the collective bargaining agreement, the authority to discipline in professional sports is not as broad as in amateur sports. The league's commissioner cannot use his disciplinary power solely to enhance the league's economic position or to restrict the competitive opportunities of a player.

One example of misbehavior in professional sports is gambling. Professional sports have always viewed gambling as contrary to the goal of maintaining the competitiveness and credibility in the sport. Gambling will diminish the fans' belief in the honesty of the games. When players gamble on the outcome, there is no guarantee that any real competition exists. Leagues have a strong interest in assuring that the contest is one of pure athletic skill and not influenced by the participant's desire to have their team perform in relationship to the views of oddsmakers. In *Molinas v. NBA* (1961) (see also *Molinas v. Podoloff* (1954)), a professional basketball player was suspended for life because he gambled on the outcome of a game. The court concluded that a rule in a contract such as this was necessary for the survival of the league and a rule invoked against gambling is as reasonable as could be imagined.

There are many other ways in which players can receive penalties. In the NFL, for example, penalties will accrue for being overweight, for being ejected from a game, for failing to properly report an injury, for damaging club equipment, and for any contact which is viewed to be detrimental to the club. "Detrimental to the club" is the all encompassing phrase under which a player can be disciplined for associating with undesirables or involving themselves in criminal activities off the field or acts which in any way might exhibit qualities that could be viewed as "anti-social." Finally, it should be noted that since the league is judge and jury, there is always the possibility of bias in the disciplinary process.

CHAPTER 22

DRUG TESTING

A. GENERALLY

There are many different policies in the various sports that are promulgated to restrict drug usage by their players. These policies cover the entire range of policing activities from statutory requirements for mandatory drug testing to voluntary programs. The more dangerous sports, for example, boxing and horse racing, have had drug testing and drug testing requirements as a part of their sport for many years.

Although there are numerous policies and programs that detect and punish drug usage in sports, there are limits to the range and breadth of these various drug testing programs. These limits are established by the Constitution.

B. PROFESSIONAL SPORTS

Every professional sport has a plan to evaluate and monitor drug usage. These programs are usually developed through collective bargaining, with a system that progressively punishes drug usage in a step-by-step program, according to the amount of repeat offenses. In these processes, elements of review and due process are made a part of the procedures.

As regards the heavily regulated sports; for example, in *Shoemaker v. Handel* (1986), there was a challenge to prevailing regulations which directed jockeys to submit to testing for drug usage. In upholding these regulations, the court emphasized the nature of horse racing, which is highly regulated with people wagering on the outcome. Drug abuse by jockeys could affect public confidence in the integrity and legality of the sport.

However, the Seventh Circuit Court of Appeals enjoined a state racing board from substance abuse rules that provided for random drug testing and probable cause testing for all racing licensees whether outriders, starters, jockeys, etc. The court held that the racing board's interest in safety and integrity were insufficient to outweigh the invasion of privacy through an otherwise unconstitutional random urinalysis. The court found that urine testing possessed limited use for those purposes since it could not measure plaintiff's present impairment, and instead, only revealed that drug usage had previously occurred at some earlier time. *Dimeo v. Griffin* (1991).

The seriously regulated sports, however, will usually be allowed to maintain mandatory random drug testing. Those programs that have developed through a collective bargaining agreement in the less regulated sports, e.g., football, baseball and basketball, combine potential redemption with punishment. Their aim is education and treatment, and if that fails, punishment. These collectively bargained for agreements usually provide for some sort of amnesty for those players who voluntarily seek treatment. However, there is a heightened schedule of punishment which usually leads to a life banishment if the abuse continues.

C. AMATEUR SPORTS

The NCAA requires that all athletes annually sign a consent to drug testing as part of their statement pertaining to eligibility, recruitment, financial aid, amateur status and involvement in organized gambling activities. Failure to adhere to this statement will result in the student's ineligibility to participate. The NCAA also has a random, mandatory drug testing program in connection with post-season intercollegiate athletic activities.

A student found to be on a substance which is included in the list of banned drugs will be ineligible for post- and regular season competition for a minimum loss of one season of competition or its equivalent. If the student-athlete tests positive for the use of any drug, other than a "street drug," he/she shall lose all remaining regular-season and post season eligibility in all sports. If the student-athlete tests positive for a street drug after restoration of eligibility, the student shall be charged with the loss of a minimum of one additional season of competition in all sports.

In 1990, a California Court of Appeals granted a permanent injunction against the NCAA prohibiting testing student athletes on the grounds that their right to privacy under the California Constitution was violated. The court averred that the NCAA did not show a compelling interest which would justify an invasion of an athlete's right to keep their urine private and the right to maintain the privacy of medical history, e.g., use of birth control pills. The NCAA program was overly broad and produced results whose accuracy was doubtful. Also, the court found that other alternatives to testing that were less intrusive to a student's right to privacy were not considered by the NCAA as possible alternatives. *Hill v. NCAA* (1990) (*Hill I*). However, the California Supreme Court reversed *Hill* in 1994. *Hill v. NCAA* (*Hill II*).

After *Hill II* the NCAA's program of consent to drug testing appears to be legal. The program demands that every athlete must annually sign a statement as regards a consent to be tested. If they do not, they can be declared ineligible. The standard seems to be that the NCAA's use of monitoring urine testing to enforce drug testing is not an unreasonable infringement on a student athlete's expectation to privacy. See *O'Halloran v. University of Washington* (1988).

In a seminal 7th Circuit case dealing with a program which appears on its face consistent with NCAA policies, the court held that a high school consent program of urinalysis of prospective athletes was legal. *Schaill v. Tippecanoe County School Corporation* (1988). This case dealt with an athlete who had to sign a consent form for urinalysis before he could be eligible for participation. Although the process of safeguarding confidentially is important, the court held that a consent program, such as this, is still legal. The court stressed that there was a lessened expectation of privacy because of the general locker room ambience. The court also averred that urine samples in that particular school were already a part of the pre-participation medical examination and, thus, were established prerequisites to athletic participation. In short, participation in high school athletics is a privilege rather than a right; because of this, limited drug testing is an acceptable way to foster an important state interest. See *Vernonia School District 47J v. Acton* (1995).

Drug testing is also important to the United States Olympic Committee. Its concern is not only with street drugs, but also with performance enhancing drugs, that is, drugs taken by athletes to increase their athletic powers, e.g., steroids. The USOC's drug program has been in place since 1983 and provides for both informal and formal testing at Olympic trials. The USOC's policy stipulates that all Olympic athletes shall be drug tested at the trials and at least be disqualified from joining the Olympic team if found to be positive. In this program, there are a variety of legal considerations: for example, the list of banned drugs, informed consent, prevention of a false positive, prevention of a false negative, confidentiality, accurate information and appeal.ʹ However, this program in its application is arguably constitutional, and it is not the subject of protest at this time.

D. RIGHT OF PRIVACY

The question is whether an individual has a right to privacy as regards to urinalysis. An expectation of privacy must be one that society is prepared to recognize as legitimate. In *Schaill v. Tippecanoe County School Corporation* (1988), the court held that the students did not have a legitimate right of privacy or an expectation of privacy in a situation where high school students were forced to sign a consent form which would allow random urinalysis as a prerequisite to athletic participation.

The California Court of Appeals in *Hill v. NCAA* (1990), held that the NCAA did not show a compelling interest to substantiate an invasion of a student athlete's right to keep their urine private and to maintain privacy of medical records in a situation where the court viewed the program as overly broad and capable of producing results whose accuracy are doubtful. However, the California Supreme Court reversed *Hill I*. Even though a policy may violate some privacy rights, it will still stand if it promotes a compelling state interest. However, the California Supreme Court used the less rigorous, legitimate interest standard with the NCAA, a private, non-governmental entity. The NCAA's interests were sufficiently legitimate to overcome the athletes' privacy rights. *Hill v. NCAA* (1994) (*Hill II*). Like the California Supreme Court in *Hill II*, the United States Supreme Court in *Vernonia School District 47J v. Acton*, for high school students, concluded that student-athletes have a diminished privacy expectation, the so-called locker room mentality, for purposes of determining the reasonableness of a drug urinalysis as "search." *Vernonia School District 47J v. Acton* (1995).

Urine is a private thing. One's urine product is not normally intended to be inspected or examined by anyone other than the donor. An individual's privacy rights will vary with the context. In certain situations an individual's expectation of privacy will be diminished by a past history of significant governmental regulations. But, the governmental interest furthered by a particular search must be weighty and generally of such a nature that alternate, less intrusive means of detection would not sufficiently serve the government's ends.

E. REASONABLENESS OF SEARCH

The legality of a urinalysis will depend on the reasonableness of the search, under all the circumstances. Reasonableness is determined by whether it is justified at the beginning of the search; and whether the search as conducted was reasonably related in scope to the circumstances that justified the search in the first place. The standard for determining the legality of the asserted force of intrusion is reasonableness. *Shoemaker v. Handel*

(1986). The courts must balance the intrusiveness of the search and an individual's fourth amendment interest against a legitimate governmental interest. The test is vague and gives the courts a great deal of discretion in this matter. Before determining reasonableness, the athlete must show that he is entitled to protection; after this, the legality of the search is determined in light of fourth amendment reasonableness.

F.   DUE PROCESS AND EQUAL PROTECTION

In all programs that involve drug testing, questions arise as regards the athlete's privacy, due process and equal protection rights. The 14th Amendment protection of due process and equal protection will not extend to private contacts that abridge only individual rights. Only state action can be challenged under the 14th Amendment. It must be determined whether the action in question is either state action or comes under the color of state action. Under *NCAA v. Tarkanian* (1988), at the college level it appears that the NCAA's actions will not be construed to be state action.

In high schools, there is no fundamental right to play football. It is more privilege than right and since it is not a fundamental right, the strict scrutiny test will not apply in an equal protection claim. The relevant standard is minimal rationality. This rational basis or minimal rationality test only calls for a rational relationship between the program and a compelling state interest. In *Schaill v. Tippecanoe County School Corporation* (1988), the compelling interest was control of drugs in high school which is certainly a positive goal. All that was required was a rational basis or connection between the state's interest and the drug testing program. Whether this was the best way to achieve the interest, or whether there were other appropriate alternatives was not the question. The constitutionality of the drug testing program did not rest on whether the program was the best choice of alternatives, but only on whether it was a reasonable choice. See *Vernonia School District 47J v. Acton* (1995).

In the context of due process in drug testing, it would be a violation of a high school athlete's due process right, if, for example, he was forced to strip in public and urinate every hour. But as in *Schaill,* if the urine sampling is done in a discrete and confidential way, it usually will be held to be constitutional. Due process is provided for if there is multiple testing to assure the accuracy of the test, protection of confidentiality, the availability of an appeal of the determination at the school level, a limiting of the sanction to suspension from athletic competition and the availability of an appeal to the judiciary.

CHAPTER 23

SEX DISCRIMINATION

A. DISCRIMINATION GENERALLY

Sexism can occur in almost every aspect of sports, including different rules in girls sports and less opportunities for girls to participate in amateur sports. Men historically have felt that women are too frail to meaningfully participate in sports.

The most vital aspect of sex discrimination is the limiting of athletic opportunities for girls. Ways in which opportunities can be curtailed cover the gamut, from school regulations which exclude girls from participation in athletic programs to rules which are not per se discriminatory but discriminate in the method by which they are applied. Another form of discrimination is the failure to provide equal funding, facilities or opportunities for female athletes, their coaches and managers.

In an attempt to solve or at least ameliorate these problems, there are three basic types of athletic programs: separate but equal, mixed competition and the component approach. All the other programs which have been experimented with are variations of these approaches.

A separate but equal type of program arguably appears to be the perfect solution to the problem of discrimination. However, these programs are often not equal, especially in their application which will disclose gross inequalities. Women lack coaching, sports selection, equipment, scheduling and access to facilities which men and boys take for granted. Funding and the type of available competition also make the separate programs unequal. For example, a boy's program may have state wide competition and championships while the girls' program may not.

Another approach is to allow mixed competition in all sports that do not involve physical contact. The only criteria for participation would be the person's ability to play. Here, the outstanding female athlete would have the opportunity to participate at the most competitive level. However, this type of program has its drawbacks because females have traditionally had poor experiences in sports training; therefore, the males would be likely to dominate every sport. The end result would be that few females would be selected and participate in the particular sporting program.

The last approach would be that each school would provide a single team which could be made up of components. Each component would contribute to the success of or failure of the team in competition with other schools. The teams would win or lose based on the total score of their components. This component program has the effect of making recognition of one component contingent on the performance of another component.

All these programs have flaws that in some way may enhance discrimination. Yet they all have something to offer which would could be positive and beneficial to the interests of female athletes. The best system is one that enables the greatest number of participants to compete against those of comparable ability.

B. SEPARATE BUT EQUAL

A typical situation is one where a college has failed to provide equally between its men's and women's athletic programs. An institution can provide separate programs for men and women. The question is not so much the separateness of the separate programs but rather the equality of the different programs. Programs must exist for both sexes; there also must be opportunity to participate in intercollegiate sports.

One way in which to examine the distinctions between programs is to analyze the revenue producing capability of each program. The courts recognize that some athletic programs are intended to be revenue generating and that the monies that are produced from an individual sport will affect the financial support of the program. Still, these discrepancies must have a basis in fact.

In an attempt to ascertain if a school's action would result in a disparate effect on one sex at the expense of the other sex, one must analyze the amount of funding that is budgeted for the various female athletic endeavors as compared to the monies budgeted for the men. Another aspect of the comparison is the amount of money spent on equipment, facilities and programs. If the differences are blatant, then no other evidence is necessary to show that disparate treatment exists between the programs. In short, equal money for both male and female collegiate sports; or, to use the rallying cry of the 90s, "gender equity."

C. CONTACT AND NON-CONTACT SPORTS

Courts have traditionally differentiated between contact and non-contact sports as regards the level and commitment of participation for girls in sports.

In the majority of cases that involve non-contact sports where no women's team is available, the courts usually allow the women to participate on the men's team. If there is not a team sponsored for one sex in a particular sport and the excluded sex has had a history of limited opportunity, then the excluded sex must be permitted to try out for that team. The pertinent Health, Education and Welfare regulations, 45 CFR § 86.41 (1979), contain a general prohibition against sex-based discrimination in any school-sponsored athletic program.

When there is ample opportunity for women to compete on their own, courts appear less apt to allow them to compete with men in contact sports. (See also discussion of Title IX infra). The Health, Education and Welfare Regulations under Title IX permit an athletic department which receives federal funds to maintain separate teams if selection for those teams is based on competitive skill or if the sport involved is a contact sport. 45 CFR § 86.41(b).

Finally, the exception that provides for competitive skill applies to most programs, because sports and the competition thereof, is ultimately based on individual skills. Therefore, separate teams are permissible for most sports, contact or non-contact, if they are available.

D. TITLE IX

Under Title IX of the 1972 Education Amendments (discussed infra), contact sports include boxing, wrestling, rugby, ice hockey, football, basketball and other sports in which the purpose or preeminent activity involves bodily contact. Some courts, however, have also included baseball and soccer as contact sports.

In order to win on a constitutional claim of gender discrimination, plaintiff must show that state action was involved in the denial of a request to participate. However, if the college shows that there is potential physical harm to the female athlete due to the nature of that particular contact sport, it is constitutional to limit participation in that sport. The state must demonstrate that the preeminent concern is for the average differences between males and females and that its concern is for the health and safety of the athletes. The criteria that will be used to justify the potential harm (which the state must both allege and prove) are intimidation, safety and displacement.

1. Application

The sexual discrimination in academics called for an answer which was created in the form of Title IX of the 1972 Education Amendments, which provided that no person shall on the basis of sex be excluded from participation in, be denied the benefits of or be discriminated against, in any education program that receives federal financial assistance. 20 U.S.C.A. § 1681 et seq. This act prohibited any federally funded educational program from discrimination and intended to curtail discrimination in any program, organization or agency that received federal funds.

Title IX clearly applies to primary and secondary schools. Title IX has been viewed as an illustration of congressional intent and policy against discrimination based on stereotypical characterizations of the sexes. It was an attempt to end misguided paternalism. The objective was to give women an equal opportunity to develop the skills that they hoped to develop and to apply those skills in the way they had hoped.

Facts and situations as enforced by the Department of Health, Education, and Welfare (HEW) are limited to discrimination against participants in federally funded educational programs. Title IX applies to the admissions policies of these institutions, whether they are vocational, professional, graduate or undergraduate in nature. It also applies to policies and practices other than admissions in all educational programs, which will include athletic programs, that also receive federal funds.

Title IX protection does not cover, however, educational institutions that traditionally admit members of only one sex, institutions that train individuals for the military, and institutions under the control of religious groups whose compliance with Title IX would violate their religious beliefs.

Even though the statute and the regulations appear to be rather clear, problems have arisen regarding the scope of the act's application. The issue is whether the term "federal financial assistance" encompasses indirect federal aid, and if so, what constitutes a program or activity funded for the purposes of regulation and fund termination under § 902 of the act, the enforcement arm of Title IX. HEW regulations from 1975 determined that "federal financial assistance" include funds received indirectly by a school, including grants and loans paid directly to students but which ultimately are received by the school. 34 CFR § 106.2(G)(1)(ii). Under this analysis, indirect benefits that emanate from federal funding will be sufficient in certain cases to allow athletic departments to be characterized as Title IX recipients.

2. Grove City and Civil Rights Restoration Act of 1987

The authors of Title IX arguably intended the benefits of their reforms to reach all federally funded programs; and thus athletic participation would also receive the umbrella protection of Title IX. However, the United States Supreme Court in *Grove City College v. Bell* (1982), ruled that only those programs within an institution that receive direct financial aid from the federal government would be subjected to Title IX protection.

This case obviously limited the affect that Title IX would have in general, and more particularly, the affect that Title IX would have on female athletic participation. The issue here was whether Title IX applied only to specific departments that received direct funding or whether it extended to any department within an institution that benefit from financial aid. The Supreme Court saw Title IX as program specific.

The Supreme Court was unwilling to hold that the receipt of basic education opportunity grants (BEOG's) by particular college students subjected the entire institution to coverage under Title IX. The Supreme Court's rationale was that in order for the entire institution to be subjected to regulation there must be evidence that the college used federal funds in areas other than the college's own financial aid program. However, the Supreme Court did hold that the colleges' financial aid program was covered under the program-specific requirements of Title IX. In short, the court held that Title IX applied only to individual programs that received federal funding at an institution of higher education and not the entire institution itself.

The ruling in *Grove City College,* however, was not the intent that Congress had in mind when they established Title IX. This ruling was a narrow approach and not intended by the Title IX creators; therefore, they did the very unusual step of rewriting *Grove City College* through a federal statute: the Civil Rights Restoration Act of 1987. 29 U.S.C.A. § 1687. This act extended the definition of "program" or "activity" to include the entire program, for example, the college, as opposed to the program specific approach as established in *Grove City College.*

Haffer v. Temple University (1981), is arguably the most important Title IX case to be reviewed after the passage of the Civil Rights Restoration Act. It was alleged that the school, Temple University, failed to afford women an equal opportunity to participate in interscholastic sports. The female athletes claimed that disparities existed in the resources that were distributed to the women's athletic programs and that applicable financial aid was unequally distributed among male and female athletes. The *Haffer* plaintiffs also asserted violations of the federal equal protection clause and Pennsylvania's ERA.

In 1988, the parties in *Haffer* reached a settlement agreement that followed the court's decision in which the court ruled in favor of a reconsideration of plaintiff's claims and denied summary judgment for the defendant. The settlement, *inter alia,* contained changes in Temple's athletic program that included proportional scholarships, increased athletic opportunities, and increased budget stipends for the female programs. The agreement only applied to this school; however, it has been viewed by many as the outline for collegiate compliance with Title IX.

In this case, for example, the cost of the expensive men's football and basketball teams were included in the overall sports budget; also, the school agreed that the money spent on the female teams would be within ten percentage points of the amount spent on the men's teams. The school was required to monitor participation in the women's sports programs to guarantee that their participation to financial aid figures are proportionate to the agreed upon ratio in the men's sports programs.

E. EQUAL PROTECTION

When one brings an action founded on the equal protection clause of the 14th Amendment, there must be a finding that state action is involved. After state action is determined the next step is to ascertain whether the athletic program's provisions or the enforcement of its prohibitions violate the equal protection clause of the 14th Amendment.

When the equal protection clause was first applied to sexually discriminatory sports rules, the standard was one of a "rational relationship."

Brenden v. Independent School District (1972). The Supreme Court has since held that the applicable standard of review for sex-based classification is one in which classification based on gender must serve an important governmental objective and also be substantially related to the achievement of those objectives. *Craig v. Boren* (1976).

This standard was followed in *Dodson v. Arkansas Activities Association* (1979), where the difference of rules for girls and boys basketball was found to deprive the girls of equal protection since these changes were not justified by an important governmental objective.

In *Dodson,* a suit was brought to challenge the constitutionality of different rules for girls' and boys' high school basketball, basically, the difference was that there was full-court basketball for the boys and half-court basketball for the girls. The court held that the difference in the rules deprived the girls of their equal protection rights. The association's rationale behind the different rules was based solely on tradition. Tradition alone without some supporting substantive gender-based reason is insufficient to justify the rule variations in light of the fact that those rules placed Arkansas girl athletes at a substantial disadvantage in comparison to their male counterparts.

Sex-based classifications will be held to violate equal protection unless they are shown to rest upon a convincing factual basis that goes beyond archaic, over broad, and paternalistic generalizations about the differences between males and females. When equal protection requirements are not met, the remedy will be to allow the complainant to participate or try out for a particular athletic team. Courts have required not that new teams be created but that the existing teams be open to all qualified people.

Under equal protection the ultimate test becomes one's ability without regard to sex. Equal protection claims can be combined with a Title IX action and also a state ERA claim. In an equal protection claim in sports sex discrimination, courts have considered elements that include demonstrations that show an adverse affect by the state action and that the disparate impact was a result of an invidious intent. This test is difficult since it requires the court to guess as regards the motives behind the choices made by the school, since schools usually do not document the intent behind their regulations.

In an equal protection claim, the courts will also consider whether the sport is or is not a contact sport. Women can be excluded from a men's team as long as there is a women's team in the same sport. If there is no female equivalent, the courts are divided; however, the state's interest here is usually expressed as the protection of the participants' health and safety. Some courts, however, hold that total exclusion when there is no separate program is overly inclusive since it is based on the assumption that females are relationally fragile. However, in noncontact sports, where there is no health or safety risks, and likewise no separate female team, then the courts will hold that total exclusion violates equal protection.

The last element that courts will consider as regards equal opportunity is the requirement of separate teams or opportunities to try out for the only available team. The courts have allowed a "separate but equal" policy when there is a separate girl's team. When a separate but equal policy is upheld, the court's next determination is to ascertain if the teams are truly equal in all levels of funding, coaching and support. The court then will evaluate the intangibles as regards the quality of the resources that are provided to the women's teams.

In summary, courts will apply an intermediate standard of review in their evaluation of the constitutionality of sex-based classifications. Sex-based classifications will only be allowed if they are substantially related to an important governmental objective. This test is somewhat subjective; and, as a result, each court's analysis can produce different or mixed results.

F. STATE ERA'S

Another route to attack alleged sex discrimination in athletics is through that particular state's Equal Rights Amendment (ERA). Not all states have passed ERA's. There is no federal constitutional amendment that is enacted at this time that prohibits sexual discrimination. Thus ERA's impact athletics at the state level for the particular state but not at the federal level. If there is an applicable state ERA, it is often helpful and may be crucial to the success of sex discrimination cases.

For example, in *Blair v. Washington State University* (1987), a class action was brought under the Washington ERA. It was held that there was a substantive cause of action for victims of sex-based discrimination in intercollegiate sports, that is, Washington's ERA prohibited sex-based classifications altogether. *Blair* illustrates that state ERA's can be instrumental in overcoming discriminatory rules and practices which exclude or deny females the opportunity to participate in sports.

An important advantage of the ERA approach is that state courts now can determine under state law whether gender classifications are suspect and thus warrant strict scrutiny as a standard of review. School rules will pass this standard if the gender classification is deemed necessary to achieve a compelling state's interest. Strict scrutiny will enhance the female athlete's opportunities for success since the school must prove that the classification has a direct relationship to the purpose of the regulation and that this purpose cannot be achieved by less restrictive means. However, all states do not have an ERA; also, of the states that do have an ERA, not all utilize strict scrutiny.

CHAPTER 24

INTELLECTUAL PROPERTY

A. GENERALLY

Intellectual property law encompasses ideas and subjects such as patents, trademarks, copyrights, trade secrets, trade dress as well as other subjects that relate to topics such as publicity rights, misappropriation, false advertising and unfair competition.

B. THE NATURE OF MARKETING

The marketing of both the athlete and sports in general deal directly with the laws of intellectual property. Sports marketing has become a huge industry in the United States and the international community in the 1990's. The business of sports has become a billion-dollar industry. The growth of sports in the last decade has exposed millions of people to sports every day in one form or another. Licensed sports merchandise sales totaled $11.4 billion in the United States in 1995. The National Football League has consistently been the leader in sports merchandise sales in the United States with sales in the billions in 1998 alone.

Sports licensing and marketing agreements are now commonplace in the business of sports and are found in many different forms. Corporate sponsorships are popular ways for a company to promote company identification and product through the purchasing of television time, etc. Corporations understand that sports has a universal appeal and they attempt to use that to their advantage to assist them in expanding their presence in a global fashion. Licensing sports properties and corporate sponsorship has become commonplace in the sports world today.

The Super Bowl is the essence of sports marketing. Every year corporate behemoths vie for the right to advertise their products on commercials during the Super Bowl.

C. ATHLETES AS ENTERTAINERS

Sports has become a part of the huge entertainment landscape in America. Sports is thought of as entertainment. Athletes have become associated with the entertainment business in many different fashions ranging from the movie industry to television appearances. Athletes have always been somewhat associated with the entertainment industry (think Johnny Weismuller). In the 1970's, such noted athletes as Jim Brown, O.J. Simpson, Fred Dryer and Merlen Olsen have had notable movie and television careers. More athletes are now appearing in movies and on television. Michael Jordan, Dennis Rodman and Shaquille O'Neal have been the most recent entries as cross-over athletes into the movie arena. Athletes are now appearing in movies and television on a regular basis as endorsers for major corporations.

D. PATENTS

Patent law is governed by the Federal Patent Act. 35 U.S.C.A. § 1 et seq. (1995). If an individual discovers or invents any new machine, process, manufacture or composition of matter they may apply to obtain a patent. An individual can secure a patent by filing an application with the United States Patent and Trademark office (PTO).

The patent act defines a potential patent as any "new and useful process, machine, manufacture, or composition of matter" which includes mechanical, chemical, and electrical structures and processes. In order for an invention to be patentable, it must meet four requirements. An invention must be (1) in a subject matter category, (2) useful, (3) novel in relation to the prior art, and (4) obvious from the prior art to a person of ordinary skill in the art at the time the invention was made.

A patent confers on the owner the right to exclude others from selling or using the process or product. A patent owner may sue those individuals who directly infringe upon the patent by using or selling the invention without the proper authority to do so. A patent lasts 17 years from the date of the issuance from the PTO.

Patent law is involved in the sports industry in many different forms from golfing gizmos to football helmets to skates to rackets to lawn darts, etc., etc.

E. COPYRIGHTS

Copyright law protects original works of authorship embodied in a tangible medium of expression. See the Copyright Act, 17 U.S.C.A. §§ 101 et seq. (1998). Subject matter that may be copyrighted include music, drama, computer programs, sound recordings and the visual arts. Copyright protects the original expression of ideas, not the ideas themselves. A work may fall into more than one category. Copyright law gives exclusive rights to produce the work, to prepare derivative works based on the work, to distribute copies or photo records of the work and to publicly display or perform such work. A copyright term extends for the life of the author plus 50 years after the author's death. There are three basic conditions. A work must be within the constitutional and statutory definitions of a work of authorship; the work must be in a tangible medium of expression and it must be original.

There are a myriad of copyright concerns that entangle the sporting universe from autobiographies to instructional videos to TV broadcasts and re-broadcasts, etc., etc. A typical and increasingly frequent example of a modern sports copyright problem is the unauthorized reception (or interception) of blacked-out (see *National Football League of New Haven v. Rondor, Inc.* (1993)) or cable (see *Home Box Office v. Champs of New Haven, Inc.*

(1993)) TV sports programming by the way of a satellite dish antenna. In this type of case, the copyright holder will usually prevail and be granted a permanent injunction. Another example is *NBA v. Motorola, Inc.* (1997), in which the second circuit ruled that a sports beeper company did not misappropriate the NBA's property by transmitting real-time NBA scores and statistics taken from the broadcasts of games in progress. See also *Score Group, Inc. v. Dad's Kid Corp.* (1994) (alleged copyright infringement of hologram baseball trading cards); and *Seal–Flex v. Athletic Track & Court Construction* (1994) (copyright infringement over a rubber running track surface).

F.   TRADEMARKS

A trademark is a type of symbol used by one to identify a particular set of goods and to distinguish them from another's goods. A trademark owner can prevent others from using the same or similar marks that create a likelihood of confusion or deception. Under trademark law, an individual can establish one's manufactured goods and services from another's (think the Nike SWOOSH).

Trademark law distinguishes between the following: (1) the right to use a mark, (2) the right to exclude others from using a mark, and (3) the right to register the mark.

The Federal Trademark Act of 1946, which is commonly referred to as the Lanham Act, governs the registration and law of trademarks as well as the remedies and enforcement procedure for infringement of trademarks. Under the Lanham Act, a trademark is defined as including "any word, name, symbol, or device or any combination thereof adopted and used by manufacturer or merchant to identify his or her goods and also to distinguish from those manufactured or sold by others." The Lanham Act provides for the registration of service marks, certification marks as well as trademarks. Trademarks actually protect both the consumer and the owner. A consumer can identify the goods and services that have been satisfactory in the past because of a trademark.

In a trademark infringement action, plaintiff must meet five requirements: (1) there must have been either a reproduction or counterfeit of the mark; (2) the reproduction must have occurred without the authority of the registrant; (3) the reproduction has been used in the stream of commerce; (4) the use must have been in the sale, distribution or offering of goods or services; and (5) the use of the reproduction must be likely to cause confusion.

In sports, the most likely conundrum is whether the use of the reproduction is likely to cause confusion. See *National Football League Properties, Inc. v. Wichita Falls Sportswear Inc.* (1982); and *University of Pittsburgh v. Champion Products* (1982).

There are many recent explosions in the trademark and trade dress jihad that is festering in the sports cosmos. The battle between golf club manufacturers against knock-off artists is just one example. The problem is, to most consumers, the SWOOSH, or the Shark's Shark, or Elkington's Elk, or the Cowboys' logo, IS the product itself. And the trademark holders must enforce their property as vigorously as Coca–Cola® or any other business will, since their identity is so intricately and completely associated with the trademark.

For example, see *Indianapolis Colts v. Metropolitan Baltimore Football Club* (1994), in which Canadian Football League (CFL) team in Baltimore was restrained from using the "Colts" trademark as in the "Baltimore CFL Colts", since "Colts" was already owned by the National Football League "Indianapolis Colts" (formerly of Baltimore). See also *Board of Trustees of the University of Arkansas v. Professional Therapy Services* (1995) (trademark infringement suit for unauthorized use of the RAZORBACK name and design logo).

Three Blind Mice Designs v. Cyrk, Inc. (1995) (trademark infringement over caricatures of hockey referees in the form of three blind mice); *Fila U.S.A. v. Kim* (1995) (trademark infringement over athletic shoes); *Sports Authority v. Prime Hospitality Corp.* (1995) (trademark infringement between "The Sports Authority," a warehouse-type sporting good store and "Sports Authority Food, Spirits and Sports"); and *Time Warner Sports Merchandising v. Chicago-land Processing Corp.* (1995) (dispute over licensing of trademarks and trade names associated with the 1994 World Cup of Soccer).

G. TRADE DRESS

Trade dress protection is available for non-functional features if they distinguish the goods' origin. The Lanham Act provides protection against the creation of confusion by the simulation of a product or services "trade dress". Trade dress originally meant a products' packaging, but more recent court decisions have extended trade dress to include the configuration and ornamentation of the product.

The signature case (so to speak) is *Peeble Beach Co. v. Tour 18, Ltd.* (1996) which can be described as "the celebrated golf course design trade dress suit." Tour 18 is a local golf course outside of Houston that has purposefully attempted to emulate America's most famous golf holes from some of this nation's most prestigious golf courses. Plaintiffs, owners of three of the copied holes, filed a complaint alleging that Tour 18 violated their design proprietary rights, including infringement of their trademarks, trade dress, copyrights, and goodwill. Judge Hittner found trade dress infringement only with respect to the reproduction of the "lighthouse" hole (#18) at Harbour Town; Tour 18 was enjoined from any use of it in its promotions. Tour 18 must disclaim in all promotions, signage, etc. any association with the replicated holes. In short, only the truly distinctive signature (like Harbour Town's 18th) deserve trade dress protection; other than that, replica golf courses are legally permissible.

In *Taylor Made Golf Co., Inc. v. Carsten Sports, Ltd.* (1997), plaintiff vigorously asserted its trademark and patented golf clubs against "knock-offs" of these clubs. Among its protected registration is the trade dress of its "BURNER BUBBLE" Metal Wood. Plaintiff's motion for summary judgment was granted, along with a monetary award based on infringer's profits. See also *Taylor Made Golf Co. v. Trend Precision Golf, Inc.* (1995) (trade dress for Callaway Golf's Big Bertha Irons).

APPENDICES

NOTE

These appendices display documents that represents practical ramifications of athletic representation. These documents are an essential aspect of the practice of sports law and should be read as an adjunct to the chapters on contracts, agents and labor law.

UNIFORM PLAYER'S CONTRACT
THE NATIONAL LEAGUE
OF PROFESSIONAL
BASEBALL CLUBS

Parties

Between _____, herein called the Club, and _____ of _____, herein called the Player.

Recital

The Club is a member of the National League of Professional Baseball Clubs, a voluntary association of member Clubs which has subscribed to the Major League Rules with the American League of Professional Baseball Clubs and its constituent Clubs and to The Professional Baseball Rules with that League and the National Association of Baseball Leagues.

Agreement

In consideration of the facts above recited and of the promises of each to the other, the parties agree as follows:

Employment

1.   The Club hereby employs the Player to render, and the Player agrees to render, skilled services as a baseball player during the year(s) 19__ including the Club's training season, the Club's exhibition games, the Club's playing season, the League Championship Series and the World Series (or any other official series in which the Club may participate and in any receipts of which the Player may be entitled to share).

Payment

2.   For performance of the Player's services and promises hereunder the Club will pay the Player the sum of $_____, in semi-monthly installments after the commencement of the championship season(s) covered by this contract except as the schedule of payments may be modified by a special covenant.   Payment shall be made on the day the amount becomes due, regardless of whether the Club is "home" or "abroad."   If a monthly rate of payment is stipulated above, it shall begin with the commencement of the championship season (or such subsequent date as the Player's services may commence) and end with the termination of the

championship season and shall be payable in semi-monthly installments as above provided.

Nothing herein shall interfere with the right of the Club and the Player by special covenant herein to mutually agree upon a method of payment whereby part of the Player's salary for the above year can be deferred to subsequent years.

If the Player is in the service of the Club for part of the championship season only, he shall receive such proportion of the sum above mentioned, as the number of days of his actual employment in the championship season bears to the number of days in the championship season. Notwithstanding the rate of payment stipulated above, the minimum rate of payment to the Player for each day of service on a Major League Club shall be at the applicable rate set forth in Article VI(B)(1) of the Basic Agreement between the American League of Professional Baseball Clubs and the National League of Professional Baseball Clubs and the Major League Baseball Players Association, effective January 1, 1990 ("Basic Agreement"). The minimum rate of payment for National Association service for all Players (a) signing a second Major League contract (not covering the same season as any such Player's initial Major League contract) or a subsequent Major League contract, or (b) having at least one day of Major League service, shall be at the applicable rate set forth in Article VI(B)(2) of the Basic Agreement.

Payment to the Player at the rate stipulated above shall be continued throughout any period in which a Player is required to attend a regularly scheduled military encampment of the Reserve of the Armed Forces or of the National Guard during the championship season.

Loyalty

3. (a) The Player agrees to perform his services hereunder diligently and faithfully, to keep himself in first-class physical condition and to obey the Club's training rules, and pledges himself to the American public and to the Club to conform to high standards of personal conduct, fair play and good sportsmanship.

Baseball Promotion

3. (b) In addition to his services in connection with the actual playing of baseball, the Player agrees to cooperate with the Club and participate in any and all reasonable promotional activities of the Club and its League, which, in the opinion of the Club, will promote the welfare of the Club or professional baseball, and to observe and comply with all reasonable requirements of the Club respecting conduct and service of its team and its players, at all times whether on or off the field.

Pictures and Public Appearances

3. (c) The Player agrees that his picture may be taken for still photographs, motion pictures or television at such times as the Club may designate and agrees that all rights in such pictures shall belong

to the Club and may be used by the Club for publicity purposes in any manner it desires. The Player further agrees that during the playing season he will not make public appearances, participate in radio or television programs or permit his picture to be taken or write or sponsor newspaper or magazine articles or sponsor commercial products without the written consent of the Club, which shall not be withheld except in the reasonable interests of the Club or professional baseball.

PLAYER REPRESENTATIONS

Ability

4. (a) The Player represents and agrees that he has exceptional and unique skill and ability as a baseball player; that his services to be rendered hereunder are of a special, unusual and extraordinary character which gives them peculiar value which cannot be reasonably or adequately compensated for in damages at law, and that the Player's breach of this contract will cause the Club great and irreparable injury and damage. The Player agrees that, in addition to other remedies, the Club shall be entitled to injunctive and other equitable relief to prevent a breach of this contract by the Player, including, among others, the right to enjoin the Player from playing baseball for any other person or organization during the term of his contract.

Condition

4. (b) The Player represents that he has no physical or mental defects known to him and un-

known to the appropriate representative of the Club which would prevent or impair performance of his services.

Interest in Club

4. (c) The Player represents that he does not, directly or indirectly, own stock or have any financial interest in the ownership or earnings of any Major League Club, except as hereinafter expressly set forth, and covenants that he will not hereafter, while connected with any Major League Club, acquire or hold any such stock or interest except in accordance with Major League Rule 20(e).

Service

5. (a) The Player agrees that, while under contract, and prior to expiration of the Club's right to renew this contract, he will not play baseball otherwise than for the Club, except that the Player may participate in post-season games under the conditions prescribed in the Major League Rules. Major League Rule 18(b) is set forth herein.

Other Sports

5. (b) The Player and the Club recognize and agree that the Player's participation in certain other sports may impair or destroy his ability and skill as a baseball player. Accordingly, the Player agrees that he will not engage in professional boxing or wrestling; and that, except with the written consent of the Club, he will not engage in skiing, auto

racing, motorcycle racing, sky diving, or in any game or exhibition of football, soccer, professional league basketball, ice hockey or other sport involving a substantial risk of personal injury.

Assignment

6. (a) The Player agrees that his contract may be assigned by the Club (and reassigned by any assignee Club) to any other Club in accordance with the Major League Rules and the Professional Baseball Rules. The Club and the Player may, without obtaining special approval, agree by special covenant to limit or eliminate the right of the Club to assign this contract.

Medical Information

6. (b) The Player agrees that, should the Club contemplate an assignment of this contract to another Club or Clubs, the Club's physician may furnish to the physicians and officials of such other Club or Clubs all relevant medical information relating to the Player.

No Salary Reduction

6. (c) The amount stated in paragraph 2 and in special covenants hereof which is payable to the Player for the period stated in paragraph 1 hereof shall not be diminished by any such assignment, except for failure to report as provided in the next subparagraph (d).

Reporting

6. (d) The Player shall report to the assignee Club promptly (as provided in the Regulations) upon receipt of written notice from the Club of the assignment of this contract. If the Player fails to so report, he shall not be entitled to any payment for the period from the date he receives written notice of assignment until he reports to the assignee Club.

Obligations of Assignor and Assignee Clubs

6. (e) Upon and after such assignment, all rights and obligations of the assignor Club hereunder shall become the rights and obligations of the assignee Club; provided, however, that

(1) The assignee Club shall be liable to the Player for payments accruing only from the date of assignment and shall not be liable (but the assignor Club shall remain liable) for payments accrued prior to that date.

(2) If at any time the assignee is a Major League Club, it shall be liable to pay the Player at the full rate stipulated in paragraph 2 hereof for the remainder of the period stated in paragraph 1 hereof and all prior assignors and assignees shall be relieved of liability for any payment for such period.

(3) Unless the assignor and assignee Clubs agree otherwise, if the assignee Club is a National Association Club, the assignee Club shall be liable only to pay the Player at the rate usually paid by said assignee Club to other Players of similar skill

and ability in its classification and the assignor Club shall be liable to pay the difference for the remainder of the period stated in paragraph 1 hereof between an amount computed at the rate stipulated in paragraph 2 hereof and the amount so payable by the assignee Club.

Moving Allowances

6. (f) The Player shall be entitled to moving allowances under the circumstances and in the amounts set forth in Articles VII(F) and VIII of the Basic Agreement.

"Club"

6. (g) All references in other paragraphs of this contract to "the Club" shall be deemed to mean and include any assignee of this contract.

TERMINATION

By Player

7. (a) The Player may terminate this contract, upon written notice to the Club, if the Club shall default in the payments to the Player provided for in paragraph 2 hereof or shall fail to perform any other obligation agreed to be performed by the Club hereunder and if the Club shall fail to remedy such default within ten (10) days after the receipt by the Club of written notice of such default. The Player may also terminate this contract as provided in subparagraph (d)(4) of this paragraph 7. (See Article XV(H) of the Basic Agreement.)

By Club

7. (b) The Club may terminate this contract upon written notice to the Player (but only after requesting and obtaining waivers of this contract from all other Major League Clubs) if the Player shall at any time:

(1) fail, refuse or neglect to conform his personal conduct to the standards of good citizenship and good sportsmanship or to keep himself in first-class physical condition or to obey the Club's training rules; or

(2) fail, in the opinion of the Club's management, to exhibit sufficient skill or competitive ability to qualify or continue as a member of the Club's team; or

(3) fail, refuse or neglect to render his services hereunder or in any other manner materially breach this contract.

7. (c) If this contract is terminated by the Club, the Player shall be entitled to termination pay under the circumstances and in the amounts set forth in Article IX of the Basic Agreement. In addition, the Player shall be entitled to receive an amount equal to the reasonable traveling expenses of the Player, including first-class jet air fare and meals en route, to his home city.

Procedure

7. (d) If the Club proposes to terminate this contract in accordance with subparagraph (b) of this paragraph 7, the procedure shall be as follows:

(1) The Club shall request waivers from all other Major League Clubs. Such waivers shall be good for three (3) business days only. Such waiver request must state that it is for the purpose of terminating this contract and it may not be withdrawn.

(2) Upon receipt of waiver request, any other Major League Club may claim assignment of this contract at a waiver price of $1.00, the priority of claims to be determined in accordance with the Major League Rules.

(3) If this contract is so claimed, the Club shall, promptly and before any assignment, notify the Player that it had requested waivers for the purpose of terminating this contract and that the contract had been claimed.

(4) Within five (5) days after receipt of notice of such claim, the Player shall be entitled, by written notice to the Club, to terminate this contract on the date of his notice of termination. If the Player fails to so notify the Club, this contract shall be assigned to the claiming Club.

(5) If the contract is not claimed, the Club shall promptly deliver written notice of termination to the Player at the expiration of the waiver period.

7. (e) Upon any termination of this contract by the Player, all obligations of both Parties hereunder shall cease on the date of termination, except the obligation of the Club to pay the Player's compensation to said date.

Regulations

8.   The Player accepts as part of this contract the Regulations set forth herein.

Rules

9.   (a) The Club and the Player agree to accept, abide by and comply with all provisions of the Major League Agreement, the Major League Rules, the Rules or Regulations of the League of which the Club is a member, and the Professional Baseball Rules, in effect on the date of this Uniform Player's Contract, which are not inconsistent with the provisions of this contract or the provisions of any agreement between the Major League Clubs and the Major League Baseball Players Association, provided that the Club, together with the other clubs of the American and National Leagues and the National Association, reserves the right to modify, supplement or repeal any provision of said Agreement, Rules and/or Regulations in a manner not inconsistent with this contract or the provisions of any then existing agreement between the Major League Clubs and the Major League Baseball Players Association.

Disputes

9.   (b) All disputes between the Player and the Club which are covered by the Grievance Procedure as set forth in the Basic Agreement shall be resolved in accordance with such Grievance Procedure.

Publication

9. (c) The Club, the League President and the Commissioner, or any of them, may make public the findings, decision and record of any inquiry, investigation or hearing held or conducted, including in such record all evidence or information given, received, or obtained in connection therewith.

Renewal

10. (a) Unless the Player has exercised his right to become a free agent as set forth in the Basic Agreement the Club may, on or before December 20 (or if a Sunday, then the next preceding business day) in the year of the last playing season covered by this contract, tender to the Player a contract for the term of the next year by mailing the same to the Player at his address following his signature hereto, or if none be given, then at his last address of record with the Club. If prior to the March 1 next succeeding said December 20, the Player and the Club have not agreed upon the terms of such contract, then on or before ten (10) days after said March 1, the Club shall have the right by written notice to the Player at said address to renew this contract for the period of one year on the same terms, except that the amount payable to the Player shall be such as the Club shall fix in said notice; provided, however, that said amount, if fixed by a Major League Club, shall be an amount payable at a rate not less than as specified in Article VI, Section D, of the Basic Agreement. Subject to the Player's

rights as set forth in the Basic Agreement, the Club may renew this contract from year to year.

10. (b) The Club's right to renew this contract, as provided in subparagraph (a) of this paragraph 10, and the promise of the Player not to play otherwise than with the Club have been taken into consideration in determining the amount payable under paragraph 2 hereof.

Governmental Regulation—National Emergency

11. This contract is subject to federal or state legislation, regulations, executive or other official orders or other governmental action, now or hereafter in effect respecting military, naval, air or other governmental service, which may directly or indirectly affect the Player, Club or the League and subject also to the right of the Commissioner to suspend the operation of this contract during any national emergency during which Major League Baseball is not played.

Commissioner

12. The term "Commissioner" wherever used in this contract shall be deemed to mean the Commissioner designated under the Major League Agreement, or in the case of a vacancy in the office of Commissioner, the Executive Council or such other body or person or persons as shall be designated in the Major League Agreement to exercise the powers

and duties of the Commissioner during such vacancy.

Supplemental Agreements

The Club and the Player covenant that this contract, the Basic Agreement and the Agreement Re Major League Baseball Players Benefit Plan effective April 1, 1990 and applicable supplements thereto fully set forth all understandings and agreements between them, and agree that no other understandings or agreements, whether heretofore or hereafter made, shall be valid, recognizable, or of any effect whatsoever, unless expressly set forth in a new or supplemental contract executed by the Player and the Club (acting by its President or such other officer as shall have been thereunto duly authorized by the President or Board of Directors as evidenced by a certificate filed of record with the League President and Commissioner) and complying with the Major League Rules and the Professional Baseball Rules.

Special Covenants

_____

_____

_____

Approval

This contract or any supplement hereto shall not be valid or effective unless and until approved by the League President.

Signed in duplicate this ___ day of ___, A.D. 199___

_____   _____
(Player)   (Club)

_____ By _____
(Home address of Player)   (Authorized Signature)

Social Security No. _____

Approved _____, 199___

_____
President, The National
League of Professional
Baseball Clubs

REGULATIONS

1. The Club's playing season for each year covered by this contract and all renewals hereof shall be as fixed by The National League of Professional Baseball Clubs, or if this contract shall be assigned to a Club in another League, then by the League of which such assignee is a member.

2. The Player, when requested by the Club, must submit to a complete physical examination at

the expense of the Club, and if necessary to treatment by a regular physician or dentist in good standing. Upon refusal of the Player to submit to a complete medical or dental examination, the Club may consider such refusal a violation of this regulation and may take such action as it deems advisable under Regulation 5 of this contract. Disability directly resulting from injury sustained in the course and within the scope of his employment under this contract shall not impair the right of the Player to receive his full salary for the period of such disability or for the season in which the injury was sustained (whichever period is shorter), together with the reasonable medical and hospital expenses incurred by reason of the injury and during the term of this contract or for a period of up to two years from the date of initial treatment for such injury, whichever period is longer, but only upon the express prerequisite conditions that (a) written notice of such injury, including the time, place, cause and nature of the injury, is served upon and received by the Club within twenty days of the sustaining of said injury and (b) the Club shall have the right to designate the doctors and hospitals furnishing such medical and hospital services. Failure to give such notice shall not impair the rights of the Player, as herein set forth, if the Club has actual knowledge of such injury. All workmen's compensation payments received by the Player as compensation for loss of income for a specific period during which the Club is paying him in full, shall be paid over by the

Player to the Club. Any other disability may be ground for suspending or terminating this contract.

3. The Club will furnish the Player with two complete uniforms, exclusive of shoes, unless the Club requires the Player to wear non-standard shoes in which case the Club will furnish the shoes. The uniforms will be surrendered by the Player to the Club at the end of the season or upon termination of this contract.

4. The Player shall be entitled to expense allowances under the circumstances and in the amounts set forth in Article VII of the Basic Agreement.

5. For violation by the Player of any regulation or other provision of this contract, the Club may impose a reasonable fine and deduct the amount thereof from the Player's salary or may suspend the Player without salary for a period not exceeding thirty days or both. Written notice of the fine or suspension or both and the reason therefor shall in every case be given to the Player and the Players Association. (See Article XII of the Basic Agreement.)

6. In order to enable the Player to fit himself for his duties under this contract, the Club may require the Player to report for practice at such places as the Club may designate and to participate in such exhibition contests as may be arranged by the Club, without any other compensation than that herein elsewhere provided, for a period beginning not earlier than thirty-three (33) days prior to the start of the championship season, provided, however, that

the Club may invite players to report at an earlier date on a voluntary basis in accordance with Article XIV of the Basic Agreement. The Club will pay the necessary traveling expenses, including the first-class jet air fare and meals en route of the Player from his home city to the training place of the Club, whether he be ordered to go there directly or by way of the home city of the Club. In the event of the failure of the Player to report for practice or to participate in the exhibition games, as required and provided for, he shall be required to get into playing condition to the satisfaction of the Club's team manager, and at the Player's own expense, before his salary shall commence.

7. In case of assignment of this contract the Player shall report promptly to the assignee Club within 72 hours from the date he receives written notice from the Club of such assignment, if the Player is then not more than 1,600 miles by most direct available railroad route from the assignee Club, plus an additional 24 hours for each additional 800 miles.

Post–Season Exhibition Games. Major League Rule 18(b) provides:

(b) EXHIBITION GAMES. No player shall participate in any exhibition game during the period between the close of the Major League championship season and the following training season, except that, with the consent of his club and permission of the Commissioner, a player may participate in exhibition games for a period of not less than thirty (30) days, such period to be designated annually by the Commissioner. Players who participate in barnstorming during this period cannot engage in any Winter League activities. Player conduct, on and off the field, in connection with such post-season exhibition games shall be subject to the discipline of the Commissioner. The Commissioner shall not approve of more than three (3) players of any one club on the same team. The Commissioner shall not approve of more than three (3) players from the joint membership of the World Series participants playing in the same game. No player shall participate in any exhibition game with or against any team which, during the current season or within one year, has had any ineligible player or which is or has been during the current season or within one (1) year, managed and controlled by an ineligible player or by any person who has listed an ineligible player under an assumed name or who otherwise has violated, or attempted to violate, any exhibition game contract; or with or against any team which, during said season or within one (1) year, has played against teams containing such ineligible players, or so managed or controlled. Any player violating this Rule shall be fined not less than Fifty Dollars ($50.00) nor more than Five Hundred Dollars ($500.00), except that in no event shall such fine be less than the consideration received by such player for participating in such game.

PRINTED IN U.S.A.   REVISED AS OF MAY 1990

MINOR LEAGUE UNIFORM
PLAYER CONTRACT

I. Parties

The parties to this Minor League Uniform Player Contract are those identified in paragraphs I and 2 of Addendum A.

II. Definitions

A. As used in this Minor League Uniform Player Contract, the term "Player" shall refer to the individual identified in paragraph I of Addendum A.

B. The term "Major League" shall refer to the American League of Professional Baseball Clubs, the National League of Professional Baseball Clubs and any other professional baseball league that is granted Major League status pursuant to the Major League Agreement (MLA).

C. The term "Major League Club" shall refer to a professional baseball club that is a member in good standing of a Major League.

D. The term "Major League Player" shall refer to a professional baseball player who is on an Active List, Disabled List or other Inactive List of a Major League Club.

E. The term "Minor League" shall refer to any domestic or foreign professional baseball league that, either directly or through membership in an association or other entity, is party to an agreement with the Major Leagues and that recognizes the authority of the Commissioner.

F. The term "Minor League Club" shall refer to any professional baseball club that is a member in good standing of a Minor League.

G. The term "Minor League Player" shall refer to any professional baseball player who is on a Minor League under control list and/or a Minor League Reserve List of a Major League Club and/or any professional baseball player who is on the Active List, Disabled List or other Inactive List of a Minor League Club.

H. The term "Commissioner" shall refer to the individual who holds the office of Commissioner of Baseball pursuant to Article I of the MLA (or, in the absence of a Commissioner, any person or entity succeeding to the powers and duties of the Commissioner pursuant to the MLA) or the Commissioner's designee.

I. The term "Club" shall refer to the professional baseball club identified in paragraph 2 of Addendum A, and any other Major League Club or Minor League Club to which this Minor League Uniform Player Contract may be assigned, loaned, leased or otherwise transferred. The term "Club" also shall refer to any Major League Club or Minor League Club for which Player is directed to perform.

J. The terms "Minor League Reserve List" and "Minor League under control list" shall refer to the lists filed pursuant to the Major League Rules of all Minor League Uniform Player Contracts to which that Club holds title.

K.   The terms "Major League Reserve List" and "Major League under control list" shall refer to the lists filed pursuant to the Major League Rules of all Major League Uniform Player Contracts that Club holds title to and that Club has placed on the Major League roster.

L.   The term "championship paying season" shall refer to the full schedule of regular-season games that has been approved for Club.

M.   The term "Minor League Association" shall refer to any association of Minor League Clubs and/or Minor Leagues that is party to an agreement with the Major Leagues and that recognizes the authority of the Commissioner.

III.   Recital

The Major Leagues have jointly subscribed to the Major League Agreement (MLA) and the Major League Rules (MLR). The parties agree that they and this Minor League Uniform Player Contract are therefore subject to and governed by the MLA and MLR, which are fully incorporated in this Minor League Uniform Player Contract as if set forth herein verbatim. The Major Leagues are currently party to the Professional Baseball Agreement (PBA) with the National Association of Professional Base-ball Leagues (National Association). To the extent that this Minor League Uniform Player Contract is assigned, loaned, leased or otherwise transferred to a Minor League Club which is a member of a National Association League (or the player is directed by the Club to perform for, or report to, such Minor League Club), the parties acknowledge (A) that they and this Minor League Uniform Player Contract are bound by, subject to and governed by the then-existing PBA and any subsequent amendments to that document, and (B) that the then-existing PBA (and any subsequent amendments to that document) are fully incorporated in this Minor League Uniform Player Contract as if set forth herein verbatim.

To the extent that this Minor League Uniform Player Contract is assigned, loaned, leased or otherwise transferred to a Minor League Club which is not a member of a National Association League (or the Player is directed by the Club to perform for, or report to, such Minor League Club), the parties acknowledge (A) that they and this Minor League Uniform Player Contract are bound by, subject to and governed by any agreement(s) and any subsequent amendments to any present or future agreements then in effect between the Major Leagues and the Minor League or Minor League Association of which the Minor League Club is a member and (B) that any such agreements (and any subsequent amendments to any such agreements) are fully incorporated in this Minor League Uniform Player Contract as if set forth herein verbatim.

IV. Scope

Subject to the provisions of the Basic Agreement applicable to Major League Players performing for Minor League Clubs and/or in Minor Leagues, this Minor League Uniform Player Contract shall set the terms and conditions of Player's employment during all periods in which Player is employed by Club as a Minor League Player. The Basic Agreement and the Major League Uniform Player Contract shall exclusively govern the terms and conditions of Player's employment during all periods in which he is performing services for Club as a Major League Player. This Minor League Uniform Player Contract therefore shall have no application during any period in which Player is on Club's Major League Active, Disabled or other Inactive List.

V. Agreement

In consideration of the foregoing Recital and Scope provisions, for the mutual representations, promises, covenants and agreements contained herein (including in Addenda A, B and C) and for other good and valuable consideration, the receipt of which is hereby acknowledged, the parties, intending to be legally bound, promise, covenant and agree as follows.

VI. Duration And Conditions Of Employment

A. Unless a different term of this Minor League Uniform Player Contract is set forth in Addendum A, Club hereby employs Player to render, and Player agrees to render, skilled services as a Minor League Player in seven (7) separate championship playing seasons, commencing with the beginning of the championship playing season identified in paragraph 3 of Addendum A, or the portion of that regular championship playing season remaining after the execution date of this Minor League Uniform Player Contract, as specified in paragraph 4 of Addendum A, whichever date is later. Unless this Minor League Uniform Player Contract is terminated pursuant to Paragraph XIX, the term of employment shall extend until Player has performed services for Club as a Minor League Player in the requisite total of separate championship playing seasons. For purposes of determining whether Player has performed in the requisite total of separate championship playing seasons, Player shall not be deemed to have performed services as a Minor League Player during any championship playing season in which he is on either the Major League Active List, the Major League Disabled List or other Major League Inactive List (or combination of the foregoing) for the entire season. Player also shall not be deemed to have performed services as a Minor League Player in any championship playing season in which he is on the Restricted List, Disqualified List, Suspended List, Ineligible List, Voluntarily Retired List or Military List (or combinations of the foregoing) for the entire season. Player also shall not be deemed to have performed services as a Minor League Player in any championship season in which he withholds his services for any portion of the championship playing season or play-off games at the conclusion of that championship playing season. For purposes of determining whether Player has performed services in the requisite total of separate championship playing seasons, service in winter league play shall be excluded.

B.   This Minor League Uniform Player Contract obligates Player to perform professional services on a calendar year basis, regardless of the fact that salary payments are to be made only during the actual championship playing season. The salary paid is in part based on considerations in addition to the actual performance of services during the championship playing season. Player therefore understands and agrees that his duties and obligations under this Minor League Uniform Player Contract continue in full force and effect throughout the calendar year, including Club's championship playing season, Club's training season, Club's exhibition games, Club's instructional, post-season training or winter league games, any official play-off series, any other official post-season series in which Club shall be required to participate, any other game or games in the receipts of which Player may be entitled to a share, and any remaining portions of the calendar year. Player's duties and obligations shall continue in full force and effect until October 15 of the calendar year of the last championship playing season covered by this Minor League Uniform Player Contract.

C.   Player and Club also agree to comply with all decisions of the Commissioner pursuant to the provisions of the MLA and MLR and, to the extent applicable, the PBA or other agreement in effect between the Major Leagues and one or more Minor Leagues or Minor League Associations.

D. Player's physical condition is important to the safety and welfare of Player and to the success of Club. Thus, to enable Player to fit himself properly for his duties under this Minor League Uniform Player Contract, Club may require Player to maintain his playing condition and weight during the off-season and to report for practice and conditioning at such times and places as Club may determine and may require Player to participate in such exhibition games prior to the championship playing season as Club may arrange. Club shall reimburse Player for expenses incurred in traveling from Player's home city to Club's training place and Club shall have the right to select the mode and class of transportation to be used and the route to be taken by Player. In the event Player fails to report for practice and conditioning as required, or fails to participate in exhibition games, Club may impose a reasonable fine upon Player in accordance with Paragraph XX and also require Player to fit himself for his duties to the satisfaction of Club at Player's own expense.

E. Player represents that he is aware of the Commissioner's Office Policy (the Policy) prohibiting Minor League Players and other Minor League Personnel from using or possessing tobacco or similar products on ballpark premises or during Club travel. Player also agrees that all Policy provisions (and any subsequent amendments, revisions or additions) shall be incorporated in this Minor League Uniform Player Contract as if set forth herein verbatim.

Player further promises that he will comply fully with all Policy provisions and that his obligation to do so is a material term of this Minor League Uniform Player Contract Player understands and agrees that any violation of the Policy may subject him to discipline (including, but not limited to, a monetary fine and/or a suspension) under the terms of this Minor League Uniform Player Contract, the MLA and the MLR. Moreover, Player stipulates and agrees that all disputes concerning the Policy and/or Player's compliance with the Policy shall be resolved in accordance with this Minor League Uniform Player Contract, the MLA and the MLR.

VII. Payment

A. For the performance of all of the skilled services by Player and for Player's other promises herein contained, Club will pay Player at the monthly rate set out in Addendum C–I during the first championship playing season covered by this Minor League Uniform Player Contract. The Player and Club shall attempt annually to negotiate an applicable monthly salary rate for the next subsequent championship playing season covered by this Minor League Uniform Player Contract. Such negotiations shall be in accordance with the applicable provisions of the MLA and, if applicable, the PBA or other agreement in effect between the Major League and one or more Minor Leagues or Minor League Associations. If the Player and Club reach agreement, the agreed-upon monthly salary rate shall be set out in a new Addendum C, and Player agrees to execute same. If the Player and Club do not reach agreement, then the Player's monthly salary rate for the next championship playing season shall be set by the Club, but shall not be less than eighty percent (80%) of the monthly salary rate set out in the most recently executed Addendum C. If the Player's monthly salary rate is set by the Club, that monthly salary rate shall be set out in a new Addendum C, and Player agrees to execute same. Any monthly salary rate set out in any Addendum C shall conform to any applicable minimum salary requirements contained in the MLR. If Player is a foreign national with a nonimmigrant visa, monthly salary rates Set out in any Addendum C shall be adjusted upward as necessary to conform with the minimum required salary levels. The various Addenda C for this Minor League Uniform Player Contract shall be numbered consecutively, for example, Addendum C–1, Addendum C–2, et cetera.

B. The monthly payments under this Minor League Uniform Player Contract will be made in two (2) semi-monthly installments on the 15th day and last day of the month after the beginning of Club's championship playing season. The obligation to make such payments to Player shall start with the beginning of Club's championship playing season or such later date as Player reports for championship season play. The obligation to make such payments shall end with the termination of Club's championship playing season and any official playoff series in which Club shall participate, or upon the termination of this Minor League Uniform Player Contract, whichever shall occur first. Player shall not be entitled to any payment under this Minor League Uniform Player Contract for any period that he is on a Major League Active, Disabled or other Inactive List. If Player is in the service of Club for part of Club's championship playing season only, he shall receive such proportion of the rate set forth above as the number of days of his actual employment in any month compares to the number of days in said month.

VIII.   Disability Of Player

A.   If Player is disabled during Club's training season and if this Minor League Uniform Player Contract is terminated during Club's training season as a result of that disability, or if this Minor League Uniform Player Contract is later terminated during the first fourteen days of Club's championship playing season while Player is so disabled, Player shall be paid by Club at the rate of compensation set out in the most recently executed Addendum C for a period of released on or before the fourteenth day of Club's championship playing season, Club shall continue to be obligated to pay Player at Addendum C until the conclusion of Club's championship playing season, or until an earlier date on which Club may give Player an unconditional release.

B. If Player is disabled during Club's championship playing season, that disability shall not impair Player's rights to receive the compensation set forth in subparagraph A of Paragraph VII for a period of fourteen days from the date of such disability if that disability continues for all of such period. It is specifically provided, however, that said fourteen days' period shall not be considered for purposes of determining whether any additional payments may be due Player under any Special Covenants to this Minor League Uniform Player Contract. However, if Player is not released during or at the end of the fourteen days' period, Club shall continue to be obligated to Player for compensation under the terms of subparagraph A of Paragraph VII to the conclusion of Club's championship playing season. or to such earlier date on which Club may give Player an unconditional release.

C. Club also shall pay all of Player's necessary and reasonable hospital and medical expenses incurred during the term of this Minor League Uniform Player Contract by reason of said disability, which expenses are not paid by workmen's compensation insurance or other surgical, medical or hospitalization insurance policy, for the number of days in the period of disability or 180 days, whichever is less. Club, however shall always have the right to select the physician or dentist to perform professional services to be rendered to Player as well as the place of delivery of said services, including hospital, offices or clinic, or to approve the person tendering such services or the place where such services are to be performed if selected by Player.

D.   The following conditions are expressly established as conditions precedent to Club's obligation to pay any of the salary provided for in subparagraphs A and B of this Paragraph Vlll, or to pay any of the medical or hospital expenses provided for in subparagraph C of this Paragraph VIII:

1.   Player's disability must have been a direct and proximate result of an injury sustained in the course and within the scope of Player's employment under this Minor League Uniform Player Contract; and

2.   Player must give Club written notice of the place, time, cause and nature of Player's injuries within five (5) days from the date of receiving such injuries or prior to the termination of this Minor League Uniform Player Contract, whichever is earlier. The failure of Player to give such notice shall not impair the rights of Player, as set forth herein, if Club has actual knowledge of such injury to Player; and

3.   Player, if requested by Club, must provide Club with written medical proof of Player's disability.

E.   Any workmen's compensation payments, or any surgical, medical or hospitalization insurance payments received by Player for the period for which Club is paying Player, as specified in this Paragraph VIII, shall be immediately paid by Player to Club. If Player fails or refuses to pay these monies to Club, Club shall deduct the same from any compensation due Player.

IX. Allowance

Club will provide Player during Club's training season and while Club is "abroad" with lodging (if Player is required to remain "abroad" overnight) and the meal allowance required by the MLR. If while "abroad" Club elects to require Player to remain "home" and he is on Club's Active or Disabled List, Club shall pay Player the meal allowance required by the MLR. No such meal allowance shall be due Player, however, if his permanent residence is located in the home city of Club or if Player returns to his permanent residence while Club is abroad. The terms "home" and "abroad" mean, respectively, at and away from the city in which Club has its home baseball park.

X. Transportation

Club will provide Player with the mode and class of transportation of its choice from "home" to "abroad" games and back. Player agrees to use the mode of transportation furnished by Club to and from all "abroad" games at all times. Club will provide Player return transportation to his home city at the conclusion of the championship playing season or playoffs, or if unconditionally released

prior thereto. Mode and class of transportation shall
be at the Club's discretion.

XI.   Uniform

Club will select and furnish Player with necessary
baseball uniforms, excluding shoes, but including all
numerals, emblems, logos or devices to be worn on
the uniform or affixed thereto. Additionally, Club
may, if it wishes to do so, provide shoes or other
personal equipment items or apparel, such as batting gloves or fielding gloves. Player shall wear
uniforms, personal equipment items and apparel as
furnished and shall not alter or disfigure them. At
the end of the championship playing season, or at
the end of any post-season series games, or upon
the assignment or other transfer of this Minor
League Uniform Player Contract, or upon the unconditional release of Player from this Minor
League Uniform Player Contract, or upon any direction by Club to perform services for a different
Club, Player immediately shall return to Club such
uniforms, personal equipment items, apparel and
any and all other property of Club in the possession
of Player. Player shall not wear or use any personal
equipment item, article of apparel or any other item
with or upon his uniform which is not approved by
Club, or which is not in accordance with the MLR.

XII.   Loyalty

Player agrees to serve Club diligently and faithfully, to keep himself in first-class condition, and to
observe and comply with all rules and regulations of

Club. Further, Player agrees to conform to high standards of personal conduct (before, during and after working hours), fair play and good sportsmanship.

XIII. Promotion of Baseball

In addition to the furnishings of professional baseball services to Club, Player agrees, beginning with the date that this Minor League Uniform Player Contract is executed, to cooperate with Club and to participate in any and all promotional activities of Club which, in the sole opinion of Club, will promote the welfare of Club or of professional baseball.

XIV. Pictures Of Player

Player agrees, beginning with the date that this Minor League Uniform Player Contract is executed, that current or future photographs, whether still or action, and motion pictures may be taken and any form of broadcasts or telecasts of Player, individually or with others, may be made at such times or places as Club may designate and agrees that all rights therein and all rights to Player's name, voice, signature, biographical information and likeness shall belong to Club and that they may be used, reproduced, sold, licensed, or otherwise disseminated or published by Club or its licensees, assignees, and/or other designees directly or indirectly in any medium whatsoever for any purpose (including but not limited to in broadcast, in print, on trading cards, posters and other merchandise of any kind, in electronics, in audio, in video or in connection with any media), in any manner and at any time, including after the term of this Minor League Uniform Player Contract, that Club desires. Player acknowledges that the foregoing rights include, without limitation, all related copyright, trademark, trade name, service mark, right of publicity and/or right of privacy rights. Club may exploit each of the rights granted to it by Player pursuant to this Paragraph XIV without additional payment or other compensation to Player. Player further agrees that during the term of this Minor League Uniform Player Contract he will not make public appearances, participate in radio or television programs, or on-line computer forums or any public conferences of any sort, permit his picture to be taken while in Club's uniform or a part thereof, sponsor or permit his name, voice, signature, biographical information and/or likeness to be used in conjunction with any commercial purpose, including but not limited to the sale, rental or advertising or promotion of products or services, or write or sponsor newspaper, magazine or any other article for publication, without the express prior written consent of Club.

XV.   Player's Representations

As a further inducement to Club to enter into this Minor League Uniform Player Contract, Player represents to Club as follows:

A.   Player has no physical or mental defects which would prevent or impair the performance of Player's skilled services as a professional baseball player for Club. Player is capable of and will perform his services and such other duties as may be required of him pursuant to this Minor League Uniform Player contract with expertness, diligence and fidelity.

B. Player does not own, directly or indirectly, stock or have any financial interest in the ownership or earnings of any Minor League Club or Major, League Club except as hereinafter expressly set forth, and covenants that he will not hereafter, while under this Minor League Uniform Player Contract, acquire or hold any such stock or interest.

C. Player has exceptional and unique skill and ability as a baseball player, and Player's services to be rendered to Club are of a special and extraordinary character which gives Player his peculiar value which cannot be reasonably or adequately compensated for in damages at law. Therefore, Player agrees that Player's breach of this Minor League Uniform Player Contract will cause Club great and irreparable injury and damage. Accordingly, Player agrees that, in addition to other remedies, Club shall be entitled to injunctive and other equitable relief to prevent a breach of this Minor League Player from playing professional baseball for any other person or organization during the term of this Minor League Uniform Player Contract.

D. Player is not a party to, and will not enter into, any contract or any contractual obligation to render skilled services as a professional baseball player with any person or organization other than

Club. Additionally, Player is not a party to, and will not enter into, any contract or any contractual obligation that conflicts with any of his obligations under this Minor League Uniform Player Contract or limits (as determined by the Club in the sole exercise of its discretion) the rights granted Club under this Minor League Uniform Player Contract or that impairs Club's ability to fully exercise such rights.

E.   Player's name, as set forth in this Minor League Uniform Player Contract, and of which his signature to this Minor League Uniform Player Contract consists, is his proper and legal name and is not a fictitious or assumed name.

F.   All personal information concerning Player in Addendum A is true and accurate.

G.   Player is eligible, in accordance with the MLR, to execute this Minor League Uniform Player Contract.

I.   Player represents and warrants that:

1.   he has the full authority to grant the rights contained in this Minor League Uniform Player Contract and to execute, deliver and perform the obligations under this Minor League Uniform Player Contract,

2.   the execution and delivery of this Minor League Uniform Player Contract will not conflict with or result in any breach of any agreement to which he is a part or by which he is bound, and

3. this Minor League Uniform Player Contract is duly executed and delivered by him.

XVI. Playing For Others

A. For the purpose of avoiding physical injuries, Player agrees that during the term of this Minor League Uniform Player Contract, Player will not play baseball other than for Club, without the written consent of the Club. If Club consents to Player's participation in a winter league, the terms and conditions of Player's employment during winter league play shall be governed by this Minor League Uniform Player Contract, except that Player and Club shall agree on the amount of monetary compensation for Player's participation in winter league play.

B. Player and Club agree and recognize that Player's participation in any other sport may impair or destroy Player's ability and skill as a professional baseball player. Accordingly, from and after the date of execution of this Minor League Uniform Player Contract, Player agrees that he shall not engage in automobile or motorcycle racing, hang gliding, fencing, parachuting, skydiving, boxing, wrestling, karate, judo, football, basketball, skiing, hockey, or any other sport or activity involving a substantial risk of personal injury. Player also agrees that, except with the written consent of Club, he will not participate in amateur, intramural, intercollegiate or professional athletics in any sport whatsoever.

XVII.   Physical Examination

A.   When requested by Club, Player shall submit to a complete physical, psychiatric, psychological and/or dental examination at the expense of Club, and, if necessary, to medical, surgical, psychiatric or dental treatment at Player's own expense, except as otherwise provided in this Minor League Uniform Player Contract. Upon the failure or refusal of Player to do so, Club may take such action against Player as it deems advisable in the manner agreed to between the parties and set forth at Paragraph XX.

B.   It is specifically provided, however, that if Player signed this Minor League Uniform Player Contract as a free agent (whether or not previously party to a Major League or Minor League Uniform Player Contract), within ninety days subsequent to the execution of this Minor League Uniform Player Contract by Player, Club may require Player to undergo a complete physical, psychiatric, psychological and/or dental examination by a physician and/or dentist of Club's choosing and at Club's expense. If such examination reveals the presence of any physical and/or dental defect, congenital or otherwise, which in the judgment of the physician or dentist would or might substantially impair Player's ability to play professional baseball and was present at the time of execution of this Minor League Uniform Player Contract by Player, Club may terminate this Minor League Uniform Player Contract without further payment to Player of any bonus, benefits or other compensation provided for in this Minor League Uniform Player Contract or any Special Covenants to this Minor League Uniform Player Contract. Such a termination, however, must be effected (including notification to the Commissioner's Office) within one hundred and five (105) days subsequent to the execution of this Minor League Uniform Player Contract by Player. In the event of a termination pursuant to this subparagraph B of Paragraph XVII, this Minor League Uniform Player Contract shall be void and of no force or effect between the Parties and Player shall repay any bonus, benefits or other compensation provided pursuant to any Special Covenants to this Minor League Uniform Player Contract.

XVIII.   Assignments, Transfers And Directions To Perform For Minor Or Major League Clubs

A.   Player specifically agrees and understands that this Minor League Uniform Player Contract may be freely assigned by Club, and re-assigned by any assignee Club, to any other Major League Club or Minor League Club.

B.   Upon assignment of this Minor League Uniform Player Contract, the assignee Club shall be liable to Player only for payments accruing from the date Player reports to the Club for which he is directed to perform by assignee Club. Assignor Club shall remain liable to Player for all payments accrued as of the date of the assignment. In addition, if Player reports to the Club for which he is directed to perform by assignee Club as soon as the mode of transportation authorized or furnished to player permits, assignor Club shall be liable to Player for the travel time required to reach the city to which Player is directed to report to join the Club for which he is directed to perform by assignee Club.

C. In the event this Minor League Uniform Player Contract is assigned, following his receipt of written or telegraphic notice of the assignment, Player shall report to the Club for which he is directed to perform by the assignee Club as soon as the mode of transportation authorized or furnished to Player permits. If Player fails or refuses to report as soon as the mode of transportation authorized or furnished to Player permits, Player shall not be entitled to any payment for the period from the date upon which he received written or telegraphic notice of the assignment to the date on which Player reports to the Club for which he is directed to perform by the assignee Club.

D. Player also specifically agrees and understands that this Minor League Uniform Player Contract (and the Club's exclusive rights to his services under this Minor League Uniform Player Contract) may be freely loaned, leased or otherwise transferred to any Minor League Club. In the event this Minor League Uniform Player Contract is loaned, leased, or otherwise transferred, following his receipt of written or telegraphic notice of the loan, lease or transfer, Player shall report to the Club to which this Minor League Uniform Player Contract is loaned, leased or otherwise transferred as soon as the mode of transportation authorized or furnished to Player permits. If Player fails or refuses to report as soon as the mode of transportation authorized or furnished to Player permits, Player shall not be entitled to any payment for the period from the date upon which he received written or telegraphic notice of the loan, lease or transfer to the date on which Player reports to the Club to which this Minor League Uniform Player Contract is loaned, leased or otherwise transferred.

E. Player also specifically agrees and understands that Club may freely direct him to perform services for any Major League or Minor League Club. Further, following his receipt of written or telegraphic notice of the direction to perform, Player specifically agrees and understands that his obligation under this Minor League Uniform Player Contract to perform services for the directed Club shall be the same as his obligation to perform services for Club under this Minor League Uniform Player Contract. If Club directs Player to perform services for a Club, Player agrees to report to the Club as soon as the mode of travel authorized or provided permits, and to perform all services for such Club in a diligent and faithful manner. If Player fails or refuses to report as soon as the mode of transportation authorized or furnished to Player permits, Player shall not be entitled to any payment for the period from the date upon which he received written or telegraphic notice of the direction to perform to the date on which Player reports to the directed Club.

F.   Player agrees that he will execute the standard form Major League Uniform Player Contract then in effect in the Major Leagues if Player is placed (following an assignment, direction to perform or otherwise) on a Major League roster, Major League under control list or Major League Reserve List at any point during the term of this Minor League Uniform Player Contract.

G.   If Player agrees, this Minor League Uniform Player Contract may be assigned, loaned, leased or otherwise transferred to (or Player directed to perform for) a Minor League Club or other professional baseball club participating in winter league play. The terms and conditions of Player's employment during winter league play shall be as stated in Subparagraph A of Paragraph XVI.

XIX.   Termination

A.   If Club is in arrears to Player for any payments due Player under this Minor League Uniform Player Contract for more than fifteen (15) days, or if Club fails for more than fifteen (15) days to perform any other obligations agreed or required to be performed by Club, Player shall be entitled to apply to the Commissioner to terminate this Minor League Uniform Player Contract. Thereafter, if Club fails to remedy the default as to the payment or other obligation within such time as the Commissioner may fix, the Commissioner shall terminate this Minor League Uniform Player Contract by a declaration of Player's free agency. It is specifically provided, however, that Club shall remain liable to Player for all payments due him as of the date of the termination of this Minor League Uniform Player Contract and the declaration of Player's free agency.

B. Club may terminate this Minor League Uniform Player Contract upon the delivery of written or telegraphic notice to Player if Player at any time shall:

1. Fail, refuse or neglect to conform Player's personal conduct to high standards of good citizenship and good sportsmanship;

2. Fail, refuse or neglect to keep himself in first-class physical condition;

3. Fail, refuse or neglect to obey Club's requirements respecting Player's conduct and service;

4. Fail in the judgment of Club to exhibit sufficient skill or competitive ability to qualify or to continue as a professional baseball player as a member of Club's team; or

5. Fail, refuse or neglect to render Player's services hereunder, or in any other manner to materially breach this Minor League Uniform Player Contract.

C. If Player becomes disabled, Club may also terminate this Minor League Uniform Player Contract in accordance with Paragraph VIII above.

XX. Disputes

A. For the violation by Player of any of the obligations or duties of Player as set forth in this Minor League Uniform Player Contract, or for the violation by Player of any of Club's rules or regulations, Player agrees that Club may impose a reasonable fine upon Player and deduct the amount thereof from Player's compensation, or may suspend Player without compensation, or both. Player also agrees that Club may place him on any disciplinary list or lists prescribed by the MLR or any other applicable Major League or Minor League rules.

B. In the event of any dispute or claim between Player and Club arising under any of the provisions of this Minor League Uniform Player Contract, the decision of Club regarding the dispute or claim shall be subject exclusively to Player's rights of appeal to the Commissioner which Player may exercise by filing a written, itemized and detailed appeal form with the Commissioner within 120 days of the maturity of the claim. The decision of the Commissioner shall be final and binding and the Player agrees and understands that the decision of the Commissioner may not be challenged in any federal or state court or any other tribunal.

C. Player specifically consents that either Club or the Commissioner may make known to the public the findings, decisions or record of any inquiry, investigation or hearing, including all evidence, information or testimony given, received, obtained or elicited as the result of any such inquiry, investigation or hearing.

XXI. Contingent Bonus

A. Any Special Covenants to this Minor League Uniform Player Contract which entitle Player to receive bonus payments if he is retained by Club on a designated date or for a designated period shall be subject to the following: In the event Player is placed on the Restricted, Voluntarily Retired, Military, Disqualified or Ineligible List prior to the date upon which the bonus payment becomes due and payable to Player, payment of the bonus shall be suspended by Club until Player is reinstated to an Active List and reports to and is retained by Club for the number of days required by this Minor League Uniform Player Contract, including any special covenants.

B. In the event the official date of placement on any of the lists enumerated in subparagraph A of this Paragraph XXI is later than the date Player ceased to be an active Player, the earlier date shall apply in determining the new date for payment of the Contingent Bonus following Player's reinstatement to an Active List of Club.

XXII. Special Covenants

If Player is to receive or has received any additional payment whatsoever from Club or from any other source in connection with this Minor League Uniform Player Contract, it must be fully described on Addendum B, giving name of payor, amount and nature of payment, when paid or to be paid, et cetera.

XXIII.   Legislation And Suspension

This Minor League Uniform Player Contract is subject to federal and state legislation, regulations, executive or other official orders and other governmental action, now or hereafter in effect, which may affect directly or indirectly Player or Club. Additionally, this Minor League Uniform Player Contract is subject to the authority of the Commissioner to suspend the operation of this Minor League Uniform Player Contract, including the payment of compensation to Player, during any national emergency or any cessation or suspension of play in the Major Leagues. In the event that this Minor League Uniform Player Contract is suspended pursuant to the terms of this paragraph, it is specifically agreed between Player and Club that the compensation provisions of Paragraph VII shall be modified and the compensation paid to Player at the monthly rate set forth in Paragraph VII shall be paid only for the portion of the championship playing season actually played by Player. Moreover, in the event that this Minor League Uniform Player Contract is suspended pursuant to the terms of this Paragraph XXIII, it is also specifically agreed between Player and Club that the Club's exclusive right to the Player's services shall remain in effect and that this Minor League Uniform Player Contract shall continue in full force and effect for the remainder of its term once the suspension ends.

XXIV.   Entire Agreement

Club and Player covenant that this Minor League Uniform Player Contract fully sets forth all understanding and agreements by and between them and agree that no understandings or agreements, whether heretofore or hereafter made, shall be valid, recognized, or of any effect whatsoever, unless and until they are set forth in a subsequent Minor League Uniform Player Contract executed by Player and Club, filed with and approved by the Commissioner of Baseball and complying with the MLR.

XXV.   Governing Law

This Minor League Uniform Player Contract shall be governed by and interpreted in such a manner as to be effective and valid under New York law. However, if any provisions of this Minor League Uniform Player Contract shall be prohibited by or invalid under applicable law, such provision shall be ineffective to the extent of such prohibition or invalidation only, without invalidating the remainder of such provisions or the remaining provisions of this Minor League Uniform Player Contract.

XXVI.   Approval Required

This is the only Minor League Uniform Player Contract form prescribed by the MLR. No different form shall be used and no clause shall be added or eliminated without the specific written approval of the Commissioner. Any written or oral agreement between Player and Club not contained in this Minor League Uniform Player Contract shall subject both parties to discipline. No such agreement shall be recognized or enforced by the Commissioner. This Minor League Uniform Player Contract, including any addenda or attachments, shall not be valid, recognized or enforced unless filed with and approved by the Commissioner.

XXVII. Player Information and Notices

Player will immediately provide Club and any Club to which this Minor League Uniform Player Contract is assigned, loaned or leased (and any Club for which Player is directed to perform services) with his current home address and telephone number, and will keep such information current. Any written notice required to be given by the Club to the Player under this Minor League Uniform Player Contract may be accomplished, at Club's option, by sending the notice via registered mail to the Player's last known address and/or by physically delivering the notice to the Player. The effective date of any written notice shall be the date on which the notice is mailed or physically delivered, whichever is earlier. The effective date of any telegraphic notice by the Club to the Player will be the date on which the telegram is sent.

This Minor League Uniform Player Contract must be received at the Commissioner's Office within 20 days from the date SIGNED by Player. Player must sign NAME, including all INITIALS, and must DATE in OWN HANDWRITING on Addendum A. Player's social security number, date of birth, street address, city, state, country, zip code and telephone number must be included. If Player has not previously signed a professional contract, Player's position, height, weight, batting hand, throwing hand, high school, high school graduation date, college, college graduation date and place of birth must be included.

ASSIGNMENTS OF THIS MINOR LEAGUE
UNIFORM PLAYER CONTRACT

1. On _____, this contract was assigned from
        (Date)

_____ to _____
        (Assignor Club)   (Assignee Club)

2. On _____, this contract was assigned from
        (Date)

_____ to _____
        (Assignor Club)   (Assignee Club)

3. On _____, this contract was assigned from
        (Date)

_____ to _____
        (Assignor Club)   (Assignee Club)

4. On _____, this contract was assigned from
        (Date)

_____ to _____
        (Assignor Club)   (Assignee Club)

ADDENDUM A

1. Player's
   Information:

Name	(First)	(Middle)	(Last)

   Street Address

City	State	Country	Zip

   Social Security No.   Telephone No.   Date of Birth

2. Club's Name: _____

3. First championship playing season covered by this Minor League Uniform Contract: 19__

4. Execution Date of this Minor League Uniform Player Contract: _____
   Month/Day/Year

5. Pursuant to subparagraph E of Paragraph XVIII, and subject to change at any time, Club initially directs Player to perform for the _____ Club of the _____ League.

STATUS OF PLAYER

First Minor League Contract	Previous Contract
□ Non-drafted Amateur Free Agent	□ Assigned from Major League Club
□ Summer Free Agent Draftee	□ Completed Previous Minor League Contract
Draft: Year___ Round____	□ Released/Nontendered Player
Selection Overall: Sel. No.___	
	□ Major League Re-entry Free Agent
	□ Other (explain)

PLAYER INFORMATION (MUST BE COMPLETED FOR FIRST MINOR LEAGUE CONTRACTS)

POS_____HGT_____WGT_____BATS_____THROWS_____

HIGH SCHOOL_____ _____ GRAD DATE _____
                                    STATE   (M/Y)

COLLEGE_____ _____ GRAD DATE _____
                                    STATE   (M/Y)

PLACE OF
BIRTH_____
    (City)   (State)   (Country)

CONTRACT TERM
(FOR PREVIOUSLY-SIGNED PLAYERS ONLY)

If Player has previously signed a Minor League or Major League contract, this Minor League Uniform Player Contract shall be, consistent with the MLR, for the term set forth below:

1 2 3 4 5 6 7 (circle one)_____(write out) championship playing seasons.

EXECUTION OF THIS CONTRACT

By affixing their signatures below, Player and Club indicate their understanding of, and agreement to, all of the provisions of this Minor League Uniform Player Contract, including pages one through six, Addendum A, Addendum B, Addendum C-1, and any other attachments.

CLUB DATE AND SIGN HERE

AS TO CLUB:_____   By:_____

            Date   Authorized Club Representative
                                         Signature

                                         Title:_____

PLAYER DATE AND SIGN HERE

AS TO PLAYER:_____   _____

              Date   Player's Signature

PARENTS OR GUARDIAN CONSENT

Irrevocable consent is given to the performance and execution of this Minor League Uniform Player Contract (including all Addenda and attachments) by the minor Player party hereto. Such consent shall be effective as to all provisions, including (but not limited to) any assignment, loan, lease or direction to perform under Paragraph XVIII hereof, and any compensation and any restrictions thereon that are hereinafter negotiated or set by the Club pursuant to Paragraph VII hereof. Consent is irrevocably given for the duration of this contract to the payment of all earnings, bonuses and other consideration personally to the minor Player party. Player's parents or guardian further agree to hold Club harmless for any injury suffered by Player during the term of this Minor League Uniform Player Contract. These consents and promise to hold harmless are expressly given as an inducement to enter into this contract.

_____   _____
Date   Signature of Father-Mother-Guardian(circle one)

_____   _____
Date   Signature of Father-Mother-Guardian(circle one)

FOR   Approved and recorded:
COMMISSIONER'S
OFFICE USE ONLY Date:_____ By:_____
                                                             Commissioner of Baseball

ADDENDUM B

Special Covenants: In accordance with Paragraph XXII of this Minor League Uniform Player Contract, all additional payments or consideration whatsoever that Player is to receive or has received from Club or from any other source in connection with this Minor League Uniform Player Contract are fully described below:

ADDENDUM C

In accordance with Paragraph VII of the Minor League Uniform Player Contract to which the undersigned Player is a party, Player's monthly salary rate during the 19___

championship playing season shall be $_____/month
(_____ dollars per month.)

If a Player and Club have agreed on a different monthly salary rate if Player is on the Active or Disabled List of a Club in a particular classification, that monthly salary rate, classification and any restrictions, contingencies, minimum service requirements, and other agreements concerning salary are fully set out below:

_____	_____
Player's Name (print or type)	Club's Name (print of type)
_____	_____
Player's Signature	Club Representative's Name/Position
_____	_____
Street Address	Club Representative's Signature
_____	_____
City State Country Zip	Date
_____	
Telephone No.	
_____	
Social Security No.	
_____	
Date	

FOR COMMISSIONER'S OFFICE USE ONLY
Date: _____

Approved and recorded:

By: _____
Commissioner of Baseball

ADDENDUM C

In accordance with Paragraph VII of the Minor League Uniform Player Contract to which the undersigned Player is a party, Player's monthly salary rate during the 19__ championship playing season shall be:

CLASSIFICA-TION OR SUBCLASSIFI-CATION	**MONTHLY SALARY**	**EXAMPLE OF CLUB**

If Player is on the Active or Disabled Lists of Clubs in more than one subclassification or classification during the same pay period and is entitled to different salary rates for the different subclassifications or classifications, his salary shall be prorated in accordance with his number of days of employment in each subclassification or classification compared to the number of days in that pay period. All other restrictions, contingencies, minimum service requirements, and other agreements concerning salary are fully set out below:

Player's Name (print or type)

Club's Name (print of type)

Player's Signature

Club Representative's Name/Position

Street Address

Club Representative's Signature

City State Country Zip

Date

Telephone No.

Date

Soc. Security No.

FOR COMMISSIONER'S OFFICE USE ONLY

Approved and recorded:
Date: _____

By: _____
Commissioner of Baseball

ADDENDUM D

In accordance with subparagraph A of Paragraph XVI and subparagraph G of Paragraph XVIII and all other terms of the Minor League Uniform Player Contract to which the undersigned Player is a party, Player's monthly salary rate during the 19__ championship playing season of the _____ League shall be $_____/month (_____ dollars per month).

_____

Team Player has agreed to perform for

_____

Team Representative's Name/Position

_____	_____
Player's Name (print or type)	Major League Club's Name (print or type)
_____	_____
Player's Signature	Major League Club Representative's Name/ Position (print or type)
_____	_____
Parent or Guardian Signature (if Player is a minor)	Major League Club Representative's Signature
_____	_____
Date	Date
FOR COMMISSIONER'S OFFICE USE ONLY	Approved and recorded:

Date: _____
By: _____
Commissioner of Baseball |

ATTACHMENT 12

NOTICE TO PLAYER OF
RELEASE OR TRANSFER

(National) (American) League _____, 19_____

To Mr. _____

You are hereby notified as follows:

1.   That you are unconditionally released.

2.   That your contract has been assigned to the _____

_____ Club of _____ League.

(a)   Without right of recall.

(b)   With right of recall.

(Cross out parts not applicable. In case of optional agreement, specify all conditions affecting player.)

_____

Corporate Name of Club

_____

President

A copy must be delivered to the player and must also be forwarded to the President of the League of which Club is a member and to the Commissioner.

THE FOLLOWING INSTRUCTIONS are given for the guidance of Club officials executing this form:

(1) If the player is unconditionally released, cross out all of paragraph 2, including subparagraphs (a) and (b).

(2) If the player is transferred outright to another Club, insert the name of that Club and of that Club's League in paragraph 2, and cross out the following:

(i) paragraph I; and

(i) subparagraph (b) of paragraph 2.

(3) If the player is transferred by an optional agreement to another Club, insert the name of that Club and that Club's League in paragraph 2, and cross out the following:

(i) paragraph I; and

(i) subparagraph (a) of paragraph 2.

Also specify all conditions affecting the player (date recall option is to be exercised, etc.).

NFL PLAYER CONTRACT

THIS CONTRACT is between _____, hereinafter "Player," and
_____, a _____

____ corporation (limited partnership) (partnership), hereinafter "Club" operating under the name of the _____

_____ as a member of the National Football League, hereinafter "League." In consideration of the promises

made by each to the other, Player and Club agree as follows:

1. TERM. This contract covers _____ football season(s), and will begin on the date of execution or March 1, _____, whichever is later, and end on February 28 or 29, _____, unless extended, terminated, or renewed as specified elsewhere in this contract.

2. EMPLOYMENT AND SERVICES. Club employs Player as a skilled football player. Player accepts such employment. He agrees to give his best efforts and loyalty to the Club, and to conduct himself on and off the field with appropriate recognition of the fact that the success of professional football depends largely on public respect for and approval of those associated with the game. Player will report promptly for and participate fully in Club's official mandatory mini-camp(s), official preseason training camp, all Club meetings and practice sessions, and all pre-season, regular season, and post-season football games scheduled for or by Club. If invited, Player will practice for and play in any all-star football game sponsored by the League. Player will not participate in any football game not sponsored by the League unless the game is first approved by the League.

3. OTHER ACTIVITIES. Without prior written consent of the Club, Player will not play football or engage in activities related to football otherwise than for Club or engage in any activity other than football which may involve a significant risk of personal injury. Player represents that he has special, exceptional and unique knowledge, skill, ability, and experience as a football player, the loss of which cannot be estimated with any certainty and cannot be fairly or adequately compensated by damages. Player therefore agrees that Club will have the right, in addition to any other right which Club may possess, to enjoin Player by appropriate proceedings from playing football or engaging in football-related activities other than for Club or from engaging in any activity other than football which may involve a significant risk of personal injury.

4. PUBLICITY AND NFLPA GROUP LICENSING PROGRAM. (a) Player grants to Club and the League, separately and together, the authority to use his name and picture for publicity and the promotion of NFL Football, the League or any of its member clubs in newspapers, magazines, motion pictures, game programs and roster manuals, broadcasts and telecasts, and all other publicity and advertising media, provided such publicity and promotion does not constitute an endorsement by Player of a commercial product. Player will cooperate with the news media, and will participate upon request in reasonable activities to promote the Club and the League. Player and National Football League Players Association, hereinafter "NFLPA," will not contest the rights of the League and its member clubs to telecast, broadcast, or otherwise transmit NFL Football or the right of NFL Films to produce, sell, market, or distribute football game film footage, except insofar as such broadcast, telecast, or transmission of footage is used in any commercially marketable game or interactive use. The League and its member clubs, and Player and the NFLPA, reserve their respective rights as to the use of such broadcasts, telecasts or transmissions of footage in such games or interactive uses, which shall be unaffected by this subparagraph.

(b) Player hereby assigns to the NFLPA and its licensing affiliates, if any, the exclusive right to use and to grant to persons, firms, or corporations (collectively "licensees") the right to use his name, signature facsimile, voice, picture, photograph, likeness, and/or biographical information (collectively "image") in group licensing programs. Group licensing programs are defined as those licensing programs in which a licensee utilizes a total of six (6) or more NFL player images on products that are sold at retail or used as promotional or premium items. Player retains the right to grant permission to a licensee to utilize his image if that licensee is not concurrently utilizing the images of five (5) or more other NFL players on products that are sold at retail or are used as promotional or premium items. If Player's inclusion in a particular NFLPA program is precluded by an individual exclusive endorsement agreement, and Player provides the NFLPA with timely written notice of that preclusion, the NFLPA will exclude Player from that particular program. In consideration for this assignment of rights, the NFLPA will use the revenues it receives from group licensing programs to support the objectives as set forth in the By-laws of the NFLPA. The NFLPA will use its best efforts to promote the use of NFL player images in group licensing programs, to provide group licensing opportunities to all NFL players, and to ensure that no entity utilizes the group licensing rights granted to the NFLPA without first obtaining a license from the NFLPA. This paragraph shall be construed under New York law without reference to conflicts of law principles. The assignment in this paragraph shall expire on December 31 of the later of (a) the third year following the execution of this contract, or (b) the year in which this contract expires. Neither Club nor the League is a party to the terms of this paragraph, which is included herein solely for the administrative convenience and benefit of Player and the NFLPA. The terms of this subparagraph apply unless, at the time of execution of this contract, Player indicates by striking out this subparagraph (b) and marking his initials adjacent to the stricken language his intention not to participate in the NFLPA Group Licensing Program. Nothing in this subparagraph shall be construed to supersede or any way broaden, expand, detract from, or otherwise alter in any way whatsoever, the rights of NFL Properties, Inc. as permitted under Article V (Union Security), Section 4 of the 1993 Collective Bargaining Agreement.

5. COMPENSATION. For performance of Player's services and all other promises of Player, Club will pay Player a yearly salary as follows:

$_____ for the 19____ season;

$_____ for the 19____ season;

$_____ for the 19____ season;

$_____ for the 19____ season;

$_____ for the 19____ season.

In addition, Club will pay Player such earned performance bonuses as may be called for in this contract; Player's necessary traveling expenses from his residence to training camp; Player's reasonable board and lodging expenses during pre-season training and in connection with playing pre-season, regular season, and post-season football games outside Club's home city; Player's necessary traveling expenses to and from pre-season, regular season, and post-season football games outside Club's home city; Player's necessary traveling expenses to his residence if this contract is terminated by Club; and such additional compensation, benefits, and reimbursement of expenses as may be called for in any collective bargaining agreement in existence during the term of this contract. (For purposes of this contract, a collective bargaining agreement will be deemed to be "in existence" during its stated term or during any period for which the parties to that agreement agree to extend it.)

6. PAYMENT. Unless this contract or any collective bargaining agreement in existence during the term of this contract specifically provides otherwise, Player will be paid 100% of his yearly salary under this contract in equal weekly or bi-weekly installments over the course of the applicable regular season period, commencing with the first regular season game played by Club in each season. Unless this contract specifically provides otherwise, if this contract is executed or Player is activated after the beginning of the regular season, the yearly salary payable to Player will be reduced proportionately and Player will be paid the weekly or bi-weekly portions of his yearly salary becoming due and payable after he is activated. Unless this contract specifically provides otherwise, if this contract is terminated after the beginning of the regular season, the yearly salary payable to Player will be reduced proportionately and Player will be paid the weekly or bi-weekly portions of his yearly salary having become due and payable up to the time of termination.

7. DEDUCTIONS. Any advance made to Player will be repaid to Club, and any properly levied Club fine or Commissioner fine against Player will be paid, in cash on demand or by means of deductions from payments coming due to the Player under this contract, the amount of such deductions to be determined by Club unless this contract or any collective bargaining agreement in existence during the term of this contract specifically provides otherwise.

8. PHYSICAL CONDITION. Player represents to Club that he is and will maintain himself in excellent physical condition. Player will undergo a complete physical examination by the Club physician upon Club request, during which physical examination Player agrees to make full and complete disclosure of any physical or mental condition known to him which might impair his performance under this contract and to respond fully and in good faith when questioned by the Club physician about such condition. If Player fails to establish or maintain his excellent physical condition to the satisfaction of the Club physician, or make the required full and complete disclosure and good faith responses to the Club physician, then Club may terminate this contract.

9. INJURY. Unless this contract specifically provides otherwise, if Player is injured in the performance of his services under this contract and promptly reports such injury to the Club physician or trainer, then Player will receive such medical and hospital care during the term of this contract as the Club physician may deem necessary, and will continue to receive his yearly salary for so long, during the season of injury only and for no subsequent period covered by this contract, as Player is physically unable to perform the services required of him by this contract because of such injury. If Player's injury in the performance of his services under this contract results in his death, the unpaid balance of his yearly salary for the season of injury will be paid to his stated beneficiary, or in the absence of a stated beneficiary, to his estate.

10. WORKERS' COMPENSATION. Any compensation paid to Player under this contract or under any collective bargaining agreement in existence during the term of this contract for a period during which he is entitled to workers' compensation benefits by reason of temporary total, permanent total, temporary partial, or permanent partial disability will be deemed an advance payment of workers' compensation benefits due Player, and Club will be entitled to be reimbursed the amount of such payment out of any award of workers' compensation.

11. SKILL, PERFORMANCE AND CONDUCT. Player understands that he is competing with other players for a position on Club's roster within the applicable player limits. If at any time, in the sole judgement of Club, Player's skill or performance has been unsatisfactory as compared with that of other players competing for positions on Club's roster, or if Player has engaged in personal conduct reasonably judged by Club to adversely affect or reflect on Club, then Club may terminate this contract. In addition, during the period any salary cap is legally in effect, this contract may be terminated if, in Club's opinion, Player is anticipated to make less of a contribution to Club's ability to compete on the playing field than another player or players who Club intends to sign or attempts to sign, or another player or players who is or are already on Club's roster, and for whom Club needs room.

12. TERMINATION. The rights of termination set forth in this contract will be in addition to any other rights of termination allowed either party by law. Termination will be effective upon the giving of written notice, except that Player's death, other than as a result of injury incurred in the performance of his services under this contract, will automatically terminate this contract. If this contract is terminated by Club and either Player or Club so requests, Player will promptly undergo a complete physical examination by the Club physician.

13. INJURY GRIEVANCE. Unless a collective bargaining agreement in existence at the time of termination of this contract by Club provides otherwise, the following injury grievance procedure will apply: If Player believes that at the time of termination of this contract by Club he was physically unable to perform the services required of him by this contract because of an injury incurred in the performance of his services under this contract, Player may, within 60 days after examination by the Club physician, submit at his own expense to examination by a physician of his choice. If the opinion of Player's physician with respect to his physical ability to perform the services required of him by this contract is contrary to that of the Club's physician, the dispute will be submitted within a reasonable time to final and binding arbitration by an arbitrator selected by Club and Player or, if they are unable to agree, one selected in accordance with the procedures of the American Arbitration Association on application by either party.

14. RULES. Player will comply with and be bound by all reasonable Club rules and regulations in effect during the term of this contract which are not inconsistent with the provisions of this contract or of any collective bargaining agreement in existence during the term of this contract. Player's attention is also called to the fact that the League functions with certain rules and procedures expressive of its operation as a joint venture among its member clubs and that these rules and practices may affect Player's relationship to the League and its member clubs independently of the provisions of this contract.

15. INTEGRITY OF GAME. Player recognizes the detriment to the League and professional football that would result from impairment of public confidence in the honest and orderly conduct of NFL games or the integrity and good character of NFL players. Player therefore acknowledges his awareness that if he accepts a bribe or agrees to throw or fix an NFL game; fails to promptly report a bribe offer or an attempt to throw or fix an NFL game; bets on an NFL game; knowingly associates with gamblers or gambling activity; uses or provides other players with stimulants or other drugs for the purpose of attempting to enhance on-field performance; or is guilty of any other form of conduct reasonably judged by the League Commissioner to be detrimental to the League or professional football, the Commissioner will have the right, but only after giving Player the opportunity for a hearing at which he may be represented by counsel of his choice, to fine Player in a reasonable amount; to suspend Player for a period certain or indefinitely; and/or to terminate this contract.

16. EXTENSION. Unless this contract specifically provides otherwise, if Player becomes a member of the Armed Forces of the United States or any other country, or retires from professional football as an active player, or otherwise fails or refuses to perform his services under this contract, then this contract will be tolled between the date of Player's induction into the Armed Forces, or his retirement, or his failure or refusal to perform, and the later date of his return to professional football. During the period this contract is tolled, Player will not be entitled to any compensation or benefits. On Player's return to professional football, the term of this contract will be extended for a period of time equal to the number of seasons (to the nearest multiple of one) remaining at the time the contract was tolled. The right of renewal, if any, contained in this contract will remain in effect until the end of any such extended term.

17. ASSIGNMENT. Unless this contract specifically provides otherwise, Club may assign this contract and Player's services under this contract to any successor to Club's franchise or to any other Club in the League. Player will report to the assignee Club promptly upon being informed of the assignment of his contract and will faithfully perform his services under this contract. The assignee club will pay Player's necessary traveling expenses in reporting to it and will faithfully perform this contract with Player.

18. FILING. This contract will be valid and binding upon Player and Club immediately upon execution. A copy of this contract, including any attachment to it, will be filed by Club with the League Commissioner within 10 days after execution. The Commissioner will have the right to disapprove this contract on reasonable grounds, including but not limited to an attempt by the parties to abridge or impair the rights of any other club, uncertainty or incompleteness in expression of the parties' respective rights and obligations, or conflict between the terms of this contract and any collective bargaining agreement then in existence. Approval will be automatic unless, within 10 days after receipt of this contract in his office, the Commissioner notifies the parties either of disapproval or of extension of this 10-day period for purposes of investigation or clarification pending his decision. On the receipt of notice of disapproval and termination, both parties will be relieved of their respective rights and obligations under this contract.

19. DISPUTES. During the term of any collective bargaining agreement, any dispute between Player and Club involving the interpretation or application of any provision of this contract will be submitted to final and binding arbitration in accordance with the procedure called for in any collective bargaining agreement in existence at the time the event giving rise to any such dispute occurs.

20. NOTICE. Any notice, request, approval or consent under this contract will be sufficiently given if in writing and delivered in person or mailed (certified or first class) by one party to the other at the address set forth in this contract or to such other address as the recipient may subsequently have furnished in writing to the sender.

21. OTHER AGREEMENTS. This contract, including any attachment to it, sets forth the entire agreement between Player and Club and cannot be modified or supplemented orally. Player and Club represent that no other agreement, oral or written, except as attached to or specifically incorporated in this contract, exists between them. The provisions of this contract will govern the relationship between Player and Club unless there are conflicting provisions in any collective bargaining agreement in existence during the term of this contract, in which case the provisions of the collective bargaining agreement will take precedence over conflicting provisions of this contract relating to the rights or obligations of either party.

22. LAW. This contract is made under and shall be governed by the laws of the State of _____.

23. WAIVER AND RELEASE. Player waives and releases any claims that he may have arising out of, related to, or asserted in the lawsuit entitled White v. National Football League, including, but not limited to, any such claim regarding past NFL Rules, the College Draft, Plan B, the first refusal/compensation system, the NFL Player Contract, pre-season compensation, or any other term or condition of employment, except any claims asserted in Brown v. Pro Football, Inc. This waiver and release also extends to any conduct engaged in pursuant to the Stipulation and Settlement Agreement in White ("Settlement Agreement") during the express term of that Settlement Agreement or any portion thereof. This waiver and release shall not limit any rights Player may have to performance by the Club under this Contract or Player's rights as a member of the White class to object to the Settlement Agreement during its review by the court in Minnesota. This waiver and release is subject to Article XIV (NFL Player Contract), Section 3(c) of the 1993 Collective Bargaining Agreement (CBA).

24. OTHER PROVISIONS. (a) Each of the undersigned hereby confirms that (i) this Contract, renegotiation, extension or amendment sets forth all components of the player's remuneration for playing professional football (whether such compensation is being furnished directly by the Club or by a related or affiliated entity); and (ii) there are not undisclosed agreements of any kind, whether expressed or implied, oral or written, and there are no promises, undertakings, representations, commitments, inducements, assurances of intent, or understandings of any kind that have not been disclosed to the NFL involving consideration of any kind to be paid, furnished or made available to Player or any entity or person owned or controlled by, affiliated with, or related to Player, either during the term of this contract or thereafter.

(b) Each of the undersigned further confirms that, except insofar as any of the undersigned may describe in an addendum to this contract, to the best of their knowledge, no conduct in violation of the Anti-Collusion rules of the Settlement Agreement took place with respect to this contract. Each of the undersigned further confirms that nothing in this contract is designed or intended to defeat or circumvent any provisions of the Stipulation and Settlement Agreement in White v. NFL, including but not limited to the Rookie Pool and Salary Cap provisions; however, any conduct permitted by the CBA and/or the Settlement Agreement shall not be considered a violation of this confirmation.

(c) The Club further confirms that any information regarding the negotiation of this contract that it provided to the Neutral Verifier was, at the time the information was provided, true and correct in all material respects.

25. SPECIAL PROVISIONS.

THIS CONTRACT is executed in six (6) copies. Player acknowledges that before signing this contract he was given the opportunity to seek advice from or be represented by persons of his own selection.

PLAYER	CLUB
Home Address	By
	Club Address
Telephone Number	
Date	Date

PLAYER'S CERTIFIED AGENT

Address

Telephone number

Date

Copy Distribution: White–League Office   Yellow–Player   Green–Member Club
                        Blue–Management Council   Gold–NFLPA   Pink–Player Agent

Excerpts from the

NFL
Collective
Bargaining
Agreement
1993-2003

COLLECTIVE BARGAINING AGREEMENT
BETWEEN
THE NFL MANAGEMENT COUNCIL
AND
THE NFL PLAYERS ASSOCIATION
As Amended June 6, 1996

ARTICLE XXIV GUARANTEED LEAGUE– WIDE SALARY, SALARY CAP & MINIMUM TEAM SALARY

Section 1. Definitions: For purposes of this Article, and anywhere else specifically stated in this Agreement, the following terms shall have the meanings set forth below:

(a) **Defined Gross Revenues**.

(i) "Defined Gross Revenues" (also referred to as "DGR7) means the aggregate revenues received or to be received on an accrual basis, for or with respect to a League Year during the term of this Agreement, by the NFL and all NFL Teams (and their designees), from all sources, whether known or unknown, derived from, relating to or arising out of the performance of players in NFL football games, with only the specific exceptions set forth below. The NFL and each NFL Team shall in good faith act and use their best efforts, consistent with sound business judgement, so as to maximize Defined Gross Revenues for each playing season during the term of this Agreement. Defined Gross Revenues shall include, without limitation:

(1) Regular season, pre-season, and post-season gate receipts (net of admission taxes, and surcharges paid to stadium or municipal authorities which are deducted for purposes of calculating gate receipts subject to revenue sharing), including ticket revenue from "luxury boxes," suites and premium seating subject to gate receipt sharing among NFL Teams; and

(2) Proceeds including Copyright Royalty Tribunal and extended market payments from the sale, license or other conveyance of the light to broadcast or exhibit NFL pre-season, regular season and play-off games on radio and television including, without limitation, network, local, cable, pay television, satellite encryption, international broadcasts, delayed broadcasts (which shall not include any broadcast of an NFL pre-season, regular season or play-off game occurring more than 72 hours after the live exhibition of the game, unless the broadcast is the first broadcast in the market), and all other means of distribution, net of any reasonable and customary NFL expenses related to the project; and

(3) Proceeds from the sale or conveyance of any right to receive any of the revenues described above.

(ii) The following is a nonexclusive list of examples of revenues received by the NFL and/or NFL Teams which are not derived from, and do not relate to or arise out of the performance of players in NFL football games (and are therefore not "DGR"): proceeds from the assignment, sale or trade of Player Contracts, proceeds from the sale of any existing NFL franchise (or any interest therein) or the grant of NFL expansion franchises, dues or capital contributions received by the NFL, fines, "revenue sharing" among NFL Teams, interest income, insurance recoveries, and sales of interests in real estate and other property.

(iii) Notwithstanding subsection 1(a)(i) above, the following shall be considered "Excluded DGR" and not included in Defined Gross Revenues: revenues derived from concessions, parking, local advertising and promotion, signage, magazine advertising, local sponsorship agreements, stadium clubs, luxury box income other than that included in subsection 1(a)(i)(1) above, sales of programs and novelties, and any categories of revenue (other than those listed in subsections 1(a)(i)(1)–(3) above) currently included under NFL Films and NFL Properties, Inc. and its subsidiaries.

(iv) In calculating Defined Gross Revenues, the amount of Excluded DGR divided by the sum of Excluded DGR plus DGR from all sources except network television revenues shall not exceed the percentage resulting from dividing 1992 Excluded DGR by the sum of 1992 Excluded DGR plus 1992 DGR from all sources except network television revenues. In the event Excluded DGR for any season exceeds the percentage resulting from the above calculation, any excess Excluded DGR shall be included in DGR. For purposes of the calculations described in this subsection (iv), Excluded DGR shall not include any revenues referred to in subsection l(a)(ii).

(v) Notwithstanding the provisions of subsection 1(a)(i)(2) above, for the purposes of calculating Defined Gross Revenues for the 1993 League Year only, revenues derived from national network television shall be deemed to be $35 million per NFL Team. Any actual amounts received in excess of that amount shall be included pro rata in DGR for the 1994 and 1995 seasons.

(vi) It is acknowledged by the parties hereto that for purposes of determining Defined Gross Revenues:

(1) NFL Teams may, during the term of this Agreement, be owned and controlled by persons or entities that will receive revenues for a grant of rights encompassing both (a) rights from the NFL Team so owned or controlled (the revenue from which is includable in Defined Gross Revenues) and (b) other rights owned or controlled by such persons or entities (the revenue from such other rights not being includable in Defined Gross Revenues), and that, in such circumstances, allocations would therefore have to be made among the rights and revenues described in this Section 1(a); and

(2) NFL Teams may, during the term of this Agreement, receive revenue for the grant of rights to third parties which are owned or controlled by the persons or entities owning or controlling such NFL Teams (hereinafter "Related Entities").

(vii) The reasonableness and includability in DGR of such allocations and transactions between Related Entities shall be determined by the nationally recognized accounting firm jointly retained by the parties, in accordance with the procedures described in Section 10 below.

(viii) For the purposes of any amounts to be calculated or used pursuant to this Agreement with respect to DGR, Excluded DGR, Benefits, Player Costs, Projected DGR, Projected Benefits, Required Tenders, Qualifying Offers, Minimum Salaries, Minimum Act/Inactive List Salaries, Team Salary, or Salary, such amounts; shall be rounded to the nearest $1,000.

(ix) In calculating Defined Gross Revenues, each League Year up to $5 million per year shall be deducted from DGR to the extent that such sums are received that League Year by the NFLPA pursuant to Paragraphs 5, 12, 29 and 30 of the Stipulation and Settlement Agreement in *NFLPA v. NFL Properties, Inc.,* No. 90–CV–4244 (MJL) (S.D.N.Y).

(x)(1) Without limiting the foregoing, except as specified in subsections (x)(2) through (x)(7) below, DGR shall include all revenues from Personal Seat Licenses ("UPSLs") received by, or received by a third party and used, directly or indirect, for the benefit of, the NFL or any Team Affiliate, without any deduction for taxes or other expenses Such revenues shall be allocated in equal portions, commenc-

ing in the League Year in which they are received, over the remaining life of the PSL, subject to a maximum allocation period of fifteen years; provided, however, that interest from the League Year the revenues are received until the League Years the revenues are allocated into DGR shall be imputed and included in DGR, in equal portions over such periods, calculated on an annual compounded basis using the Treasury Bill rate published in The Wall Street Journal of February 1 during the League Year in which the revenues are received. Each equal portion of PSL revenues allocated into DGR, plus an equal portion of the imputed interest specified above, shall be referred to as the "Maximum Annual Allocation Amount."

(x)(2) To the extent that PSL revenues are used to pay for the construction of a new stadium or for stadium renovation(s) that increase DGR (regardless of whether the stadium is owned by a public authority or a private entity (including, but not limited to, the NFL any Team or any Team Affiliate)), and if such PSL revenues have received a waiver of any League requirement of sharing of "gross receipts," then such PSL revenues will not be included in a particular League Year in DGR or in Excluded DGR. Notwithstanding the foregoing, the maximum exclusion of PSL revenues each League Year from DGR shall be equal to any increase in DGR that directly results from such stadium construction or renovation (including through any spillover from Excluded DGR) as calculated in subsections (x)(3) through (x)(7) below.

(x)(3) Until the first full League Year the new stadium or the renovated facilities are put into service, the amount of PSL revenues excluded each League Year shall be equal to the Maximum Annual Allocation Amount. If the actual increase in DGR directly resulting from such stadium construction or renovations during the first full League Year in which such stadium or renovations are put into service (the "First Year PSL Increases") is less than any, Maximum Annual Allocation Amount for that League Year or any prior League Year (the "PSL Difference"), then the aggregate PSL Difference for every such League Year (assuming for purposes of calculating such PSL Difference, that the First Year PSL Increase had been received in each such League Year) shall be credited to DGR in the immediately following League Year.

(x)(4) Commencing with the first full League Year the new stadium or the renovated facilities are put into service, the jointly retained Accountants (set forth in Article XXIV, Section 10(a)(ii) below) shall determine the increase in DGR that directly results each League Year from a stadium construction or renovation funded, in whole or in part, by PSL revenues. In the case of a new stadium, such calculation shall be made by comparing the DGR directly generated by the old stadium during the last full League Year in which the old stadium was in service with the DGR directly generated by the new stadium during the League Year in question.

In the case of stadium renovations, such calculation shall be made by comparing the DGR directly generated by those specific stadium facilities which are renovated, with the DGR directly generated by those facilities prior to their renovation (where new facilities, such as completely new luxury suites or premium seats, are constructed, the DGR directly generated by any facilities that were replaced by the renovation). If the NFL or the NFLPA agree that a renovation is substantial enough to increase revenues throughout the stadium (e.g., significant renovations throughout the stadium which enable the Club to attract more fans and/or increase ticket prices) then the Accountants shall consider any increase in DGR throughout the stadium (e.g., increased concession, parking or novelty revenues spilling into DGI) as being directly generated by the renovation.

(x)(5) If the calculations set forth in (x)(4) above result in an exclusion of PSL revenues from DGR that is less than the Maximum Annual Allocation Amount, the Accountants shall report the amount not excluded from DGR as a "Carryover PSL Credit." Such Carryover PSL Credits, if any, shall be deducted from a Team's DGR in the first future League Year in which the amount of DGR directly

*generated by the new stadium or the renovated facil-
ities exceeds the Maximum Annual Allocation
Amount (the "PSL Excess"), but only up to the
amount of the PSL excess. Each dollar of Carryover
PSL Credit may be deducted from a Team's DGR
only once, and only to the extent of any PSL Excess
existing at the time of such deduction.*

*(x)(6) Any applicable deduction from DGR or Ex-
cluded DGR for any expenses (i.e., interest, rent,
taxes or depreciation) that are attributable to premium seats or luxury suites included in any new
stadium or stadium renovation project funded, in
whole or in part, by PSL revenues excluded from
DGR and Excluded DGR pursuant to subsection
(x)(2) above shall be reduced, in any League Year, by
an amount equal to the result obtained by multiplying (a) the gross deduction for such expenses that
would otherwise be available under this Agreement
in respect of such League Year; only a fraction, the
numerator of which is (1) the total PSL revenues
described in the first sentence of subsection (x)(2),
and the denominator of which is (2) the total costs
for construction of the new stadium or renovations.*

*(x)(7) For purposes of this paragraph, the term
"PSL" shall include any and all instruments of any
nature, whether of temporary or permanent duration, that give the purchaser the right to acquire or
retain tickets to NFL games and shall include without limitation, seat options and bonds giving pur-
chasers the right to acquire NFL tickets. PSL revenues shall also include revenues from any other
device (e.g., periodic payments such as surcharges,*

loge maintenance fees, etc.) that the NFL and the NFLPA agree constitutes a PSL.

(xi)(1) Notwithstanding Section 1(a)(i)(iv), above, premium seat revenues that otherwise would be included in Excluded DGR shall not be so included in a particular League Year to the extent that such revenues are used to pay for, or to pay financing costs for; the construction of a new stadium or for stadium renovation(s) that increase DGR (regardless of whether the stadium is owned by a public authority or a private entity (including, but not limited to, the NFL, any Team or any Team Affiliate)), and if such revenues have received a waiver of any League requirement of sharing of "gross receipts." The maximum exclusion of premium seat revenue from Excluded DGR each League Year shall be equal to any increase in DGR that directly results from such stadium construction or renovation including through any spillover from Excluded DGR) as calculated in subsections (xi)(2) through (xi)(6) below.

(xi)(2) Until the first Full League Year the new stadium or the renovated facilities are put into service, the amount of premium seat revenues excluded each League Year shall be equal to the amount that receives a waiver of any League requirement of sharing of gross receipts (the "Non–Shared Amount"). If the actual increase in DGR during the first full League Year in which the new stadium or the renovated facilities are put into service (the "First Year Premium Seat Increase") is less than any Non–Shared Amount for that League Year or any prior League Year (the "Premium Seat Difference), then

the aggregate Premium Seat Difference for every such League Year (assuming for purposes of calculating such Premium Seat Difference that the First Year Premium Seat Increase had been received in each such League Year) shall be credited to Excluded DGR in the immediately following League Year.

(xi)(3) Commencing with the first full League Year the new stadium or the renovated facilities are put into service, the jointly retained Accountants (set forth in Article XXIV Section 10(a)(ii) below) shall determine the increase in DGR that directly results each League Year from the stadium construction or renovation funded, in whole or in part, with premium seat revenues. In the case of a new stadium, such calculation shall be made by comparing the DGR directly generated by the old stadium during the last full League Year in which the old stadium was in service with the DGR directly generated by the new stadium during the League Year in question. In the case of stadium renovations, such calculation shall be made by comparing the DGR directly generated by those specific stadium facilities which are renovated, with the DGR directly generated by those facilities prior to their renovation (where new facilities, such as completely new luxury suites or premium seats, are constructed, the DGR directly generated by the facilities prior to their renovation would equal either zero, or the amount of DGR directly generated by any facilities that were replaced by the renovation). If the NFL and the NFLPA agree that a renovation is substantial enough to increase revenues throughout the stadium (e.g., significant reno-

vations throughout the stadium which enable the Club to attract more fans and/or raise ticket prices) then the Accountants shall consider any increase in DGR throughout the stadium (e.g., increased concession, parking or novelty revenues spilling into DGR) as being directly generated by the renovation.

(xi)(4) If the calculations set forth in (xi)(3) above result in an exclusion of premium seat revenues from Excluded DGR that is less than the Non–Shared Amount, the Accountants shall report the amount not excluded from Excluded DGR as a "Carryover Premium Seat Credit." Such Carryover Premium Seat Credits, if any, shall be deducted from a Team's Excluded DGR in the first future League Year in which the amount of DGR directly generated by the new stadium or the renovated facilities exceeds the Non–Shared Amount (the "Premium Seat Excess"), but only up to the amount of the Premium Seat Excess, Each Carryover Premium Seat Credit may be deducted from a Team's DGR only once, and only to the extent of any Premium Seat Excess existing at the time of such deduction.

(xi)(5) Any applicable deduction from DGR or Excluded DGR for any expenses (i.e., interest, rent, taxes or depreciation) that are attributable to premium seats or luxury suites included in any new stadium or stadium renovation project funded, in whole or in part, by premium seat revenues excluded from Excluded DGR pursuant to subsection (xi)(1) above shall be reduced, in any League Year by an amount equal to the result obtained by multiplying (a) the gross deduction for such expenses that would

otherwise be available under this agreement in respect of such League Year, by a fraction, the numerator of which is (1) the total premium seat Non–Shared Amount dedicated to funding the project during the allocation period, and (2) the denominator of which is the total costs for construction of the new stadium or renovations.

(xi)(6) For purposes of this paragraph, the term "Premium Seat Revenue" shall include revenue from any periodic change in excess of the ticket price that is required to be paid to acquire or retain any ticket to NFL games (other than PSL revenues and charges for purchase or rental of luxury suites), including charges in respect of any amenities required to be purchased in connection with any ticket.

* Extension Agreement 6/6/96

(b) **Benefits.** "Benefits" and "Player Benefit Costs" mean the aggregate for a League Year of all sums paid (or to be paid on a proper accrual basis for a League Year) by the NFL and all NFL Teams for; to or on behalf of present or former NFL players, but only for:

(i) Pension funding, including the Bert Bell NPL Player Retirement Plan (as described in Article XLVII), the Pete Rozelle NFL Player Retirement Plan (as described in Article XLVII), the Bert Bell/ Pete Rozelle NFL Player Retirement Plan (as described in Article XLVII), the National Football League Pre–59er Special Benefit Program, and the Second Career Savings Plan (as described in Article XLVIII);

(ii) Group insurance programs, including, life, medical, and dental coverage (as described in Article XLIX or as required by law), and the Supplemental Disability Plan (as described in Article LI);

(iii) Injury protection (as described in Article XII);

(iv) Workers' compensation, payroll, unemployment compensation, and social security taxes;

(v) Pre-season per diem amounts (as described in Sections 3 and 4 of Article XXVID and regular season meal allowances (as described in Article XXXIX);

(vi) Moving and travel expenses (as described in Sections 2, 3, and 4 of Article XLI, and Section 8 of Article XXXVII);

(vii) Post-season pay (as described in Article XLII and Article XLIII);

For purposes of the Salary Cap in the 1996 and 1997 League Years, salary paid to practice squad players pursuant to a practice squad contract during the post-season will be a Benefit under article XXIV, Section 1(b)(vii), unless the practice squad player contract is executed or renegotiated after December 1 for more than the minimum practice squad salary, in which case all salary paid to a practice player during the post-season will be counted as Salary.

* Side Letter 10/8/96

(viii) Player medical costs (i.e., fees to doctors, hospitals, and other health care providers, and the drugs and other medical cost of supplies, for the treatment of player injuries), but not including salaries of trainers or other Team personnel, or the cost of Team medical or training equipment (in addition, the amount of player medical costs included in Benefits may not increase by more than ten percent (10%) each League Year beginning with the 1993 League Year, which may not increase more than ten percent (10%) over the 1992 League Year); and

(ix) Severance pay (as described in Article L).

Benefits will not include salary reduction contributions elected by a player to the Second Career Savings Plan described in Article XLVIII. Benefits also will not include any tax imposed on the NFL or NFL Clubs pursuant to section 4972 of the Internal Revenue Code for the Bert Bell NFL Player Retirement Plan, the Pete Rozelle NFL Player Retirement Plan, and/or Bert Bell/Pete Rozelle NFL Player Retirement Plan. Benefits for a League Year will be determined by adding together all payments made and amounts properly accrued by or on behalf of the NFL and all NFL Clubs for the above purposes during that League Year except that Benefits for pension funding and the Second Career Savings Plan will be deemed to be made in a League Year for purposes of this Article if made in the Plan Year beginning in the same calendar year as the beginning of such League Year.

(c) **Salary**.

(i) "Salary" means the compensation in money, property, investments, loans or anything else of value to which an NFL player (including Rookie and Veteran players and players .hose contracts have been terminated) or his Player Affiliate is entitled in accordance with a Player Contract, but not including Benefits. Salary with respect to any period shall include all Salary actually payable with respect to such period under the terms of a Player Contract and all Salary attributable to such period under the terms of this Agreement.

(ii) A player's Salary shall also include any and all consideration received by the player or his Player Affiliate, even if such consideration is ostensibly paid to the player for services other than football playing services, if the NFL can demonstrate before the Impartial Arbitrator that the consideration paid to the player or Player Affiliate for such non-football services does not represent a reasonable approximation of the fair market value of such services as performed by such player. The Impartial Arbitrator's determination may take into account, among other things: (1) any actual dollar amounts the player or Player Affiliate received for similar non-football playing services from an independent third party; and (2) the percentage of total compensation for non-football services received from third parties versus the Team or Team Affiliate.

(iii) For purposes of this Article, Salary shall be computed pursuant to the additional rules below.

***Section 2*. Trigger for Guaranteed League-wide Salary, Salary Cap, and Minimum Team Salary**: There shall be no Guaranteed League-wide Salary, Salary Cap, or Minimum Team Salary for NFL Teams during the 1993 League Year. If in the 1993 League Year or any subsequent League Year the total Player Costs for all NFL Teams equals or exceeds 67% of actual Defined Gross Revenues, there shall be a Guaranteed League-wide Salary, Salary Cap, and Minimum Team Salary in the amounts set forth below for the next League Year and all subsequent League Years, unless the Salary Cap is removed pursuant to Section 4(b)(ii)(4) below. Notwithstanding the immediately preceding sentence, there will be no Guaranteed League-wide Salary, Salary Cap or Minimum Team Salary in the Final League Year.

* Extension Agreement 6/6/96

***Section 3*. Guaranteed League-wide Salary**: In any League Year in which a Salary Cap is in effect there shall be a Guaranteed League-wide Salary of 58% of actual Defined Gross Revenues. In the event that the Player Costs for all NFL Teams during any League Year in which a Salary Cap is in effect are less than 58% of actual Defined Gross Revenues for such season, then, on or before April 15 of the next League Year, the NFL shall pay an amount equal to such deficiency directly to players who played on NFL Teams during such season pursuant to the reasonable allocation instructions of the NFLPA.

Section 4. **Salary Cap Amounts**:

(a) Subject to the adjustments set forth below, the amount of the Salary Cap for each NFL Team in years that it is in effect shall be (1) in the first League Year, 64% of the Projected Defined Gross Revenues, less League-wide Projected Benefits, divided by the number of Teams playing in the NFL during such year; (2) in the 1995 and 1996 League Years, 63% of the Projected Defined Gross Revenues, less League-wide Projected Benefits, divided by the number of teams playing in the NFL during such year; (3)in the 1997 League Year, 62% of the Projected Defined Gross Revenues, less League-wide Projected Benefits, divided by the number of Teams playing in the NFL during such year; and (4) in the remaining League Years of this Agreement until the Final League Year; or until the Cap is removed pursuant to subsection 4(b)(ii)(4) below, as specified in Section 4(c) below.

* Extension Agreement 6/6/96

(b) The foregoing Salary Cap amounts shall be adjusted as follows:

(i) The actual dollar amount of the Salary Cap shall not be less than the actual dollar amount of any Salary Cap in effect during the preceding League Year; provided, however, that at no time shall the Projected Benefits, plus the amount of the Salary Cap multiplied by the number of Teams in the NFL, exceed 70% of the Projected Defined Gross Revenues.

(ii) If the total Player Costs of the NFL Teams during any League Year in which the Salary Cap is in effect falls below:

(1) 59% of actual Defined Gross Revenues, then the Salary Cap percentage for the next League Year shall be increased by 1% of Projected Defined Gross Revenues;

(2) 58% of actual Defined Gross Revenues, then the Salary Cap percentage for the next League Year shall be increased by 2% of Projected Defined Gross Revenues;

(3) 57% of actual Defined Gross Revenues, then the Salary Cap percentage for the next League Year shall be increased by 3% of Projected Defined Gross Revenues;

(4) 56% of actual Defined Gross Revenues, then there shall be no Salary Cap for the next League Year or any succeeding League Year unless and until the Salary Cap again becomes effective in accordance with Section 2 of this Article.

(c)(i) If neither party has provided notice by December 1, 1997 cancelling the extension set forth in Article LXI Extension of Agreement), Section 1, the amount of any Salary Cap for each NFL Team in the 1998 League Year and any remaining Capped Years shall be 63% of the Projected Defined Gross Revenues, less League-wide Projected Benefits, divided by the number of teams playing in the NFL during such year.

(ii) If the NFLPA has provided notice by December 1, 1997 cancelling the extension set forth in Article LXI (Extension of Agreement), Section 1, the amount of any Salary Cap for each NFL Team in the 1998 League Year and any remaining Capped Years shall be 62% of the Projected Defined Gross Revenues, less League-wide Projected Benefits, divided by the number of teams playing in the NFL during such year.

(iii) If the NFLPA has provided notice by December 1, 1998 cancelling the extension set forth in Article LXI (Extension of Agreement), Section 2, the amount of any Salary Cap for each NFL Team in the 2000 League Year shall be 62% of the Projected Defined Gross Revenues, less League-wide Projected Benefits, divided by the number of Teams playing in the NFL during such year, and the amount of any Salary Cap for each NFL Team in the 2000 League Year shall be 62% of the Projected Defined Gross Revenues, less League-wide Projected Benefits, divided by the number of Teams playing in the NFL during such year.

(iv) If the NFL has provided notice by December

1, 1997 cancelling the extension set forth in Article LXI (Extension of Agreement), Section 1, the amount of any Salary Cap for each NFL Team in the 1998 League Year shall be 62% of the Projected Defined Gross Revenues, less League-wide Projected Benefits, divided by the number of Teams playing in the NFL during such year, and the amount of any Salary Cap for each NFL Team in the 1999 League Year shall be 63% of the Projected Defined Gross Revenues, less League-wide Projected Benefits, divided by the number of Teams playing in the NFL during such year.

(v) If the NFL has provided notice by December 1, 1998 cancelling the extension set forth in Article LXI (Extension of Agreement), Section 2, the amount of any Salary Cap for each NFL Team in the 1999 League Year shall be 62% of the Projected Defined Gross Revenues, less League-wide Projected Benefits, divided by the number of Teams playing in the NFL during such year, and the amount of any Salary Cap for each NFL Team in the 2000 League Year shall be 63% of the Projected Benefits, divided by the number of Teams playing in the NFL during such year.

(vi) A summary of the above percentages is set forth in Appendix K hereto.

* Extension Agreement 6/6/96

Section 5. **Minimum Team Salary**:

(a) With respect to each League Year for which a Salary Cap is in effect, there shall be a guaranteed Minimum Team Salary for each Team of the Projected Defined Gross Revenues, less League-wide Projected Benefits, divided by the then current number of teams in the NFL. Each Team shall be required to have a Team Salary of at least the Minimum Team Salary at the end of each League Year.

(b) Nothing contained herein shall preclude a Team from having a Team Salary in excess of the Minimum Team Salary, provided it does not exceed the Salary Cap.

(c) Any shortfall in the Minimum Team Salary at the end of a League Year shall be paid, on or before April 15 of the next League Year, by the Teams having such shortfall, directly to the players who were on such Teams' roster at any time during the season, pursuant to reasonable allocation instructions of the NFLPA.

(d) If the NFL agrees, or a judgment or award is entered by the Special Master, that a Team has failed by the end of the then current League Year to make the payments required to satisfy a Team's obligations to pay the Minimum Team Salary required by this Agreement, then, in the event the Team fails promptly to comply with such agreement, judgment or award, the NFL shall make such payment on behalf of that Team (such funds to be paid as salary directly to the players on such Team at the direction of and pursuant to the reasonable allocation instructions of the NFLPA).

Section 6. **Computation of Team Salary**: During any League year in which the Salary Cap is in effect, all of the following amounts shall be included every day in determining a Team's Team Salary:

(a) **Player Contracts**. Subject to the rules below in Section 7 of this Article, all amounts the Team has paid or is obligated to pay as set forth in all Player Contracts of current and former players covering a particular League Year, including exercised, options, shall be included in Team Salary.

(b) **Tenders**.

(i) Drafted Rookies' Salaries shall be tendered automatically at the Rookie Minimum Active List Salary as of the day of the Draft and shall be included in Team Salary until (1) the player is signed, (2) the Team's rights are relinquished through waivers, or (3) the Tuesday following the tenth week of the regular season (if the player is unsigned).

(ii) For players with less than three Accrued Seasons whose contracts have expired, the Minimum Active List Salary will be included in Team Salary when tendered until the player is signed, or the Team's rights are relinquished.

(iii) For players who are Restricted Free Agents, the Qualifying Offer will be included in Team Salary when tendered until the player is signed, the Qualifying Offer is withdrawn, or a "June 1 tender" (which may be made on or before June 1) is made. If the player is unsigned and the Team makes a June 1 tender or June 15 tender, such tender will be included until the player is signed, the Team's rights are relinquished, or the Tuesday following the tenth week of the regular season (if the player is unsigned).

(iv) For players who are Unrestricted Free Agents, the June l tender, if made, will be included in Team Salary as of July 15 and thereafter until the player is signed, the tender is withdrawn, the Team's rights are relinquished or extinguished, or the Tuesday following the tenth week of the regular season (if the player is unsigned).

(v) For Transition Players and Franchise Players, the tender will be included in Team Salary when made until the player is signed, the tender is withdrawn, the Team's rights are relinquished, or the Tuesday following the tenth game of the regular season (if the player is unsigned).

(vi) All Offer Sheets will be included in Team Salary when tendered until the player is signed to a Player Contract by any NFL Team, or the Offer Sheet is withdrawn.

(c) **Practice Squad Contracts**. Any Practice Squad contract Salaries shall be included in Team Salary.

(d) **Termination Pay**. Any type of Termination Pay liability will be included in Team Salary at the time the player is released, except to the extent the Team is relieved of any such liability.

(e) **Grievances**. When a player salary grievance is filed against a Team, 50% of the amount claimed will be counted in Team Salary until the grievance is resolved or until the end of the League Year, whichever comes first; at the end of the League Year, if any grievances have been settled or awards have been made, if the net total grievance amounts paid by the Team are more than the original 50% attributions and put the Team over the Salary Cap, the excess will be deducted from the Team's Salary Cap in the following League Year; if the net total grievance amounts paid are less than the original 50% attributions and the Team finishes the season at the Salary Cap or below the Salary Cap by less than the amount of the unawarded attributions, the difference will be added to the Team's Salary Cap for the following League Year. If an award or settlement is made for a grievance in a League Year after the grievance was filed, and the grievance amount paid is more than the original 50% attribution, the excess shall be included in Team Salary when paid; if the grievance amount is less than the original 50% attribution, the difference shall be deducted from Team Salary when the award is made.

(f) **Expansion Bonuses**. Except as set forth in Article M1 (Expansion), any expansion bonuses paid to players shall be included in Team Salary.

(g) **Other Amounts**. Any other Salary not listed above paid to players shall be included in Team Salary.

Section 7. **Valuation of Player Contracts**: Notwithstanding any provision in a Player Contract to the contrary or when such payments are actually made, the following rules shall apply in determining the amount of a player's Salary that is to be included in Team Salary in a particular League Year for purposes of the Salary Cap:

(a) **Paragraph 5**.

(i) The highest applicable Salary set forth in Paragraph 5 of the NFL Player Contract shall be included in Team Salary in the year earned, except that, between March 1 and the first day of the regular playing season, only the following amounts from Paragraph 5 shall be included for players whose Player Contracts are not among the Team's 51 highest valued Player Contracts, tenders and Offer Sheets (as determined under this Section 7):

(1) Any amount that exceeds the Minimum Active/Inactive List Salary for Undrafted Rookie Free Agents; and

(2) Any amount that exceeds twice the applicable Minimum Active/Inactive List Salary for all other players.

(ii) **Deferred Salary**. Any Paragraph 5 Salary to be earned in a particular year but not to be paid until after the next League Year shall be considered "Deferred Salary" and will be included in Team Salary during the League Year earned at its present value based on the Treasury Bill rate published in The Wall Street Journal on March 1 in the year earned. Salary to be paid any time before the end of the League Year after it is earned shall not be considered Deferred Salary and will be included fully in the Team's Salary during the year earned.

(b) **Signing Bonuses**.

(i) **Proration**. The total amount of any signing bonus shall be prorated over the term of the Player Contract in determining Team and Player Salary, except that:

(1) Signing bonuses in contracts negotiated in a Capped Year may not be prorated more than three years beyond *the Final Capped Year*.

*Extension Agreement 6/6/96

(2) Any contract year in which the player has the right to terminate based upon events within his sole control shall not be counted as a contract year for purposes of proration. In the event the NFL and the NFLPA cannot agree upon whether an option is within the player's sole control, such issue shall be resolved by the Impartial Arbitrator.

* With respect to the proration of signing bonuses for Player Contracts entered into by Rookie players in which the player has the right to terminate based solely upon reporting, making the roster and/or playtime, such conduct shall automatically be deemed "within his sole control," as set forth in Article X, Paragraph G.2.(a)(ii) of the Stipulation and Settlement Agreement and in Article XXIV, Section 7(b)(i)(2) of the Collective Bargaining Agreement, unless the exercise of the right to terminate is also conditioned upon the following playtime requirements: (1) for players drafted in the first round, at least 35% of the plays if the triggering condition occurs in the first year of the Player Contract, and at least 45% of the

plays if in any subsequent year; (2) for all other Rookie players, at least 15% of the plays if the condition occurs in the first year of the Player Contract, and at least 30% of the plays if in any subsequent year The playtime requirements set forth above do not affect the signing bonus allocation for any contract entered into by players other than Rookies.

* Side Letter 9/21/93: Sec. 15

*[A]ny multi-year Player Contract not unconditionally approved by the Commissioner as of the date hereof other than any multi-year Player Contract executed in the last Capped Year of this Agreement, that extends from a Capped Year into any Uncapped Year (hereinafter "Subject Contract") For purposes of determining Team Salary, if (i) the sum of the player's Paragraph 5 Salary, roster bonuses that are based upon the player making any of the Club's roster categories without limitation, and reporting bonuses during all Capped Years of the Subject Contract (but, if there are fewer than three remaining Capped Years, during the first three years of the Subject Contract) in the aggregate less than (ii) the portion of the Subject Contract's signing bonus that would be allocated to those League Years if the signing bonus were prorated equally over the term of the Subject Contract, then: the difference between the amounts calculated pursuant to (ii) and (i) of this sentence, up to 50% of the portion of the

signing bonus that would otherwise be allocated to the Uncapped Years ("the Difference"), shall be deducted in equal portions from those Uncapped Years and reallocated[1] in equal portions over the Capped Years of the Subject Contract (or, if there are fewer than three Capped Years within the term of the Subject Contract, over the first three years of the Subject Contract).

For purposes of this Paragraph, a renegotiation shall be treated as if it is an entirely new Player Contract. Notwithstanding the above, any Subject Contract executed prior to November 15, 1995 for which there is a Difference as a result of the calculation set forth above shall have the 1995 portion of such Difference allocated to 1995 Team Salary to the extent of the Club's current and any future Room during the 1995 regular season (except such Room that results from the termination or renegotiation of a 1995 Player Contract after October 30, 1995), with the balance to be allocated to the 1996 League Year Further, any Subject Contract executed between November 15, 1995 and the end of the 1995 League Year shall have the 1995 portion of any Difference allocated to the 1996 League Year.

* Side Letter 11/1/95: Sec. I

(3) If a Player Contract provides for an increase in Salary upon the assignment of such contract to another NFL Team, such increase shall be included

1. This sentence incorporates the language of the Side Letter dated 11/22/95.

in the player's Salary upon such assignment and be attributable to the Team paying the bonus.

* For the purposes of the Salary Cap, any signing bonus given in connection with a contract extension entered into before the expiration of the player's existing contract will be prorated over the remaining years of the unexpired contract together with its extension. The parties agree that, pursuant to the Collective Bargaining Agreement, the player shall always have the right to receive such a signing bonus at the time that the extension is executed, unless the player expressly agrees in the contract to defer payment of the extension bonus, in which case only the present value of the deferred payment, calculated in accordance with the method set forth in Article X, Paragraph G.1.(b) of the Stipulation and Settlement Agreement and Article XXIV, Section 7(a)(ii) of the Collective Bargaining Agreement, shall he prorated (unless the extension is executed within one year of the execution of the contract being extended, in which case the gross amount of the extension bonus shall be prorated).

* Side Letter 9/21/93: Sec. 17

(i) **Acceleration**.

(1) For any player removed from the Team's roster on or before June any unamortized signing bonus amounts will be included in Team Salary (or such League Year. If such acceleration puts a Team

over the Salary Cap the Team will have seven days
to conform with the Salary Cap but may not sign
any players until there is Room to do so under the
Salary Cap.

(2) For any player removed from the Team's roster after June 1 any unamortized signing bonus
amounts for future years will be included fully in
Team Salary at the start of the next League Year.

** During any League Year immediately preced-
ing an Uncapped Year; the provisions relating
to acceleration of unamortized signing bonuses
applicable on or before June 1 of that League
Year shall apply during that League Year after
June 1.*

* Side Letter 11/1/95: Sec. 2

(3) In the event that a player who has had a
signing bonus allocated over the years of his Player
Contract is traded or whose Contract is assigned to
another team pursuant to the NFL's waiver procedure then such signing bonus shall be accelerated as
in subsection (ii)(1) above and the assignee Team's
Team Salary will not include any portion of the
signing bonus.

(4) Any contract year that the player has the
right to terminate based upon a contingency shall
count as a contract year for purposes of proration
until the contingency is fulfilled at which time any
amounts attributed to such year shall be accelerated
and included immediately in Team Salary. To the
extent that such acceleration puts the Team over its

Salary Cap the difference shall be deducted from its Salary Cap for the following year.

With respect to a Player Contract in which the player has one or more rights to terminate based upon one or more not "likely to be earned" incentives and the player also being on the roster at a subsequent time no acceleration shall occur pursuant to Article XXIV Section 7(b)(ii)(4) of the CBA until both the incentive(s) and the roster precondition(s) have been satisfied.

* Side Letter 10/21/96: Sec. 5

(5) The unamortized portion of any signing bonus contained in an NFL Player Contract that is renegotiated to reduce the number of years of such Player Contract shall be included, to the extent attributable to such reduced year or years, in Team Salary at the time of the renegotiation.

(iii) **Prior Signing Bonuses.** All signing bonuses from League Years prior to 1993 will be prorated over the term of the original Player Contracts and included in Team Salary in the 1993 League Year and thereafter.

(iv) **Amounts Treated as Signing Bonuses**. For purposes of determining Team Salary under the foregoing, the term "signing bonus" shall include:

(1) Any amount specifically described in a Player Contract as a signing bonus;

(2) Any guaranteed reporting bonus;

(3) Any consideration, when paid, or guaranteed, for option years, contract extensions, contract modifications, or individually negotiated rights of first refusal;

(4) Any option buyout amount, when paid or guaranteed; and

(5) In the event that a Player Contract calls for a Salary in the second year of such Contract that is less than half the Salary called for in the first year of such Contract, the difference between the Salary in the second contract year and the first contract year shall be treated as a signing bonus.

* In a contract signed after the start of training camp, a reporting bonus for that season will be counted as a signing bonus. In a contract signed after the last pre-season game, a roster bonus for that season will be counted as a signing bonus.

* Side Letter 9/21/93: Sec. 18

* Any salary advance paid on a guaranteed basis will be counted as a signing bonus.

* Side Letter 9/21/93: Sec. 19

* For purposes of the Salary Cap and Entering Player Pool, any guaranteed bonus tied to workouts shall be treated as a Signing Bonus.

* Side Letter 6/23/93: Sec. 3

* For purposes of the Salary Cap and Entering Player Fool, any salary advance which a player is not obligated to re-pay shall be treated as a Signing Bonus.

* Side Letter 6/23/93: Sec. 4

* For purposes of the Salary Cap and Entering Player Pool, any roster or reporting bonus which is earned or paid before the start of the Club's pre-season training camp shall be treated as a signing bonus.

* Side Letter 6/23/93, Sec. 6

Except as set forth in [the] Paragraph [to follow], the full non-guaranteed amount of any Salary advance, off-season work-out bonus, off-season roster bonus, or off-season reporting bonus shall be included in Team Salary only in the League Year in which it is earned by the player, without any pro-ration. For purposes of this paragraph only, "guaranteed" means Salary that is fully guaranteed, prior to being earned, for skill, for injury, and regardless of any termination of the contract by the Club. The definition of "guaranteed" other purpose.

* Side Letter 10/21/96: Sec. 1

With respect to any Player Contract, or any renegotiation or extension of a Player Contract, that is executed in the Final Capped Year, each of the following shall be treated as a signing bonus, at the time of execution, if it is to be earned or paid to the player in the final League Year (which is an Uncapped Year): (a) any Salary advance which the player is not and cannot be obligated to repay; (b) any off-season workout bonus that is contingent upon the player's participation in less than 32 days of the Club's off-season work-out program; (c) any off-season roster bonus; and (d) any off-season reporting bonus.

*Side Letter 10/21/96: Sec. 2

* [A]ny bonus to be paid to a player solely for fulfilling his obligations to play under his Player Contract without seeking to renegotiate and/or "holding out" (i. e., a "completion bonus"), and which bonus is otherwise guaranteed for skill and injury, shall be considered to be a "signing bonus" under Article XXIV of the CBA, except that the amount of any such completion bonus shall be calculated at its present value, computed at the Treasury Bill rate published in The Wall Street Journal on March 1 of the League Year in which the Player Contract is executed. Further, if any event occurs which extinguishes the player's right to receive such completion bonus, any amount of the bonus that has previously been included in Team Salary shall be immediately added to the Team's Salary Cap for the current League Year, if such

event occurs prior to June 1, or for the remainder of the bonus that has been allocated to Team Salary for future League Years immediately extinguished.

* Side Letter 1/18/94: Sec. 3

Any relocation bonus which is individually negotiated between a player and a Club shall be treated as a signing bonus.

* Side Letter 5/24/95: Sec. 9

Through the 1997 League Year, if a Club and a player renegotiate or extend a contract and increase the player's Salary for the current League Year, the increase will be counted as Salary for that League Year if the NFL Management Council receives, prior to 4:00 p.m. on the Monday of the tenth week of the regular season, notice of the salary terms of such an executed extended or renegotiated contract. In any other circumstance through the 1997 League Year the increase in Salary will be treated as a signing bonus that is allocated over the remaining years of the Player contract (including the "current" year of that contract) to the extent that such allocation is permitted by the CBA.

* Side Letter 5/24/95: Sec. 14

(v) **Credit for Signing Bonuses Refunded**. In the event that a Team receives a refund from the player of any previously paid portion of a signing bonus, or the Team fails to pay any previously allocated portion of a signing bonus, such amount as has previously been included in Team Salary shall be added to the Team's Salary Cap for the next League Year.

(c) **Incentives**.

(i) Any and all incentive amounts, including but not limited to performance bonuses, shall be included in Team Salary if they are "likely to be earned" during such League Year based upon the player's and/or Team's performance during the prior year. In the case of a Rookie, or a Veteran who did not play during the prior season, in the event that the NFL and the NFLPA cannot agree as to whether such performance bonus is "likely to be earned," such disputes shall be referred to the Impartial Arbitrator. Any incentive within the sole control of the player (e.g., non-guaranteed reporting bonuses, off-season workout and weight bonuses) shall be deemed "likely to be earned."

(ii) At the end of a season, if performance bonuses actually earned resulted in a Team's paying Salary in excess of the Salary Cap, then the amount by which the Team exceeded the Salary Cap as a result of such actually paid performance bonuses shall be subtracted from the Team's Salary Cap for the next League Year.

(ii) At the end of a season, if performance bonuses previously included in a Team's Team Salary but not actually earned performance bonuses actually earned but not previously included in Team Salary, an amount shall be added to the Team's Salary Cap for the next League Year equalling the amount, if any, by which such overage exceeds the Team's Room under the Salary Cap at the end of a season.

> * *Any team performance will be automatically deemed to be "Likely to be earned" if the Team met or exceeded the specified performance during the prior League Year, and will be automatically deemed to be "not likely to be earned" if the Team did not meet the specified performance during the prior League Year.*
>
> * *Side Letter 2/22/96: Sec. 1*

> *Any incentive bonus that depends on team performance in any category not identified in Exhibit A hereto automatically will be deemed "likely to be earned."*
>
> * *Side Letter 9/21/93: Sec. 8*

> *Any incentive bonus that depends on a player's individual performance in any category not identified in Exhibit B hereto automatically will be deemed "likely to be earned." Any incentive bonus that depends on a player's individual performance in categories other than those used to assess performance at the player's primary position automatically will be deemed "likely to be earned."*
>
> * *Side Letter 9/21/93: Sec. 11*

ARTICLE XXV ENFORCEMENT OF THE SALARY CAP AND ENTERING PLAYER POOL

Section 1. **Undisclosed Terms**: At the time a Club and a player enter into any Player Contract, or any renegotiation, extension or amendment of a Player Contract, there shall be no undisclosed agreements of any kind, express or implied, oral or written, or promises, undertakings, representations, commitments, inducements, assurances of intent, or understandings of any kind, between such player and any Club involving consideration of any kind to be paid, furnished or made available or guaranteed to the player, or Player Affiliate, by the Club or Club Affiliate either during the term of the Player Contract or thereafter.

Section 2. **Circumvention**: Neither the parties hereto, nor any Club or player shall enter into any agreement, Player Contract, Offer Sheet or other transaction which includes any terms that are designed to serve the purpose of defeating or circumventing the intention of the parties as reflected by (a) the provisions of this Agreement with respect to Defined Gross Revenues, Salary Cap, Entering Player Pool, and Minimum Team Salary, and (b) any other term and provision of this Agreement. However, any conduct permitted by this Agreement shall not be considered to be a violation of this provision.

Section 3. **Special Master Action**: Any individual player or the NFLPA acting on that player's or any number of players' behalf, the NFL, and any Club may bring an action before the Special Master alleging a violation of Article XVll (Entering Player Pool) and/or Article XV (Guaranteed League-wide Salary, Salary Cap & Minimum Team Salary) of this Agreement. Issues of relief and liability shall be determined in the same proceeding. The complaining party shall bear the burden of demonstrating by a clear preponderance of the evidence that the challenged conduct was in violation of Article XVІl (Entering Player Pool) and/or Article XXlV (Guaranteed League-wide Salary, Salary Cap Minimum Team Salary).

Section 4. **Commissioner Disapproval**: In the event the Commissioner disapproves any Player Contract as being in violation of Article XVII (Entering Player Pool) and/or Article XXlV (Guaranteed League-wide Salary, Salary Cap & Minimum Team Salary), he shall at the time of such disapproval notify the NFLPA, all affected Clubs, and all affected players of such disapproval in writing and the reasons therefor. Except as required by the terms of this Agreement. Nothing in this Agreement is intended to affect (i) any authority of the Commissioner to approve or disapprove Player Contracts and (ii) the effect of the Commissioner's approval or disapproval on the validity of such Player Contracts.

Section 5. **Special Master Review**: In the event that the Commissioner approves a Player Contract pursuant to Section above, the NFLPA, any affected Club, and any affected player shall have the right within thirty (30) days of such person's notice of such disapproval to initiate a proceeding before the Special Master to determine whether such contract is in violation of Article XVII (Entering Player Pool) and/or Article XXIV (Guaranteed League-wide Salary, Salary Cap & Minimum Team Salary). The Special Master shall review the dispute de novo, and shall have the authority to approve such Player Contracts in lieu of the Commissioner's approval, or confirm the Commissioner's disapproval, In the event the Commissioner's disapproval is upheld, the player and the Club shall have ten (10) days to attempt to renegotiate such Player Contract notwithstanding any other time period set forth in this Agreement. The Special Master does not have the authority to impose any revisions to such Player Contract on the player or the Club.

Section 6. **Sanctions**: In the event that the Special Master finds a violation of this Section 1 of this Article, the Commissioner shall be authorized to impose a fine of up to $2,000,000 payable to the NFL, upon any Club found to have committed such violation, and shall be authorized to void any Player Contract(s) that was (or were) the direct cause of such violation.

Section 7. **Prior Conference**: Prior to the initiation of a proceeding under this Article by the NFLPA, the parties shall confer in person or by telephone to attempt to negotiate a resolution of the dispute.

INDEX

References are to Pages

ABANDONMENT OF CONTRACTS, 3

ACCEPTANCE
See Offeror and Offeree

AGENTS
Generally, 15–18
Conflicts of interest, 18, 19
Criminal liability, 23, 24
Registration, 19
NCAA, 22, 23
State legislation, 19, 20
Union, 21, 22
Representation, 24, 25
Standard representation agreements, 15, 16

AIDS, 233, 234

AMATEUR SPORTS, 201
Administration, 201, 202
NCAA, 204–206
Rule-making, 203
Status of athlete, 202, 203

AMATEUR SPORTS ACT, 249–252

AMERICANS WITH DISABILITIES ACT, 233–234

ANTI–MARRIAGE RULES, 218, 219

ANTITRUST
Generally, 52–55
Amateur sports, 68
Cable TV, 66–68
Collegiate draft, 61–62
Exemptions, 56
Baseball, 56, 57
Labor, 57, 58
NFL, 58
Nonstatutory labor, 58–61
Franchise movement, 62 64
League versus league, 64, 65
Per se, 53, 54
Player restraints, 61–62
Rule of reason, 5355
Tie-ins, 69
TV packaging, 65–66

ARBITRATION AND MEDIATION, 47–50
Grievance, 50
Salary, 50, 51
Vacating an award, 49

ASSIGNMENTS
Contracts, 9–10
Income, 28

ASSUMPTION OF RISK, 156–161
Expressed, 159, 160
Implied, 160, 161
Jockeys and car racers, 161–163
Minors, 166
Skiing, golf and baseball, 163–166

BARGAINING UNIT, 41, 42

BASEBALL
Assumption of risk, 16–166
Exemption, 56, 57
Salary grievance,
See Arbitration and Mediation
Spectators, 105–108

BATTERY, 198

BLOOD DOPING, 254

BOYCOTTS, 252, 253

CABLE TV, 66–68

CANADA
Criminal liability, 199, 200
  Self-defense, 199, 200

CAR RACES
Assumption of risk, 161–163
Spectators, 109–111
Waivers, 176, 177

CHARITABLE IMMUNITY, 184
See also Sovereign Immunity

CIVIL RIGHTS RESTORATION ACT OF 1987, pp. 278–281

CLAUSES, SPECIALTY
See Specialty Clauses

COACHES
Duty to warn, 131
Failure to hire competent, 118
Liability, 122–125
Preparation of participants, 128–132
Qualifications, 125–128
Supervision, 132, 133

COLLATERAL AGREEMENTS, 8–9

COLLECTIVE BARGAINING, 44, 45
Agreement, 45
  See also Appendix
  Discipline and penalties, 260, 261

COLLEGES
  See also Schools
Collegiate draft, 61, 62
Scholarships,
  See Scholarships

COMMISSIONER'S SIGNATURE, 1
Condition precedent, 1
Material breach, 1
Player's signature as revocable offer, 1

COMPARATIVE NEGLIGENCE, 169

CONCERTED ACTIONS, 45
Lockouts, 46, 47
Strikes, 46

CONFLICTS OF INTEREST
Agents, 18, 19

CONTACT SPORTS, 100, 101
Sex discrimination, 275, 276

CONTRACTS
See also Offeror and Offeree
Abandonment,
    See Abandonment of Contracts
Defenses,
    See Defenses, Contract
Interpretation,
    See Interpretation of Contracts
Negotiation, 13–14
Scholarships, 238–242
Standard player's,
    See Standard Player's Contract

CONTRIBUTORY NEGLIGENCE, 167–169

COPYRIGHTS, 289, 290

COUNTER–OFFER, 1

CRIMINAL LIABILITY
Generally, 195, 196
Agents, 23, 24
Battery, 198
Canadian approach, 199–200
    Self-defense, 199–200
Inherently violent sports, 196–198

"DEATH PENALTY", 258–259

DEFAMATION
Defenses, 151–155
    Fair comment, 151, 152
    Opinions, 152–155
Per se, 141–143
Public figures, 143–147
Rule of repose, 148, 149
Sportswriters, 140, 141

DEFENSES, CONTRACT, 11–13
Mutuality, 13
Unclean hands, 12
Unconscionability, 12–13

DEFERRALS
Contracts, 29
Pension plans, 29–31
Substantially non-vested property, 31–32

DISABLED ATHLETE, 227, 228
AIDS, 233, 234
Americans with Disabilities Act, 233, 235
Eligibility, 228–233
§ 504, Rehabilitation Act, 231–233

DISCIPLINE AND PENALTIES
Generally, 256, 257
High school sports, 259, 260
NCAA, 257–258
"Death penalty", 258–259
Power to sanction, 257, 258
Professional sports, 260–262

DISCRIMINATION, SEX
See Sex Discrimination

DRAFT, COLLEGIATE, 61–62

DRUG TESTING
Generally, 263
Amateur sports, 265–268
Due process and equal protection, 270, 271
NCAA, 265, 266, 268–270
Olympics, 253–255
Professional sports, 263–265
Reasonableness of search, 269, 270
Right of privacy, 268, 269

DUE PROCESS, 213–216
Drug testing, 270–271
Power to discipline, 256, 257

DUTY OF FAIR REPRESENTATION, 43, 44

EDUCATION AMENDMENTS, 1972, TITLE IX
See Sex Discrimination, Title IX

ELIGIBILITY, 207
Due process and equal protection, 213–216
Disabled athletes, 227, 228
Right or privilege, 208–210
Scope of rules, 207, 208
State actors, 211–212
Types of rules, 216
    Anti-marriage, 218, 219
    "No agent" rates, 219–221
    No transfer rules, 217, 218
    Red shirting, 216, 217

EQUAL PROTECTION, 213–216
Drug testing, 270, 271
Sex discrimination, 281–284

EQUAL RIGHTS AMENDMENTS, 284, 285

ESTATE PLANNING
    Generally, 36–38
Estate tax, 37
Generation skipping tax, 38
Life insurance, 38
Revocable trusts, 37
"Unified credits", 38

EXEMPTIONS, ANTITRUST, 56
Baseball, 56, 57
Labor, 57, 58
NFL, 58
Non-statutory labor, 58–61

FACILITY LIABILITY
Design, construction, maintenance and repair, 93, 94
Invitees, 91–92
Minors, 92, 93
Status of injured party, 90, 91
Unreasonably dangerous conditions, 93

FAILURE TO REFER, 86

FAIR REPRESENTATION, DUTY OF
See Duty of Fair Representation

FINANCIAL PLANNING, 34
Estate planning, 36–38
    Estate tax, 37
    Generation skipping tax, 38

FINANCIAL PLANNING, 34—Cont'd
Estate planning—Cont'd
Life insurance, 38
Revocable trusts, 37
"Unified credits," 38
Preservation of capital, 34, 35
Protection against risk, 36
Tax minimalization, 35
Keogh contributions, 35

FRAUDULENT CONCEALMENT, 79–82

FRANCHISE MOVEMENT, 62–64

GAMBLING, 5
Power to discipline, 261, 262

GENERATION SKIPPING TAX, 38

GIRLS AND WOMEN
See Sex Discrimination

GOLF
Assumption of risk, 163–166
Spectators, 108, 109

GOOD FAITH BARGAINING, 42, 43

GRIEVANCE ARBITRATION, 50

HANDICAPPED ATHLETES
See Disabled Athletes

HIGH SCHOOL SPORTS
See also Schools
Discipline and penalties, 259, 260
Drug testing, 266, 267

HOCKEY SPECTATORS, 109–111

INCOME ASSIGNMENT, 28

INCOME DEFERRALS
See Deferrals

INCORPORATION, 33, 34

INFORMED CONSENT, 77, 78

INJUNCTIONS, 4, 10, 11

INSTRUCTION
Failure to, 118

INSURANCE, LIFE, 38

INTELLECTUAL PROPERTY
   Generally, 286
Athletes as entertainers, 287, 288
Copyrights, 289, 290
Marketing, 286, 287
Patents, 288, 289
Trade dress, 293, 294
Trademarks, 290–292

INTERNATIONAL OLYMPICS COMMITTEE (IOC), 248, 249
Drug testing, 253, 254

INTERNATIONAL SPORTS, 248

INTERPRETATION OF CONTRACTS
Abandonment, 3
Ambiguous terms, 2
   "Player-manager," 2, 3

INVASION OF PRIVACY, 149–151

INVESTMENT, TAX–SHELTERED
See Taxation, Tax–Sheltered Investments

JOCKEYS
Assumption of risk, 161–163
Drug testing, 264

KEOGH CONTRIBUTIONS, 35

LIBEL AND SLANDER, 141, 142

LIFE INSURANCE, 38

LOCALITY RULE, 124, 125

LOCKOUTS
See Concerted Actions

MARKETING, 286, 287

MEDIATION AND ARBITRATION
See Arbitration and Mediation

MEDICAL MALPRACTICE
Doctor-patient relationship, 75, 76
Duty of care, 76, 77
Duty to disclose, 77, 78
Failure to refer, 85, 86
Fraudulent concealment, 79–82
Informed consent, 77, 78
Preparticipation physical exams, 83–85
Team physicians, 82–86
Vicarious liability, 86

MINORS
Assumption of risk, 166
Facility liability, 92, 93
Spectators, 111–113
Waivers, 177, 178

MUTUALITY, 13

NATIONAL GOVERNING BODY (NGB), 250–252

NATIONAL LABOR RELATIONS ACT, 39–41
Bargaining unit, 41, 42
Duty to bargain, 42, 43
Good faith, 42, 43
Jurisdiction, 40

NCAA, 204, 205
Amateurism, 219
"Death penalty", 258, 259
Drug testing, 265, 266, 268, 269
Legislative process, 206
"No-agent" rules, 219–221
Power to sanction, 257, 258
Proposition 42, p. 222
Proposition 48, pp. 221, 222
Proposition 16, pp. 222, 223

NEGLIGENCE
Generally, 71, 72
Breach of duty, 73
Damages, 74, 75
Duty of care, 72
Proximate cause, 74
Schools, 115–117
Standard of care, 72, 73

NEGOTIATIONS, CONTRACT
See Contracts, Negotiation

"NO AGENT" RULES, 219–221

NO–CUT CLAUSE, 7, 8

NO–DUTY RULE, 106

NO PASS, NO PLAY, 210, 215, 223–226

NO–TAMPERING CLAUSE, 5

NO TRANSFER RULES, 217, 218

NON–STATUTORY LABOR EXEMPTION, 58–61

OFFEROR AND OFFEREE, 1
    See also Contracts
Acceptance, 2
Binding contracts, 2
Revocable offers, 2

OLYMPICS, 248–249
International Olympics Committee (IOC), 249
    Drug testing, 253–255
US. Olympic Committee (USOC), 247–252
    Drug testing, 253–255

OPTION CLAUSES, 6–7

PAROL EVIDENCE RULE, 4

PARTICIPANTS
Coach's preparation, 128–132
Contact sports, 100, 101
Injuries, 95–97
Professional sports, 99, 100
Referee's duty to protect, 136
Third persons, 101–103
Unsportsmanlike conduct, 98, 99
Violation of safety rules, 97, 98

PATENTS, 288, 289

PENALTIES AND DISCIPLINE
See Discipline and Penalties

PENSION PLANS
Deferrals, 29

PHYSICIANS, TEAM, 82–86

PLAYER RESTRAINTS, 61–62

PRIVACY
Drug testing, 268, 269
Invasion of, 149–151

PRODUCT'S LIABILITY, 87, 88
Dangerous products, 87
Warnings, 88

PROFESSIONAL SPORTS
Discipline and penalties, 260–262
Participant injuries, 99–100
Workers' compensation, 186–188

PROPOSITIONS 16, 42 AND 48, pp. 221–223

PUBLIC FIGURES, 143–147

REASONABLENESS OF SEARCH
Drug testing, 269, 270

RECREATIONAL USE STATUTES, 185

RED SHIRTING, 216, 217

REFEREES
Anticipating reasonably foreseeable dangers, 137, 138
Duty to enforce rules, 135, 136
Duty to protect participants, 136
Duty to warn, 136, 137
Failure to control game, 138, 139
Liability,
    Generally, 134, 135

REGISTRATION OF ATHLETES
NCAA, 22, 23
State legislation, 19, 20
Union, 20–22

REHABILITATION ACT, § 504, pp. 231–233

REMEDIES, 10–11
Specific performance, 10–11
    Injunctions, 10–11

REPRESENTING THE ATHLETE
    Generally, 15–18, 24, 25
Standard representation contracts, 15, 16

RESERVE CLAUSE, 7

REVOCABLE TRUSTS, 37

RIGHT OF PRIVACY
See Privacy

RULE OF REPOSE, 148–149

SAFETY RULES, VIOLATION OF, 97, 98

SALARY ARBITRATION, 50, 51

SCHOLARSHIPS, 236–238
Contracts, 238–242
Employee status, 246, 247
Taxation, 244–246
Workers' compensation, 242–244

SCHOOLS
See also Colleges; High School Sports
Failure to hire competent coaches, 118
Failure to instruct, 118
Failure to maintain equipment and facilities, 120–121
Failure to properly supervise, 119–120
Failure to warn, 118
Negligence, 115–117
Vicarious liability, 117–118

SEARCHES AND SEIZURES
See Reasonableness of Search

SEPARATE BUT EQUAL, 274, 275

SEX DISCRIMINATION
Generally, 272–274
Contact sports, 275, 276
Equal protection, 281–284
Separate but equal, 274, 275
State E.R.A.'s, 284, 285
Title IX, 276–281
Application, 277, 278
Grove City and Civil Rights Restoration Act of 1987, pp.
278–281

SKIING
Assumption of risk, 163–166

SLANDER AND LIBEL, 141, 142

SOVEREIGN IMMUNITY, 178–181
    See also Charitable Immunity; Recreational Use Statutes
Discretionary acts, 181–183
Governmental-private duality, 180
Policy considerations, 183

SPECIALTY CLAUSES, 6–8
No-cut, 7–8
Option, 6–7
Reserve, 7

SPECTATORS
Injuries, 104, 105
    Baseball, 105–108
    Facilities, 113, 114
    Golf, 108–109
    Hockey, car races and wrestling, 109–111
    Minors, 111–113

SPORTSWRITERS, 140, 141

STANDARD PLAYER'S CONTRACT, 3–6
    See also Appendix
Ambiguous terms, 4
Commissioner's signature, 1, 5
Discipline and penalties, 260, 261
Gambling, 5, 261, 262
Handwritten provisions, 4
Injunctive relief, 4
No-tampering clause, 5
Parol evidence rule, 4
Physical examinations, 4, 5
Termination clause, 5

STANDARD REPRESENTATION CONTRACTS, 15, 16

STATE ACTORS, 211, 212

STEROIDS, 255, 267

STRICT LIABILITY, 88, 89

STRIKES
See Concerted Actions

SUBSTANTIALLY NON–VESTED PROPERTY
Deferrals, 31–32

TAC (THE ATHLETIC CONGRESS), 249

TAXATION
Generally, 26, 27
Gross income, 27
Minimalization, 35, 36
Keogh contributions, 35
Planning, 27, 28
Scholarships, 244–246
Tax-sheltered investments,
Leveraging, 32
Positive cash flow, 33
Tax-deferral, 32, 33

TEAM PHYSICIANS, 82–86

TERMINATIONS, 5, 9

THIRD PERSONS, 101–103

TIE–INS OF TICKET PURCHASES, 69

TITLE IX, 1972 EDUCATION AMENDMENTS
See Sex Discrimination, Title IX

TRADE DRESS, 293, 294

TRADEMARKS, 290–292

TRUSTS, REVOCABLE, 37

TV PACKAGING, 66

UNCLEAN HANDS, 12

UNCONSCIONABILITY, 12–13

UNFAIR LABOR PRACTICES, 43
Failure to bargain in good faith, 43

"UNIFIED CREDITS", 38

UNIONS, 41–44

UNITED STATES OLYMPIC COMMITTEE (USOC), 202, 248–253, 255, 267
Drug testing, 255, 267

UNREASONABLY HAZARDOUS CONDITIONS, 93

UNSPORTSMANLIKE CONDUCT, 98–99

URINALYSIS, 268

VICARIOUS LIABILITY, 86, 117–118

VIOLATION OF SAFETY RULES, 97, 98

VIOLENCE, 193–195

WAIVERS, 171–174
Car races, 176, 177
Foot races, 174–176
Minors, 177, 178

WARNINGS, 170, 171
Coach's duty, 131
Failure to, 118
Referee's duty, 136, 137

WARRANTY LIABILITY, 89, 90
Express, 89, 90
Implied, 89, 90

WOMEN AND GIRLS
See Sex Discrimination

WORKERS' COMPENSATION, 186
Collegiate sports, 189
Employer-based sports, 189–191
Non-participants, 191, 192
Professional sports, 186–189
Scholarships, 242–244

WRESTLING SPECTATORS, 109–111